In Search of America's Past

In Search of America's Past

LEARNING TO READ HISTORY
IN ELEMENTARY SCHOOL

Bruce VanSledright

FOREWORD BY LARRY CUBAN

TEACHERS
COLLEGE
PRESS

Teachers College, Columbia University
New York and London

Published by Teachers College Press, 1234 Amsterdam Avenue, New York, NY 10027

Library of Congress Cataloging-in-Publication Data

VanSledright, Bruce.
  In search of America's past: learning to read history in elementary school /
  Bruce VanSledright ; foreword by Larry Cuban.
    p.   cm.
  Includes bibliographical references (p.   ) and index.
  ISBN 0-8077-4192-2 (pbk. : alk. paper)—ISBN 0-8077-4193-0 (cloth : alk. paper)
  1. United States—History—Study and teaching.   2. United States—History—Study and teaching (Elementary).   I. Title.

E175.8. V36   2002
372.89'0973—dc21   2001060351

ISBN 0-8077-4192-2 (paper)
ISBN 0-8077-4193-0 (cloth)

Printed on acid-free paper
Manufactured in the United States of America

09   8   7   6   5   4

Contents

Foreword

> We must avoid introducing what is called scientific history in the schools, for it is [a] history of doubt, criticism, examination of evidence. It tends to confuse young people. . . . What we need to study in schools is the united effort, the common thought, of bodies of men; of the men who make public opinion, that is of the uncritical and conservative rather than of the educated classes.
>
> —Woodrow Wilson

Speaking at a conference on the teaching of history, then-Princeton professor Woodrow Wilson took one side of an emerging struggle over what kind of history should be taught in American public schools. Wilson wanted students to learn the chronology and facts of the American past. He wanted children to be inspired by the stories of Founding Fathers and noble deeds. Advocates of scientific history, however, wanted elementary and secondary students to study actual documents, determine their accuracy, and interpret history. They wanted students to experience the craft of historians even if inquiry revealed less inspiring deeds. Wilson and other historians, concerned about transmitting the nation's ideals and heroes to the next generation, wanted none of that. As Professor Lucy Salmon of Vassar, a member of the American Historical Association's committee examining the study of history in public schools, said, one must avoid in any discussion of national heroes "the presentation to children of . . . blemishes the world has gladly forgiven and forgotten for the sake of a great work accomplished and a noble life lived" (quoted in Peter Novick, *That Noble Dream* [1988]).

For well over a century, social studies teachers have faced the dilemma of two competing values—seeking to inculcate a deep attachment to the nation's heritage and teaching children how to think historically. Arising at the end of the 19th century, surfacing anew in the mid-1960s with the "New Social Studies," and again emerging strongly since the early 1990s, this core dilemma about the purposes of teaching history to the young has persisted among practitioners, policy-makers, and researchers.

While the dilemma has persisted, any impartial review of the past century of the teaching of U.S. history would find that fact-filled textbooks, curricular guides laid out in chronological order, and a teacher-centered pedagogy committed to transmitting content have prevailed. Yes, there have been moments, as mentioned above, when eager reformers and researchers sought to introduce historical thinking into texts, curricula, and pedagogy. With the introduction of the U.S. History standards in the early 1990s and a small group of researchers studying how children think about the past and bring their experiences to bear on interpreting what has occurred, we are in the midst of another revival of interest in helping students understand the past by using the methods of historians.

Bruce VanSledright's study of fifth graders doing history adds nicely to the work of those historians, educational researchers, and schoolteachers then and now who believe that citizenship is best cultivated when students learn the critical skills of historical investigation and draw their own conclusions supported by evidence drawn from primary sources. That 10-year-olds can do historical inquiry can be traced back to the work of Dewey, Piaget, and Bruner. In the past decade, contemporary researchers interested in the teaching and learning of history have reworked the ground plowed by earlier generations of colleagues and practitioners. They believe that children and youth are capable of such classroom work, can learn critical skills from the historian's craft, and can come to relish the activities. Beyond their personal beliefs, however, is a small but growing body of research studies that document instances of young children doing historical inquiry. It is to that literature that VanSledright has added his full measure.

And he has done so by teaching fifth graders to do inquiry. In conducting the research by actually teaching a group of children, VanSledright ventured into the dicey territory of conflicting roles of teaching and researching. He gathered class and individual data through interviews, observations, examination of student work, and performance assessments. All the safeguards that need to be taken in doing such complex participant-observation, VanSledright has taken. All the cautions that need to be stated in doing such research, he has stated explicitly. I am confident in the conclusions he draws about these particular 10-year-olds.

Too much investigation into teaching and learning is drive-by research; that is, it covers a few days or weeks, is survey-driven, and is nonobservational. This volume stands out for its duration, detailed observations of young children, the totality of the evidence, and measured analysis.

Because VanSledright is both a researcher and reformer, he has carefully juggled those competing roles in doing this study. Although it is only one study of one class in one school, his systematic inquiry adds nicely to the small literature that Sam Wineburg, Suzanne Wilson, Peter Seixas, Linda Levstik, Keith Barton, Jere Brophy, and others have created over the last decade raising serious questions about the teaching and learning of history. And it is exactly that literature, advancing the value of young children doing history, that continues to challenge the prized value of passing on an unexamined heritage that Woodrow Wilson, Lucy Salmon, and their current supporters endorse. Although the late 19th century dilemma over the purposes of teaching history in public schools persists into the early 21st century, Bruce VanSledright's bold venture into a fifth grade classroom underscores the vitality and the necessity of that tension by highlighting what 10-year-olds can do intellectually when they study the past.

—Larry Cuban

Preface

The pages that follow contain an account of my experience teaching 23 fifth-graders to learn history by investigating it. Not only was I their teacher, but I also served as a researcher, collecting data on my own teaching practices, on the influence a pedagogical theory of historical thinking and critical reading held over my decision-making process, and on what the fifth-graders were learning. The data I gathered from the students suggest that they learned many things. But I am quite sure that I learned much more than they. For me, it was a more powerful experience.

To situate this account within the broader sweep of history education in the United States, I describe in Chapter 1 a number of its intellectual, pedagogical, and political contours. I discuss issues that I believe currently suffocate history education's potential vitality. I also identify ways in which that vitality can be restored, some of which I pursued in this teacher-researcher project. Chapter 2 situates the project within the school and classroom in which it occurred.

For much of the middle of the book (Chapters 3 through 5), I attempt to lay bare what I was thinking about as I taught—and what I consequently learned. Despite my many years as a history teacher, the picture that emerges frequently reveals the musings and choices of one who might be construed as an anxious greenhorn. When I reread it, I occasionally found myself cringing because, in retrospect, I suspect I might have made better decisions. But it was in such places that I learned most about my teaching practice, about the way my knowledge of history both broadened and narrowed the students' educational opportunities, about how relevant the research on the historical thinking of experts and novices is for the elementary school classroom. As a means of building pedagogical wisdom, I can think of few more effective methods than engaging in such teacher-research studies. This center portion of the book, although teased apart into three chapters, represents a running narrative of my experience and thoughts as I taught the fifth-graders. Rather than tie up each chapter with a customary conclusion section, I leave them relatively open, saving conclusions for Chapters 6 and 7.

Chapter 6 is devoted initially to a general characterization of what the 23 fifth-graders learned while I taught them and then to a more specific delineation of what a subgroup of 8 learned. These 8 students served as my principal informants in the study and the source of the most robust and representative data I have on the fifth-graders' intellectual growth. In Chapter 7, I conclude by returning to several of the issues I took up in Chapter 1. I focus on how the results of my journey with the fifth-graders can be understood in pedagogical and policy-making terms.

During this project, I had the luxury—afforded few elementary school teachers—of being responsible for only one subject, American history. This made my efforts to teach and do research on what I was teaching somewhat more manageable. However, it was daunting nonetheless, in part perhaps explaining why, despite repeated calls for them, there are so few teacher-research studies in the literature. From my perspective on the completed side of this study, I want to observe that, until teachers' workloads are reconstructed to acknowledge the importance of such studies and the crucial role they can play in teachers' professional growth, they will continue to remain scarce in the research literature. We must develop and employ policies that reconfigure teachers' daily worklives, enabling them to systematically study and learn from their own practice, write about it, and thus enable other teachers to learn from it as well. I hope we can seize on this soon, so that, say, 10 years from now, the study presented here is buried under the vast weight of teacher-research projects accumulating in the educational research archives. The amassing of the wisdom of teaching practice that results would be welcome indeed.

I am deeply indebted to Ms. Proctor (a pseudonym), the teacher in whose I class I experimented, and to her 23 fifth-graders, who by now are eighth-graders and are moving, or have moved, through another exposure to American history. Proctor's warm embrace of my suggestion that I teach the students history was much appreciated, as was the time she spent with me conferring about my decisions and teaching me about "her" children. Those 23 students made indelible marks on my psyche. I can close my eyes and see each one of their faces even now, 2 years later. I hope they are doing well. I am also indebted to the then-principal of Kendall Elementary School for hosting me, to the school district for giving me permission to teach and then research my own practice, and to the students' parents for granting me access to their children's educational process.

My research assistant, Elizabeth Fasulo, was a joy to work with on this project. I owe her many thanks. At an early point, when I was attempting to obtain funding for this project and finding it difficult, Larry Cuban offered timely encouragement to pursue it, noting that persistence about a matter in which you deeply believe can be as important as the idea itself. I owe him special gratitude for that encouragement. Finally, without the support of a grant from the Spencer Foundation, this study would have never been possible. I want to convey deep appreciation to them for funding the effort. The views expressed in this account are entirely my own and do not necessarily represent the endorsement of the foundation.

In Search of America's Past

1

W(h)ither History Education?

On a warm May morning, 11-year-old Alexandra sat reading four documents dealing with the April 19, 1775, battle at Lexington Green. It was here, the historians tell us, that "the shot heard 'round the world" signaled the commencement of the American Revolutionary War. The first document, a primary source, contained testimony about the events from 34 colonial minutemen, as they gave their statement under an oath before three justices of the peace on April 25, 1775. The second document, also a primary source, was a 1782 account of those same events narrated from a different perspective by British Army Ensign Jeremy Lister. Like the minutemen, he had participated in the battle. The two remaining documents were short newspaper reports describing the confrontation, one from the *Salem Gazette*, dated April 25, 1775, and the other from the *London Gazette*, dated June 10, 1775. Alexandra thought aloud as she read, attempting to make sense of the various interpretations as she forged an understanding of who fired those first shots.

Her analysis of the testimony of the 34 minutemen (Document 1, in the Endpoint Performance Task in Appendix B) was characterized by descriptions of what she thought the text indicated about the action. She frequently summarized sections of the document as she read. As she neared the end, she began making a number of judgments about the actions of the British. For example, after reading the lines,

> We further testify . . . that about 5 o'clock in the morning, hearing our drum beat, we proceeded towards the Green, and soon found that a large body of [British] troops were marching towards us. . . . Some of our company [of Minutemen] were coming up to the Green, and others had reached it, at which time [our] company began to [break up], [and while] our backs were turned on the troops, we were fired on by them, and a number of our men were instantly killed and wounded,

she noted, "Maybe the British soldiers got a little mad because they didn't like seeing the colonists' backs, so they shot them." Then after reading the two lines that followed,

Not a gun was fired by any person in our company on the [British] regulars to our knowledge before they fired on us, and they continued firing until we made our escape,

she said, "So, the British, they must have been doing something fishy." She then scanned the title of Ensign Lister's account ("Personal Narrative of Ensign Jeremy Lister, British Army," see Appendix B), noting the date it was written (1782), and immediately responded with incredulity: "But that [pointing to the minutemen testimony] was written *before* this one, so how can this be exact to that?" As she finished the Lister account, she attempted to answer her own question by checking the time lapse between the writing of the two documents and remarked a bit testily, "Seven years, that's a long time. He [Lister] could have made this up . . . to save his own skin, so he wouldn't have to go to jail. They were probably gonna go through his stuff. I don't believe any of them yet!"

Next she turned her attention to the *Salem Gazette* and *London Gazette* accounts (see Appendix B). In analyzing and commenting on them, she cross-checked details to further augment and corroborate several inter-pretations of the event she was constructing. She was quick to comment on the sources, as a means of trying to identify partisan affiliation. *Salem Gazette*: "So they must have been for the colonists. It's all the British fault, all the soldiers fault." *London Gazette*: "It's in between [balanced?], 'cause it's actually telling a little bit about both the troops and the [colonists]."

Upon finishing with the documents, she examined two artists' depic-tions of the battle (see Appendix B), images reproduced from files in the American Memory section at the National Archives and Record Adminis-tration (www.nara.gov). Prior to looking at the two images, she reported being unclear about what had happened at Lexington Green, demanding more evidence before drawing firm conclusions. She studied the pictures. After scanning the artist's depiction in Image 1 (Figure B.4), she com-plained, "I've had evidence from primary sources and now I get a picture? And I don't even know if it's a secondary or primary source. If it's a sec-ondary source, it could be lying. Well, they [historians drawing conclu-sions based on primary sources] don't even know if the British actually shot. I'm not taking the British side, but . . ." Frustrated by the limitations of the evidence, but hardly defeated, she pressed on. She carefully con-trasted the two images and tried to understand when and where they originated. She then attempted to assess them against the documents, checking and cross-checking them. The more diligently she pursued on the analytic process, the more elusive a definitive answer to the question "Who fired those first shots?" became. She finally grew even more exas-perated. However, she seemed to understand that, like those who had studied this battle before her, a conclusive answer to the first-shot question was not to be had.

Alexandra had been through a similar prior experience. Approximately 4½ months earlier, she had read, analyzed, and thought out loud about two written accounts and three artist depictions of the Boston "Massacre." The result was similar: Arriving at a conclusive answer to the question "Who was responsible for the so-called Boston 'Massacre'?" proved just as elusive. Her attempt to answer the question at that point brought even higher levels of exasperation with the analytic task. Now, however, after more than 4 months of practice investigating history by exploring, among other things, several riddles connected with early events at Jamestown and other colonies and events leading up to the American Revolution, she had grown somewhat accustomed to seeing historical evidence trails evaporate before decisive answers were obtained. But she never got fully comfortable with the idea. Alexandra seemed driven by the need to know for certain.

Noting her earlier experience with unresolved questions about the Boston "Massacre," and now this one—where it appeared that historical investigators must make peace with not knowing what actually happened on Lexington Green that fateful April morning—I asked Alexandra, "Does that bother you about the study of history?" On the exhale of my last word, and with what seemed like a knowing glint in her eye, she replied, "Yeah! Bothers me a lot, because I'll never know the answer. You don't know [who] actually triggered the Revolutionary War. It was big! It was humongous! It's very hard [not to figure it out]. I just don't see how historians can do this." I smiled at her and she smiled back. That was all we needed to say. We both knew from spending 4 months studying American history together in classroom 23 that history was like that sometimes, perhaps more often than we wanted it to be.

Clearly Alexandra has doubts about how historians manage to do what they do. Alexandra is hardly alone. Historian Joan Wallach Scott (1996) alludes to that doubt:

> The reality to which the historian's interpretation refers is produced by that interpretation. [Y]et the legitimacy of the interpretation is said to rest on its faithfulness to a reality that lies outside, or exists prior to, interpretation. History functions through an inextricable connection between reality and interpretation which is nonetheless denied. (p. 1)

According to Scott, doing history depends on pursuing a tightly wound connection between interpretation and reality that, she notes succinctly, is denied. How are historical investigators to recapture a reality that has long since ceased to be? All they have are traces of a past reality that must be interpreted. However, the accounts historians create often give the impression that there was no interpretive process used at all, that their words directly capture the reality they depict, as though they were there, chronicling every word and action. Yet, as Scott implies and as Barthes (1968, 1986) noted more explicitly before her, this is all a referential illusion: the mirage that the text's words refer seamlessly to a past reality they describe. Historical investigators are engaged in the difficult and sometimes frustrating task of reconstructing the past from shards of evidence that sometimes lead down blind alleys and up dead-end streets. As with the battle at Lexington, the shootings in Boston in 1770, and a host of other historical events, investigators wind up not knowing for sure who fired the first shot or who gave the order to fire.

Yet if we are to learn anything about the past, *reconstruct* and *re-create* we must. In the process of filling in the missing pieces, we collide head-long with the historical investigator's reality–interpretation paradox. Scott (1996) adds, "An inescapable tension results because the two [interpretation and reality] are posited as separate and separable entities; a tension of which historians have long been aware. This tension is not a new discovery, not the product of the ravings of radical relativists, nor the by-product of some nihilistic 'deconstructionism'; *it inheres in the practice of history itself*" (p. 1; emphasis added).

If historians—ostensibly experts at the practice of doing history and thinking historically—struggle with this paradox as they encounter it repeatedly during their investigations, it would be fair to ask: How can 10- and 11-year-olds manage to do it? If 11-year-old Alexandra seems incredulous about how the experts manage to do what they do, would it be reasonable to assume that novices such as she could learn to investigate the past and wrestle successfully with the problems it entails? To do so would seem to be a tall order.

Nevertheless, if we look carefully at what Alexandra is doing when she analyzes the Lexington battle documents and images, we see that she appears to effectively engage the investigative process and thus tap into the very issues that often plague historians. Like a good detective, she wants to solve the mystery of the battle at Lexington. Like a seasoned historical investigator, she carefully studies the evidence in order to reconstruct events in her head. As her comments suggest, she desires the illusion of complete verisimilitude so that she might narrate "the reality of the confrontation" in a way that renders interpretive handiwork invisible. Yet, recapturing the reality of Lexington is a vain hope. In short order, (precocious?) Alexandra concludes that knowing who fired the infamous first shot cannot be established conclusively, at least given the evidence in front of her. She lands squarely on the tension Scott describes. She is frustrated by it, but to have seen the look in her eye and to have heard the tone in her voice would have told you that she understood its inevitability. In this sense, historian Scott and 11-year-old Alexandra appear to share some understanding of the trials and tribulations than can arise in the practice of doing history, even though they do not speak about it in quite the same vocabulary. What is going on here? A significant amount of experience and the time required to develop it separate the two of them. Yet Alexandra analyzes historical documents and images with a level of proficiency that most high school students lack (Stahl, Hynd, Britton, McNish, & Bosquet, 1996; Wineburg, 1991). How far can fifth-graders such as Alexandra be pressed in learning to employ the cognitive tools necessary to effectively investigate the past and think historically? How close can they come to approaching what the ostensible experts do?

These questions animate this book. They also animated the classroom-based research on which the book is based. In the chapters that follow, I convey an account of my 4-month experience teaching a group of 23 racially and ethnically diverse fifth-graders—of whom Alexandra was one—how to become historical investigators. I provide a narrative of what we did in the classroom and then discuss what the students learned from the experience. Evidence for the latter comes from extensive documentation I did while teaching the students and from two complex historical-analysis performance tasks I asked the students to undertake, once before my teaching began and again after I had finished. In this first chapter, I consider a rather wide swath of the intellectual, theoretical, and political landscape on which the project was undertaken. To get at it, I discuss four key challenges for the history education of young students: learning history, the subject matter itself, teaching it, and recent history education reform recommendations—all challenges I have hinted at in different ways in the preceding paragraphs.

THE CHALLENGE OF LEARNING TO THINK HISTORICALLY

Complex Cognitive Acts Required

As the foregoing suggests, learning history is no simple task. It demands some fairly sophisticated thinking processes. This thoughtfulness, at almost every turn, propels you into intellectual situations where there is considerable tension between your need to interpret, to imagine, and to understand what things were like back then, and the desire to carefully recapture and recount a reality that is no longer available to you. From among others that could be described here, consider these tough historical thinking practices.

Historical thinking that produces the sort of understanding of the past exhibited by those with deep experience sorting through it requires a complex regimen of investigative techniques. For example, investigators need to know where to find the remaining evidentiary traces—artifacts and documents—that can tell stories about the time, place, and events under scrutiny. However, the real work begins once the evidence is located; investigators must know what to do with that evidence. They must be able to classify and categorize it according to whether it represents a primary or secondary source. They must then check and cross-check the evidence as they begin to build contextualized interpretations of the events being studied. Researchers refer to this process as corroboration (Wineburg, 1991). This process of corroboration involves making a series of careful judgments about the perspective presented in, say, a diary, or an image, or eyewitness testimony. Judgments of the relative validity and reliability of perspectives also must be made. In doing so, investigators need to read the evidence for different sorts of political and sociopolitical subtexts, as a means of sorting out validity and reliability issues. From this collection of research techniques and judgments comes the construction of a viable interpretation of the events. Investigators then become authors as they make a carefully argued case—as tightly linked to the evidence as possible—for their understanding of the event or events.

As if this were not enough, investigators must also engage in "filling in the blanks" when evidence does not exist to tie important elements surrounding an event together (Shemilt, 1984; VanSledright, 2001). Here, investigators are operating at the height of their interpretive presence, the place where the tension Scott (1996) observes is most acute. This is an exceedingly difficult task because investigators must attempt to avoid imposing attitudes of their own historical era on the actions and decisions of the historical agents under analysis. As Lowenthal (1985) notes, the past is indeed a foreign country. Those ancients being studied often did not share our present-day ontological assumptions, making it difficult for investigators to "connect" with their thoughts and actions. The ancients frequently seem odd to us moderns (see Ashby & Lee, 1987a; Seixas, 1996; Shemilt, 1984; VanSledright, 2001). Yet investigators must work from some assumptions, and often all they have are their own, colored and shaped by their present place in the march of time and culture. Holding those assumptions entirely at bay is essentially impossible. Interpretive compromises are made here. Investigators strive to tell the truth about what they have found, but that truth is at some level affected by the interpretive machinery at play in the process of thinking historically and patching up the holes where evidence is thin or nonexistent. Historical theoreticians and philosophers to date have found no way around this conundrum. Attempting to blot out the contemporaneous assumptions that shape what I call our historical positionalities would render us incapable of interpreting anything at all, because we depend on those assumptions to make sense of our world, past as well as present (VanSledright, 1998).

Against this foreground of intense investigative activity lies a background set of decisions that is no less important or difficult. Investigators must choose what to investigate in the first place. To make those choices, investigators operate on some understanding of what is historically significant (see, e.g., Barton, 2001; Barton & Levstik, 1998; Epstein, 1998; Seixas, 1994). For instance, some historians research how a small and very local sociocultural milieu shaped the identity, lives, and actions of a particular group of people, say, gay men in San Francisco in the 1920s. Other historians think it trivial to study such narrowly circumscribed groups and contexts, preferring instead to focus on national leaders and political, military, and economic events that affected millions. These latter historical investigators deem the former's choice of historical circumstance to examine less significant than their own. Whether you agree or not is less crucial than understanding how what investigators choose to investigate is tied to their definitions of what is historically significant. This decision-making landscape is rocky at best for the historical investigator, because careful rationales for investigative decisions must be developed, and not everyone always agrees with them.

Children Can't Do History

These practices—however difficult and, as Wineburg (2001) observes, "unnatural"—are the building blocks of historical understanding. Without the capacity to do history, to investigate the past oneself, learning about history, particularly in school, is reduced largely to rote memorization of dates, events, and people, or, in other words, the consumption of other people's facts (see Holt, 1990). History education research demonstrates that history presented as the putative story of the past in voluminous textbooks has little appeal to students and seems to do severe injustices to an otherwise compelling subject matter (e.g., Barton, 1996; Grant, 2001; Levstik, 1996; Smith & Niemi, 2001; VanSledright, 1995). Nonetheless, these same studies frequently report that this is exactly what children get, and the younger they are, the more likely it will be the case (e.g., Cuban, 1991; Goodlad, 1984; Seixas, 1999; VanSledright, 1996, 1997). This reality is partly fueled by the largely unexamined claim that young students—say, 10- and 11-year-olds—

simply do not yet possess the intellectual capacity to practice history themselves by investigating the past.

That claim may in part be rooted in 1960s misapplications of Piagetian principles of developmental psychology to such subject matters as history and social studies. As the argument goes in its application to these subjects, young children are first concrete thinkers, who need things spelled out in systematic steps tied to objects they can touch and manipulate (see Hanna, 1963). Only later, typically in adolescence, do they acquire the capacity to deal with abstract concepts such as revolution, capitalism, democracy, and the like. Since historical study involves immersion in and understanding of a host of abstract concepts, terms, and practices, concrete thinkers—for example, 10- and 11-year-olds—simply are not presently equipped for such study and investigation (see Coltham, 1971; Hallam, 1971).

Another source for the claim that young children cannot effectively do much more with history than commit dates, events, and actors to memory is the influence of behavioristic learning principles on school organization and curricula. These principles are based on the assumption that young children learn best when information is broken up into relatively discrete bits and fed to them piecemeal as learning stimuli. If children respond by learning the information correctly (memorizing small clusters of names, dates, and events for example), their behavior—that is, their recall capacity on a test—is reinforced by good grades, thus anchoring the learning process. Only as children amass the correct clusters of historical information via the stimulus–response–reinforcement process are they ready for more in-depth exploration and analysis. An examination of the typical survey American history course sequence and pedagogical approach that students experience repeatedly in U.S. schools (in grades 5 and 8, and at some point in high school) suggests that curriculum policy makers view late high school as the point where this deeper exploration is to occur, if at all (e.g., Cuban, 1991; Goodlad, 1984; Tyack & Tobin, 1994). According to this view, it takes until then to build a large enough store of historical knowledge to do more than reproduce it on recall tests.

The influence of misapplied Piagetian ideas and shallow behavioristic learning principles on school history—and the view of children as learners they impose—makes it unlikely that students as young as 10 or 11 will get opportunities to practice history in the ways I have previously described. This creates an interesting self-fulfilling prophecy: We believe that children are incapable of difficult acts of historical thinking and investigation, so we prevent them from having opportunities to do so, which in turn reinforces our assumptions that they are incapable because we do not see them perform as such. In many ways, this may be a more serious challenge for children's learning how to think historically because it carries the weight of tradition and is codified in school curriculum and organizational practices. However, as we will see momentarily, the claim that, say, fifth-graders are too young to do history is being challenged from several different quarters, most notably from the recent research literature in history education and from the standards movement.

THE CHALLENGE OF HISTORY AS A SUBJECT MATTER

Epistemological Turmoil in the Discipline

The challenges involved in learning to think historically and investigate the past are only part of the story. It would be nice if we could turn to the discipline of history itself in order to seek guidance in addressing the learning challenges. However, the critique of knowledge production that has arisen during the current postmodern period has not left the discipline of history untouched (see Ankersmit & Kellner, 1995; Berkhofer, 1995; Cronon, 1992; Iggers, 1997; Novick, 1988; Poster, 1997). Debates about the nature of history and historical knowledge have been a mainstay of disciplinary activity recently. These debates have significant implications for history education, because the issues raised in the discipline can affect how history as a school subject matter is conceptualized (Bain, 2000; Segall, 1999; Seixas, 1993).

To illustrate several facets of this debate about the nature and validity of historical knowledge and its production, consider the following exchange between two historians. In 1988, on the pages of the venerable *American Historical Review,* critic Robert Finlay took issue with Natalie Zemon Davis's (1983) interpretation of the facts in *The Return of Martin Guerre.* Finlay (1988) accused Davis of exercising excessive interpretive license, of producing a historical account that lacked proper allegiance to the existing evidence. In doing so, he invoked what he called "the sovereignty of the sources" and "the tribunal of the documents" (p. 571) as the proper interpretive arbiters used in constructing acceptable historical accounts. He concluded that Davis's efforts in *Martin Guerre* took her well beyond the interpretive boundaries long regarded as sacrosanct within the profession.

Davis (1988) responded by defending her treatment of the Martin Guerre case as an attempt to create an account that could be read as a detective work, paralleling the way in which the story unfolded in 16th-century France. She added that this entailed using a form of conjectural logic because the so-called facts of the case were and have continued to be in dispute. She noted that there were differences between Finlay's and her "mental habits, cognitive styles, and moral tone" (p. 574). She observed, "I see complexities and ambivalences everywhere. . . . Finlay sees things in clean, simple lines; he wants absolute truth, established with no ambiguity . . . ; he makes moral judgments in terms of sharp rights and wrongs" (p. 574). In effect, she argued that their divergent readings of the Guerre case, and the differing interpretive stances they assumed that produced those readings, accounted for the dispute about the evidence. She spent the better part of her essay describing those differences.

This exchange is but one illustration. A flap over Edmund Morris's (1999) biography of Ronald Reagan, *Dutch*, is only a more recent installment (see Masur, 1999). Some historians were peeved that Morris, deploying artistic license, *invented* a character for his book (Morris himself), who "was there" to chronicle Dutch's life as he lived it. Such cases reveal how contentiousness arises in debates over the relationship between the putative facts at historians' disposal via evidentiary documents, records, and artifacts, and the interpretations of the past—or histories—that result from the analysis of those facts. This is the tension Scott (1996) was addressing. The issues raised by the Finlay–Davis exchange, for example, are surely not new to the historical profession. However, they have taken on a certain recent urgency as criticism of modernist knowledge-construction projects and their underlying epistemological assumptions continues to mount.

Heritage or History?

If historians are debating the nature of historical knowledge, this raises important questions about what the subject matter of history should look like in schools. For example, should history be considered the largely indisputable facts that historians have uncovered and recorded in history books for consumption by schoolchildren? Should it be considered the investigative result of historians' interpretations of others' interpretations of events, and thus open to endless questioning, debate, and revision by future investigators, which could include students? Or should it be considered some combination of these? If the latter, where would the line be drawn between what is considered factual on the one hand, and a set of interpretations open to question and revision on the other?

One way to examine these questions is to explore historian David Lowenthal's (1998) distinction between *heritage* and *history*. (See also Kammen, 1997, Chapter 9 especially, for a related treatment of the concept of heritage.) *Heritage*, in Lowenthal's view, is "not history at all; while it borrows from and enlivens historical study, heritage is not an inquiry into the past but a celebration of it, not an effort to know what actually happened but a profession of faith in a past tailored to present-day purposes" (p. x). He adds, "The heritage fashioner, however historically scrupulous, seeks to design a past that will fix the identity and enhance the well-being of some chosen individual or folk" (p. ix). For example, Lowenthal would think of the people at Walt Disney Productions who brought us the film *Pocahontas* as heritage fashioners.

Although Lowenthal (1998) notes that history and heritage are inextricably bound up with one another, he contrasts history with heritage by pointing to the work that historians do, work that in purpose distinguishes it from that of the heritage fashioner. "The historian, however blinkered and presentist and self-deceived, seeks to convey a past consensually known, open to inspection and proof, continually revised and eroded as time and hindsight outdate its truths" (p. xi). *History*, while sharing some common space with heritage, is nevertheless primarily about the application of rigorous method, about the counsel and judgment of peers, about exhaustive inquiry, and about attempts to overcome bias in reporting, however unsuccessful.

The goal of *heritage* is principally to use the past—as a legacy, an inheritance—to spark faith, enhance identity, and create a sense of pleasure and joy in being who we are. Take, for example, William Bennett's (1994) approach in *To Reclaim a Legacy*: "But our goal should be more than just a common culture . . . we should instead want all students to know a common culture rooted in civilization's lasting visions, its highest shared ideals and aspirations, and its heritage" (p. 10). And make no mistake: Bennett believes this "civilization"—the *only* civilization, as his words imply—is none other than the Anglo-American one, not a hybrid of aboriginal, Central American, African, Asian, *and* European descent. The story of "our civilization's common culture" is what Bodnar (1992) calls "official history."[1] Bennett's "official" heritage champions parochialism and patriotism. However, history pursues cosmopolitanism and skepticism. While occupying the same historical topography, Lowenthal (1998) argues that "the aims that animate [the] two enterprises, and their modes of persuasion, are [nonetheless] contrary to one another" (p. xi).

Schools' socialization function, the passing along of *the* inspirational "common culture" to which Bennett refers, often results in a particular version of the past being taught as a sociopolitical effort to transmit a nation's "official" heritage and to enhance identity and a form of national

---

[1] For a typical version of "official" U.S. history, see the "freedom-quest" narrative described in the opening section of Chapter 5.

commitment or patriotic spirit. By Lowenthal's (1998) definition, schools typically do not teach much history at all, nor would they necessarily want to, given the way they may perceive the importance of their socialization function. Teaching students to study the subject as history, in the Lowenthalian sense, may present a serious challenge to the "official" heritage narrative. To teach what he calls history would involve undertaking the same activities that influence the work of historians: examination of evidence, careful investigation, rigorous argument, submission of claims to a tribunal of peers, revision of claims in light of new evidence or successful challenges to their validity. Learning to think this way could undermine efforts to teach the "official" heritage story because students might develop the intellectual tools necessary to question its partisan excesses and critique its attempts to inspire a form of unexamined patriotism. This in turn would work against schools' socialization function, insofar as using school subject matter to achieve sociocultural amalgamation and identity homogenization is a goal.

Accountability and Testing in Schools

The current testing and accountability movement in U.S. education often supports and reinforces the study of feel-good, patriotic heritage in schools, creating yet another significant challenge for children and their study of history. Many high-stakes tests developed by state education agencies that students are increasingly required to take seldom assess the sorts of ideas and practices that investigating history entails. Instead, they test students' ability to recall the details and persons and events that surround heritage mythologies. Many state-mandated and even locally mandated high-stakes assessments studiously avoid test items that require the actual doing of history. Such items carry considerably higher administration and scoring expense and can involve sticky standardization and reliability issues that policy makers would rather not confront. Facing what they appear to perceive as more pressing economic and political necessities (e.g., cheaper tests, higher reliability coefficients), policy makers typically opt for assessing what children know, rather than what they can do with what they know. As Darling-Hammond (1991) ruefully observed, "testing in the U.S. is primarily controlled by commercial publishers and nonschool agencies that produce norm-referenced, multiple-choice instruments designed to rank students cheaply and efficiently" (p. 220).

Such assessments therefore often protect "official" heritage approaches in school curricula, particularly when those curricula are aligned to the test and teachers then teach to that test. Policy makers control the test items, choosing who and what is to be recalled. To the extent that they seek to use heritage mythologies to inspire patriotic commitment and a form of common national identity (and occasionally a more local version), the tests send powerful messages about who the "right" heroes and notable stories are that must be remembered and celebrated. Test items that ask students to analyze, interrogate, and investigate the past for the purpose of debating what heritage is and/or should be are perceived to be contrary to such inspiration and commitment. Although some states and localities have opted to augment their tests with performance-based assessments that invite students to practice history (New York State's document-based questions on the Regent's Test; Maryland's State Performance Assessment Program, or MSPAP), such forms of assessment are rare and there seems to be little rush to increase their use. Time will tell how widespread they will become.

Public Opinion and Understanding of History

Education is in the news. We have "education governors," "education presidents," and "education representatives" everywhere. Educational accountability is their adopted chant. To hear them tell it, the public unequivocally supports it. In most places these days, accountability translates into high-stakes test outcomes. Given the burgeoning growth of assessment efforts across the country, and given that these assessments include measures of "official" heritage commemoration and celebration more often than measures of historical thinking and understanding, it would be safe to conclude, with Lowenthal (1998), that the general public does not distinguish history from heritage. It may be reasonable to contend that the public believes that the "official" heritage narrative *is* history. To the extent that this is the case, the public supports the accountability rhetoric and favors tests that measure their children's recall of national and local heroes and the events that made them so. Although genealogical research and occasional programs about the doing of history on the History Channel are surprisingly popular today, investigating the past and practicing history in fifth grade is not something that would likely resonate with most parents. Ask history teachers what parents inquire about regarding their children's learning, and they will tell you that they are concerned most with what "official" historical knowledge they can recall. Investigating history is not something many are familiar with, at least not as part of the school curriculum.

With public understanding tied up in a view that historical knowledge is the ability to reproduce the sorts of "facts" found in heritage-inspired textbooks and asked for on many high-stakes accountability measures, the practice of history languishes in classrooms. A public that defines history as the "official" heritage narrative and supports the accountability chorus and the assessment practices tied to it serves as a further challenge to the teaching and learning of historical thinking and understanding, because it reinforces the type of policy making that keeps history, in Lowenthal's sense of it, from ever entering the classroom door.

THE CHALLENGE OF TEACHING HISTORY

All the foregoing factors mitigate against history teachers' efforts to teach history rather than heritage. They would be enough in themselves it seems. However, there are at least three additional factors that can contribute to the challenges of embracing the practice of investigating the past with young children, all hinted at in the issues noted above: (1) the deep subject-matter knowledge required to do so, (2) the complexity of teaching it well and the pedagogical dilemmas that surface during the process, and (3) increases in diverse, special-needs students in large, fiscally strapped and resource-challenged urban public schools where less well prepared teachers often work (e.g., Fordham, 1996; Kozol, 1992; Taylor, 1991). I touch on these only briefly here because they arise in a variety of forms in the chapters that follow.

Deep Subject Knowledge Required

Being able to practice history in an elementary classroom requires more than significant memory of historical events and the people involved in them. It requires a deep understanding of the processes involved in investigating the past: knowing where to obtain the sources of evidence, knowing what to do with that evidence, understanding how to read difficult texts and analyze sometimes mysterious artifacts, and honing the ability to get into the hearts and minds of people whose worlds were different from our own without unfairly imposing our contemporary assumptions on them. In other words, deep substantive knowledge of the subject matter of history must be coupled with equally deep procedural knowledge.

It is no secret that most elementary teachers are prepared to teach as subject-matter generalists. If they hold deep knowledge in any curricular area they teach, it is most likely reading, that is, the teaching of how to read in a general sense. Without the sort of deep knowledge I am describing here, fifth-grade teachers who are called on to teach history are at a distinct disadvantage. Lack of a deep understanding of the subjects teachers must teach significantly shrinks the pedagogical landscape on which learning opportunities can be offered to students (Wilson, 1990). And most teachers get few professional development opportunities to remedy the situation, to deepen their knowledge of history and its investigative processes in order to teach it in the way that it would demand if the goal were to do it intellectual justice.[2]

Pedagogical Complexities and Dilemmas

Even if teachers of upper-elementary-age children were more rigorously prepared to teach history, there is nothing to prevent the many pedagogical dilemmas that haunt any classroom from appearing in theirs. For example, history can be a controversial subject precisely because the serious investigation of it has the power to undermine cherished "common culture" heritage mythologies. Nosing around in the events that ushered in the American Revolution has led more than a few historians to conclude that colonial "patriotism" could just as easily be understood as high treason, depending on your point of view. Interpreting Truman's decision to drop the atomic bomb on Japan is no less controversial. Then there is the whole matter of slavery, the Jim Crow period, Klan activity, and the lynching of freed slaves. Children's reactions to serious examinations of these events are unpredictable, as are their parents' reactions. Practicing history invites you in deeply enough to create powerful responses that often run contrary to cherished beliefs and assumptions about who Americans are supposed to be. At the same time, this is why it is so intriguing, because most of us seem to be curious about our identities and where and how we have come to be who we are. However, at least in the study of "our" history, these curiosities can lead us to unanticipated locations and question our epistemological and ontological perspectives. History teachers have little recourse but to expect the unexpected and to learn to manage the ensuing pedagogical dilemmas as best they can (Bain, 2000; Lampert, 1985). This can be discomforting, particularly to those who view teaching as a largely routinized, procedural practice.

Student Populations in Large, Urban School Systems

Many urban schools, and even suburban schools on the fringe of large urban areas, have witnessed multiculturalization of their student populations in recent years. Although historically significant strength has been

---

[2] Although secondary teachers are required to be more expert in their subjects, most history teachers have not taken courses on the practice of history; therefore they, like their elementary counterparts, lack an understanding of the procedural and strategic knowledge components of the discipline.

found in this kind of diversity, recently it has meant a return to increases in all types of educational challenges for students in these large public school districts. In many places it is an issue of sheer density. Without reductions in class size or workload, teachers are pressed to attend to large numbers of children who are recent immigrants, who are poor, and who speak very little if any English, as well as children receiving a variety of special education services (Taylor, 1991). The growing poverty of some urban schools, where cities have been abandoned by wealthier families and businesses who take tax support with them when they depart, has brought with it significant challenges (e.g., Fordham, 1996; Kozol, 1992). The demands such schooling scenarios present increase the pedagogical dilemmas history teachers must manage.

Perhaps just as important are the challenges that arise from questions about whose history should be taught in these urban school settings. Should we teach the "common culture" heritage myths as a means of "Americanizing" the diverse immigrant students as some would contend, or the more diversified and multiculturalized heritage myths that have been argued by others as connecting more powerfully with the different backgrounds of the children being taught? In Oakland, California, where Whites are in the minority, middle school history teacher Steven Weinberg described the issue this way: "It's very hard to do this right. What makes sense to a student from Cambodia? I have a boy from Ethiopia in my class. We have people from South America. It constantly forces me to rethink, because I don't want simply to teach what I was taught. [For example,] I spent a lot of time trying to teach the Alamo accurately. The traditional view minimizes slavery in Texas" (quoted in Gitlin, 1995, p. 25). The time spent on such battles over *what* history to teach in large urban schools frequently obscures the approach that inverts the "what history/how to do it" relationship. This inversion promotes learning history through an emphasis on *historical investigation,* as advocated by Lowenthal (1998) and others (e.g., Holt, 1990; Kammen, 1997). For the teachers I have talked to who are more inclined to pursue learning history by foregrounding this investigative path, their difficulties attending to it have intensified because the conversation about what to teach diverts attention away from considering investigation's pedagogical and curricular viability.

THE CHALLENGE OF HISTORY EDUCATION REFORM

The challenges mitigating against systematically investigating history with schoolchildren seem almost insurmountable. However, there is cause for optimism if your goal is to practice history in the classroom. Despite many obstacles, a host of history education reform recommendations exist that point the entire enterprise toward teaching history in the sense Lowenthal (1998) describes it, and away from the standard heritage approaches found in many classrooms and in the voluminous textbooks written for children. There are at least three areas in which the literature on history education reform indicates support for teaching children how to investigate the past and practice history: (1) the empirical research studies whose results seriously question the assumption that children cannot do history; (2) the research work on what happens when children study the past as though it were a grocery list of dates, events, and people to be committed to memory; and (3) the appearance of curriculum and achievement standards that raise the bar for learning history. I consider each of these in turn.

Children *Can* Do History If You Show Them How

The assumption that, say, 10- and 11-year-olds cannot think historically and practice history because they lack the necessary intellectual ability has been challenged repeatedly in recent research studies. These studies—based on interviews with children, their performances on tasks that ask them to do history instead of simply recall it, and observations of them in classroom contexts—suggest that American youngsters are being shortchanged by this assumption.

In one study, six fifth-graders, who had no discernible experience being taught to investigate history, were given two documents that dealt with accounts of the Boston "Massacre" (VanSledright & Kelly, 1998). Both were secondary sources. One account contained invented dialogue. The other included actual eyewitness testimony. The first account was a rather terse summary of events that ended with a simple moral injunction against both sides, claiming that the Boston citizens and the British soldiers were clearly wrong for doing what they did. The other account painted a much more complex picture, showing how local tensions had escalated during the several days preceding the shootings and implying that there was some inevitability to what occurred given that escalation. This second account contained no moral judgments. The six fifth-graders read and thought about the texts out loud as a way of gauging the degree to which they could analyze the tragedy historically, construct an interpretation of events, and judge the status and reliability of the two sources.

Having not been taught to think analytically about such pieces of historical evidence, the students showed only some inclination to cross-examine the documents and intertextually judge their reliability. However, several students noted in a retrospective interview that they favored the second source because the eyewitness testimony in particular broad-

ened their understanding of the event, as well as cued them to the different political perspectives the opposing sides had on what was happening
to and around them. The authors of the study concluded that even young
students such as these fifth-graders appeared to understand the importance
of perspective in considering past events, as well as to demonstrate some
nascent capacity to judge the validity and reliability of sources, all despite
not having been taught to do this explicitly. They recommended that students be given more opportunities to practice historical investigation themselves as a way of building their historical thinking capabilities and enhancing their understanding of both the past and the nature of history as
subject matter and academic discipline.

In a related study, Barton (1997) spent a year observing in a fourth-
grade and a fifth-grade classroom and exploring, among other things, how
these students dealt with historical evidence as they learned about Kentucky
state history and U.S. history. He concluded that the students demonstrated
some significant strengths in understanding the reliability of sources but also
displayed a reluctance to use the evidence to draw conclusions about the
past. He noted that students often were able to critically assess the evidence
they examined but seldom did so spontaneously, needing to be prompted
in interview settings to do so. As in the preceding study, Barton observed
that the students had little practice drawing conclusions based on evidence,
which may have accounted for their reluctance. He concluded that his data
demonstrated that the fourth- and fifth-graders appeared to be ready to
handle historical sources as evidence and could, if asked, use it to render
interpretations and draw conclusions. Therefore, he recommended that
history teachers provide students with clear opportunities to wrestle with
historical sources, much as seasoned historical investigators do, and assist
them in clarifying the status of those sources and the types of inferences
and conclusions that could be drawn from them.

In another study, researchers demonstrated in a chronologically ori-
ented picture-sorting task given to children in kindergarten through grade 6
that, although the youngest struggled with the notion of historical dating,
by grade 3 children were beginning to making sense of historical chronology (Levstik & Barton, 1996). Based on their data, the researchers noted
that there was no reason to let history's chronological ordering and
periodization structure interfere with teaching even 7- and 8-year-olds how
to reason historically. They used these results and others deriving from their
extensive research program in history education to write *Doing History: Investigating with Children in Elementary and Middle Schools* (Levstik & Barton,
1997). The book, as the title suggests, champions the idea of practicing history. It contains a wide variety of helpful ideas on how to teach young children to investigate the past, using the cognitive tools experts rely on.

British researchers also have investigated the progression of children's historical thinking in England (e.g., Ashby & Lee, 1987b, 1996; Shemilt, 1980, 1987). Students there get a variety of opportunities to investigate history much earlier in school than their American counterparts, largely because of fundamental differences in how their respective history curricula are structured. As a result, these studies document that children in Great Britain tend to be more astute at investigating the past using staples of historical thinking at earlier ages. Extrapolating from these studies of progression in historical thinking among students in England points toward realizing that American children likely would show the same propensities as the British children if they were given investigative opportunities in classrooms with knowledgeable teachers to assist them. In Chapter 6, I say more about extrapolating from this British research to children in the United States and about important cautions required in doing so.

The Futility of Teaching History as a Grocery List

The research work on historical cognition has been spurred in part by the rather dismal results students attain on tests that measure their knowledge of historical details and events; that is, their ability to recall history's grocery list. Authors such as Ravitch and Finn (1987) repeatedly bemoan the fact that American students are egregiously remiss in being able to recall their nation's history. In an attempt to understand how children, adults, and experts think about history as a means of further understanding why they sometimes do not recall details very well, studies indicate that making sense of the past requires thought that is only partially based on recall. In fact, historians who were not expert in the particular historical period they were asked to examine still made good sense out of documents and evidence in front of them because they knew *how to think historically* in the ways I described earlier. Even without much background knowledge to recall and draw on in sorting out details about the period in question, these historians were not significantly hampered in their efforts to piece together a fairly sophisticated understanding of events (see Wineburg, 1998). It turns out that being able to think historically and practice doing history is more crucial to making sense of the past than having memorized a grocery list of historical details.

Understanding historical events demands the construction of explanatory contextualized interpretations that can be used as arbiters in judging historical sources. A grocery list may be helpful and perhaps necessary, but it is insufficient. Without a road map, so to speak, constructed via deliberate cognitive steps through evidentiary sources as a means of making all the details cohere, you end up where a frustrated eighth-grader once said he was: "I just don't remember—the [historical] ideas are all jumbled in my head" (VanSledright, 1995). These cognitive steps involve investigating the past and practicing deliberative acts of historical thinking. The studies conclude on this note: If it works for the experts, we should be giving children the same opportunities, assuming that we are interested in having them *understand* history as a subject matter (see also Brophy & VanSledright, 1997; Stahl et al., 1996). This line of research has helped us see why children (and, as some have noted, adults also) often do poorly when they are asked to read a history textbook, commit its "one damn thing after another" to memory, and then replay it all on the test. As such, the studies offer a prima facie challenge to those who would make history merely the study of someone else's heritage.

In a related vein, a recent line of research on how students make judgments about historically significant events and persons demonstrates that Black and White students in U.S. schools, for example, form quite different perspectives on what is important in the past (Epstein, 1998, 2000). White students often pushed traditional White heritage heroes to the top of the list (e.g., Washington, Lincoln). Black students, stating how mindful they were of a legacy of repression suffered at the hands of such heroes, elevated people such as Dr. Martin Luther King to the top of their lists of those most important. One can conclude from these studies that, despite curricular and accountability efforts to homogenize students' understanding by teaching them Anglo American heritage myths and heroes, students still construct their own interpretations based on what they perceive to be "their own heritage." How a student interprets the past appears dependent on identity factors such as class, race, ethnicity, and gender. Moral proclamations about the importance of teaching the grocery list of "our" civilization's "common cultural" heritage and about the triumphs of its heroes seem particularly naive in the light of such work. These studies also may explain why some students, who do not buy into the traditional "common culture" heritage myths, do poorly on history tests that measure their recall of them. It turns out that repeatedly overfilling the gas tank simply will not make a car with worn-out brakes stop any better. Repairs must address the source of the problem.

National Standards

History education curriculum reform groups have also weighed in on what studying history in the classroom ought to look like. For instance, the *National Standards for United States History* include a detailed section on historical thinking and analysis that appears to take its cue from the empirical research on historical thinking and understanding.

The *Standards* (National Center for History in the Schools [NCHS], 1994) were designed to revolutionize the teaching and learning of U.S. history, said co-director of the Center and co-author Gary Nash at one point. Chapter 2 of the document (pp. 17–34) is entirely devoted to historical thinking. Standard 3—Historical Analysis and Interpretation—opens by commenting on the problems associated with the typical approach to teaching history of having students seek "one right answer" found in the history textbook. The *Standards* note:

> These problems are deeply rooted in the conventional ways in which textbooks have presented history: a succession of facts marching straight to a settled outcome. To overcome these problems requires the use of more than one source: of history books other than textbooks and a rich variety of historical documents and artifacts that present alternative voices, accounts, and interpretations or perspectives on the past. [The study of history] requires following and evaluating arguments and arriving at useable, even if tentative, conclusions based on the available evidence. (p. 26)

Much of the emphasis in Chapter 2 of the *Standards* (and in the document as a whole) is placed on being able to do history, much as is done by historians themselves. The section on historical analysis and interpretation lays out 10 substandards (see p. 27) that ask students to be able to do such things as sift evidence, analyze and interpret primary and secondary sources, do research, question authors' and texts' assertions, make decisions and applications based on analyses of evidence, and construct arguments. Historical knowledge—the ostensible facts—is given somewhat lower-order status and pressed into the service of historical thinking, analysis, and interpretation. The individual content standards (a 212-page Chapter 3) are replete with historical-thinking language in what they would require of students. The world history standards, also authored at the Center, read much the way as the United States history standards do, only the content examples are obviously broader.

As a practice-based follow-up to the *National Standards for United States History*, the Center produced a volume entitled *Bring History Alive! A Sourcebook for Teaching United States History* (Ankeney, Del Rio, Nash, & Vigilante, 1996). It opens by borrowing language and intent from the *Standards*. It then reiterates the importance of emphasizing the development of historical thinking in learners and provides four brief essays that focus on topics such as engaging students in inquiry experiences, using primary sources, constructing historical arguments, and doing book reviews as historians frequently do. The remaining portion of the volume is devoted to practical advice about investigating history in the classroom using a variety of sources and research-based thinking strategies arranged by common periodization eras. The book also contains a storehouse of references—organized around the eras—to primary source material packets developed by the Center.

COMPETING CHALLENGES

By now it should be clear that the terrain on which people argue about what history ought to look like in grade school classrooms is much contested. Lined up on one side are those who continue to see history as a repository of "true" heritage mythologies—what historian Michael Kammen (1991) once called stabilized history—that children should be committing to memory. This is, in the case of the United States as a nation, *the* quintessential story of "our" history. It is largely the Anglocentric political, economic, and military *heritage* children should acquire if they are to enter ranks of educated American citizens, or so the argument goes (e.g., Bennett, 1994). The standard history textbook serves as the central vehicle by which this stabilized story is transmitted. And besides, proponents of this approach maintain, children simply are not yet intellectually equipped to handle the intricacies and machinations involved in investigating the past themselves, even if they wanted to. Here, the sociocultural and political use of history—that is, "our" common heritage—holds sway, underwritten and rationalized by a deficit model of children's capacity to learn a subject matter and a typical public perception that history and heritage are indistinguishable. Here the challenge is about controlling what is taught in history classes, largely in service of politically inspired and partisan accountability models applied to schools that are frequently supported by pitched rhetoric about higher achievement standards.

On another side are a group of educational reformers and researchers (and likely a number of ambitious history teachers) who draw heavily from a growing body of studies on children's and adults' understandings of history, the ways they make sense of it, and their capacity to engage in historical investigation. They claim (1) that this empirical research repeatedly calls into question the notion that children are not intellectually ready to investigate history themselves; (2) that the teaching of whoever's heritage demonstrates partisanship, is excessive and breeds fractiousness along political lines, teaches little about history, and must be construed as largely distinct from history; and (3) that the research studies systematically account for why students often do so poorly on tests that ask them to do little more than recall mythologies, only some of which they trust. Proponents then offer a more efficacious replacement model for learning the subject. These educational reformers and researchers argue that if we are interested in actually having students understand history, we have to begin early, inviting them to practice it themselves with all its learning, teaching, and subject-matter challenges intact. They also insist by implication that the mere capacity to recall a bag full of historical details is a lower-status form of knowledge compared to being able to reason with and argue from a deep understanding of history as a subject matter. Pressing on the former to the exclusion of the latter sells children short. The challenge engaged by this group is to tackle the obstacles that limit children's learning opportunities in history classrooms.

The history education reformers and researchers face an uphill battle. Those who seek to control the curriculum, keeping history essentially the study of "our" heritage found in textbooks, are supported by the weight of a long tradition in public schools, as the *Standards* authors allude and as historians Tyack and Tobin (1994) note. In many places this tradition is currently buoyed by the rush to implement cheap standardized tests that drive the school accountability movement. For reformers and researchers, this situation is exacerbated by the general absence of empirical research studies that systematically document how young children can be taught to practice history, how they might deal with such historical investigations in actual classroom contexts, and what they actually learn as a result.

I have no doubt that there are a number of ambitious history teachers who teach their students how to investigate the past, how to read and evaluate primary and secondary sources, make interpretations, and build historical arguments for themselves. I also have no doubt that these teachers have learned of the compelling benefits such teaching practices provide their students. What I am maintaining is that we have few design experiments (Brown, 1992) in the research literature that take the history reform recommendations seriously and attempt to demonstrate the educational efficacy, robustness, and possible limitations of systematically teaching young children to investigate history, particularly American history. The closest that we have come is an intriguing study by Wilson (1990), who taught third-graders about Michigan history. However, her efforts focused as much, perhaps more so, on geographical thinking and spatial investigation as they did on historical thinking and practicing history. We also have an anecdotal account of teaching youngsters to use primary source documents (Edinger, 2000) and an impressionistic view of investigating history in the secondary classroom (Kobrin, 1992). It is in this apparent void and amid the challenges I have noted that I conceptualized the project I describe in the chapters that follow.

2

Conducting Historical
Investigations with Fifth-Graders

On a sunny but cold January morning in 1999, I stood in front of a group of 23 fifth-graders, some of whom were rather lively and certainly chatty. This was classroom 23 of a large elementary school in a very large school district in a Mid-Atlantic state. The school district abutted a large city, but in many ways that urban core had spread its sociocultural net beyond its political and geographic boundaries to encompass this school. The children in front of me represented a racial and ethnic rainbow. Standing at the front and taking a quick count, I could not discern the existence of a racial or ethnic majority. Many of the students qualified for the free- or reduced-cost-lunch program. A couple of them spoke only rough versions of English, and one student was a recent immigrant from Peru. Her native language was Spanish, and she was still struggling mightily as an English reader. One boy was physically much larger than any of his classmates. It turned out that he had been held back two grades. Another, much smaller, boy had recently been placed on Ritalin. His body had not yet adjusted to the medication, so he often looked barely awake. I was there to teach all of them American history. They were smiling at me and I caught myself smiling back at them, despite remembering the words of one of my former teacher educators: "Don't grin until January—period!" Well, it was January, I thought.

This was a new experience for me. I had taught middle and high school American and world history in departmentalized arrangements in Colorado and Michigan, but never fifth grade. The students wanted to know who I was. They were fairly certain I was not a student intern from the local university, many of whom had taught these students in previous years. But they were asking to be sure. I told them that I was a teacher at that local university that was responsible for educating new teachers. I was not an intern, I assured them. Rather, I was the teacher who taught the teacher interns who had taught them, and now, because I was interested in doing so, I was there to teach them American history. I pointed out that I had been a school history teacher before but that I went back to graduate school, earned a Ph.D., and became a university-based teacher educa-tor and researcher with a deep interest in understanding how children learned history and what teachers did to teach it well. I explained that I had spent the better part of the preceding 9 years doing research in his-tory classrooms, observing and talking with history teachers, interview-ing students—many of them their age—about what they were learning (or not), and writing articles about it for research journals.

The more I talked, the more restless and itchy they became. It turned out what they really wanted to know was *why* I was there to teach *them* American history. Brittney blurted this out as I paused between sentences. Other children's heads nodded, approving the question. Several said, "Yeah, why?" This I thought was a wonderful question, but one I was not fully prepared to address at that point, primarily because, as with much about teaching, I was not expecting it. I thought for a moment and then observed that I was there to put my money where my mouth was, so to speak. They looked on, quizzically. Sensing that they wanted more, I ex-plained that, in articles I had written, I had made a number of statements about how I thought history should be taught to young kids like them. I was there to test those ideas. They were my guinea pigs. I am not sure they knew quite what to think of that prospect, but being excited fifth-graders, eager for new experiences (at least ones that did not hurt too much), they welcomed me. Just like that, the honeymoon—if you can call it that—was over; the hard work began.

In this brief recounting of my introduction to the fifth-graders in room 23, I believe I make my allegiances quite clear. My stake in this effort to explore the teaching and learning of history is tied to those who would change the experience, to align it more closely with the practice of investi-gating history with children. For my part, I was (and still am) convinced that children as young as fourth and fifth grade—perhaps even younger—can learn how to investigate the past themselves and benefit from the higher-status substantive and procedural knowledge such a practice can confer upon children. However, as I noted in the last chapter, the literature is largely devoid of design experiments (Brown, 1992) that systematically study the teaching of historical thinking and investigation and what children learn (and do not learn) as a result. I was in room 23 to conduct one such study. In several ways, it was a litmus test of my own research-based recommen-dations and, to the extent that mine were linked to reform documents such as the *Standards for United States History* (NCHS, 1994) (hereafter either *Stan-dards* or National History Standards), a litmus test of them also.

At the moment I explained that I was putting my money where my mouth was, the daunting nature of the responsibility I was assuming fi-nally dawned on me. Not only was I going to be their history teacher for the next several months, but I was also going to be testing my own theory of how I thought children should learn history. Was it an adequate theory? Would it fail me in this sort of classroom with students this young? Partially fail? Fully collapse? I experienced a momentary flash of abject fear, much akin to what inexperienced intern teachers must face when they take over the class for the first time. It helped me appreciate again what they go through. However, what perhaps distinguished me from those green interns was having this rather well-honed "small-*t*" theory of historical thinking and learning I had developed over 13 years of teaching middle and high school students, and then having an opportunity to further refine it as a history education researcher for 9 years. The theory should be quickly recognizable, embedded as it is in the research literature and reform recommendations discussed earlier.

A THEORY OF HISTORICAL THINKING AND LEARNING

Subject Matter and Practice-Based Origins

By theory, I am referring to a set of pedagogical understandings about the relationship among teaching, learning, and the subject matter of history. This is a theory about how those three pieces fit together in a classroom context in what Shulman (1987) calls pedagogical content knowledge. Born largely out of teaching practice in combination with a level of disciplinary wisdom, this knowledge is a cluster of ideas a teacher holds about how to make a particular form of learning occur for students. It is not a grandiose capital-*T* theory such as quantum mechanics. Teachers possess many small-*t* theories about their teaching practices. For whatever reasons, perhaps the least of which is that they are seldom asked, teachers simply do not articulate them very often. In this study, I wanted to be as clear as I could about my theory of historical thinking and its origins, largely because my research design was intentionally putting it to the test.

As a history teacher, I was frequently uncomfortable with the idea that history was something that could be packaged in a fat textbook and insinuated into the heads of my students, falling as it seemed from the sky in official, reified form and descending mysteriously through my charges' skull bones and into their cranial matter, form intact. My undergraduate degree in American history had taught me to be wary of singular accounts of the past, the so-called 1950s consensus interpretations of political, economic, and military America. My undergraduate subject-matter preparation involved reading and debating a variety of interpretations of the colonial period, the American Revolution, abolitionism, slavery, Reconstruction, and the like. My history professors instilled in me a profound respect for the thoroughly interpretive nature of historical scholarship. One professor was fond of summoning up and paraphrasing Voltaire and Nietzsche, noting that history is like a package of tricks the living play on the dead. Several of my history professors also remarked how each generation was wont to write its own history and that revisionism could be seen as historical scholarship's lifeblood.

As I began my career as a history teacher, I found myself trying to assign readings that included everything but the textbook. I drew on the scholarship I had consumed as a college student. I augmented with primary sources as frequently as I could (which was not as often as I would have liked). Mirroring some of the actions of my history professors, I tried to stir discussion and debate by purposefully giving my students competing interpretations of events. I steered away from those areas where there was considerable agreement in the field and toward those periods in American history about which historians tend to disagree regarding what happened because the evidence trails are thin and inconclusive and sources frequently conflict (see Davidson & Lytle, 1992). The more raucous the disagreements, the better. This was where I could find the best competing source material. Over time, I built up a considerable storehouse of both primary and secondary sources. As this collection grew, my use of the school-sanctioned textbook shrank to the point where my students almost never cracked the cover.

This approach met with some success, but my students—both in middle and high school—often resisted my efforts. They had "done school" long enough to be suspicious of teachers who suggested that there were multiple possible answers to questions they asked (and sometimes no conclusive answers at all). They were accustomed to hearing the multiple-answers bit, but being met instead with multiple-choice questions where only one answer counted. I tried to avoid those kinds of questions, relying more heavily on essay formats in which I asked students to take a position on a historical event we had debated in class and support their position by drawing on what we had read. Part of what sent me to graduate school was the creeping feeling that what I was doing was somehow "incorrect" pedagogically. Some of this was the result of my students' resistance and some of this came in the wake of feeling perpetually guilty for not using that expensive textbook much. A smaller part of it, but a pressing one nonetheless, revolved around the fatigue that followed my struggle to get my students to write well-supported essays and the sheer weight of grading them all year after year. I imagined that graduate school would either help me rationalize my approach and teach me how to do it more effectively (and, with luck, efficiently) or disparage what I was doing and point me toward a more pedagogically sound method. It did neither. However, it did help me clarify my fledgling theory of how I was attempting to bring together teaching practice, a view of historical subject matter, and an understanding of student learning in my classroom.

Refining the Theory Through Research

In many ways, although I only dimly knew it initially, the research agenda I undertook in graduate school and took along into my university position was designed to teach me about what I had been doing as a history teacher. Despite spending 9 years in other teachers' classrooms, researching their teaching practices and exploring what their students were learning, this process did more for me in regard to sharpening and refining my theory of historical thinking than I suspect it ever did for the participants in my studies (on this point, see Wolcott, 1995). I am greatly indebted to those teachers and students for having granted me that opportunity. It, along with the extensive reading graduate study affords, pushed me to clarify how I was thinking about what I had been doing.

At the point of beginning this fifth-grade classroom study—20-plus years after I first began teaching history—the theory of historical thinking that guided my practice looked something like the following. Children learning history develop deeper levels of historical understanding when they have opportunities to consciously use their prior knowledge and assumptions, regardless of how limited or naive. The most direct and productive method of revealing and employing prior knowledge is through actual historical investigation. This demands that children learn investigative strategies. Paying attention solely to the products of others' (historians) investigations into the past seldom assists children in acquiring a repertoire of such strategies. They need to practice what Davidson and Lytle (1992) call "the art of historical detection" themselves. To that end, they must be given clear, carefully guided opportunities to:

- Work with various forms of evidence and types of source material
- Deal with issues of interpretation, as contentious as they can often be
- Ask and arbitrate questions about the relative significance of events and the nature of historical agency
- Cultivate and use thoughtful, context-sensitive imagination to fill in gaps in evidence trails when they arise

Children also must learn to construct detailed, evidence-supported arguments about the nature of events being investigated.

Specific strategic-knowledge dispositions necessary for the development of historical understanding include the capacity to:

- Build interpretations of historical events
- Understand the nature of different kinds of sources, their strengths and limitations
- Check and cross-check details and versions of events contained in the sources
- Judge the validity and reliability of sources in order to construct defensible interpretations
- Make sense of an author's position in the account being told (Wineburg, 1991), all while taking into conscious account the way learners are also imposing their own view on these matters as they engage in interpreting the evidence (VanSledright, 2001)

In short, the theory points toward employing investigative practices closely linked to the ones historians use in order to effectively build among students the cognitive capacity to understand what happened in the past.

The design for the study was predicated on the assumption that simply because we lack systematic classroom-based research studies that document this theory in practice with children as young as 10 and 11, there is no reason to believe that they are incapable of learning to think historically as so defined. As I stood in front of those fifth-graders on that January morning, these ideas swirled about in the back of my head. The ideas also helped me more specifically frame my pedagogical goals around the investigative approach that would define classroom activity with respect to historical study into early May. I realized that in some sense I had come full circle: from theory born and tested initially in practice, to theory refined through research and analysis, back to theory tested by practice. Before describing my experiment translating this theory back into the classroom, let me say a little more about the setting in which this all occurred.

SETTING FOR THE STUDY

Kendall Elementary School

Kendall Elementary (identifying names are pseudonyms) is large as elementary schools go; approximately 750 students were in attendance when I was teaching there. And it was growing beyond its capacity, as the portable classrooms on the side of the building bore witness. Two years earlier, almost the entire building had been leveled and then rebuilt in somewhat expanded form. As a result, the building felt completely new. Paint was fresh; the tile floors and lavatory walls sparkled; Internet outlets were available in each classroom. Shiny new Macintosh computers seemed to be everywhere. A trip through the front doors brought you to a large corridor atrium, with light streaming in from three sides.

The school district of which Kendall is a part appeared to take education seriously. School board members and local politicians were relatively quick to spend on education. As the district had become more diversified racially, ethnically, and socioeconomically, pressure had mounted to attend more diligently to students with special needs, creating tension along racial and ethnic lines in recent years. As I noted in Chapter 1, Kendall had many students with unique needs, given the urban-style neighborhoods and low-income housing developments in which they lived. Kendall's student population was about as racially, ethnically, and socioeconomically heterogeneous as it could possibly be. Principally for that reason, the prospect of teaching American history to fifth-graders there held great fascination and intrigue for me. Would my theory of historical thinking and the investigative approach designed to enhance it work with students as diverse as these? How would my approach need to be tailored to meet the potentially wide range of differences I was likely to encounter?

Room 23

Room 23 was like most of the other classrooms in the building. It was large and amply supplied. Books filled a large set of shelves below broad windows along one entire side of the room. The standard chalkboard covered the front wall and whiteboard covered the back. Desks were standard fare, easy to move about into clusters so that students could work together as necessary. Two sets of storage cabinets were lined with a host of common teaching supplies. A computer sat in one corner. It was connected to the Internet and by s-video link to a large, ceiling-mounted monitor that also housed a VCR. Overall, it was a warm, bright, cheerful room that seemed to say, "Come in and learn here because that's what goes on in this place."

The Teacher and Her Students

The class's teacher, Ms. Proctor, was an African American female who had been teaching for almost 20 years, most of them in this school. I had known her for 7 years prior to the study. She had mentored a number of the teacher interns placed at Kendall for their practicum experiences. We had worked together along with other teachers at Kendall to shape it into a Professional Development School site. She was a superb teacher and a superior mentor for the university students interning in her classroom. By virtue of her longevity at Kendall and her excellent teaching reputation, she also was seen as a leader in the school. What most distinguished her was the passion she demonstrated toward learning. Her approach to her students, the interns in her room, my presence and work with her, and her dealings with fellow teachers and administrators was characterized by an undying devotion to learning more about what it means to teach. When I approached Proctor about the study and described the details, she welcomed me and the idea warmly. She indicated that her curiosity about the project was rather selfish: She might get an opportunity to learn something interesting about historical study by watching me teach. I demured, noting that I thought I would be struggling some of the time and needing to draw heavily on her classroom and pedagogical expertise, especially with regard to knowing students. I thought that her openness to having me present and her desire to learn from me while I learned from her would make for a good match. She also believed so.

This class of 23 fifth-graders in room 23 was one of four fifth-grade classes at Kendall. It was the smallest of the four, primarily because Proctor elected to take a larger number of the students with learning difficulties and behavioral issues. The deal she struck entailed a smaller class size in exchange for a higher number of individual student challenges. Two of the other three teachers were novices and untenured, still learning many of the rudiments of teaching. The third of the three was a more seasoned veteran, but she had just that year moved to fifth grade from second grade and had very little experience with older students.

Of the 23 students, 7 were African American, 7 were European American, 6 were Hispanic, and 3 were Asian American; 12 were girls and 11 were boys. This distribution virtually mirrored the population at Kendall, where approximately 30% of the students were African American, 30% were White, and 30% were Hispanic. The remainder were mostly Asian American; however, a small but growing percentage were recent immigrants from countries all over the world. Approximately 40% of the students at Kendall qualified for the free- or reduced-cost-lunch program. It was approximately the same percentage in room 23.

Eight Primary Informants

All 23 students served as sources for studying the influence of my investigative approach and theory of historical thinking. However, to acquire a more in-depth understanding of what was occurring in the classroom and how students were affected by what I did, Proctor and I identified eight students who would act as primary informants. Several criteria were employed in selecting these eight:

1. The students should represent a gender mix; thus four should be boys and four, girls.
2. They should be representative of the racial and ethnic diversity within the class.
3. Because historical study is so text-based, two should read somewhat above grade level, four roughly on grade level, and two somewhat below grade level, as determined by district criterion-referenced reading tests.

These eight included Alexandra, a European American female from an upper-middle socioeconomic-class (SEC) background, whom we heard from in Chapter 1; Ben, a Latino from a working-SEC background; Candy, a bilingual Latina from a working-SEC background who had recently immigrated from Peru and whose native language was Spanish; Coral, an African American male from a working-SEC background; Jamie, a European American male from a middle-SEC background; Jeffrey, an African American male from a middle-SEC background; Kendra, an African-American female from a middle-SEC background; and Tho, a bilingual Asian American female from a middle-SEC background, whose first language was Vietnamese.

Alexandra was a very good reader, as defined by the high scores she received on the criterion-referenced standardized reading tests. She studied very diligently, was often overprepared for class, and seemed to suffer a mild case of overachiever's anxiety. She was polite and gracious in class and in interview sessions, and incisive and precise in response to questions and classroom tasks.

Ben was one of the most curious fifth-graders I have ever met. He was fascinated by the opportunities he had to explore primary sources and investigate the questions that were posed to such events as the Jamestown Starving Time in 1609–1610 and the Boston "Massacre." His reading test scores pegged him as an average reader, reading on grade level or just a bit above.

Candy was a warm, cheerful, energetic student who worked exhaustively to learn to read English effectively. Her oral English was broken but reasonably understandable. She participated regularly in class but needed some assistance whenever activities called for reading text. Her reading scores, as one might expect for an English-as-a-second-language reader, were quite low, but she was undaunted by this in her desire to learn in general and learn history in particular.

Coral was a very bright but quiet student. He was thoughtful and articulate but seldom spoke unless he was sure of his position. Then he would argue it forcefully but undemonstratively. His reading test scores were high, placing him considerably above grade level. His father had died in a car accident about a year before the study took place. Proctor attributed some of his quietness to his attempts to deal with that loss.

Jamie was a good-natured student, frequently sporting a smile. He was occasionally witty and sarcastic, but in a jovial way. His reading test scores were at the mode for the criterion-referenced system, placing him on grade level for the district.

In many ways, Jeffrey was Coral's alter ego. He was exceptionally vocal, opinionated, bright, and highly articulate. He also was judgmental, frequently staking out positions before he had mustered enough information to support them consistently. He loved to argue with his classmates, sometimes me, and occasionally Proctor. His confrontations with Proctor seldom resulted in his winning his case. This would put him in a somewhat sullen mood for an hour or so. He was reading on grade level, according to his reading test scores. He was interesting to have in class because you could always count on him to spur discussion. However, his style always threatened to overwhelm things.

Kendra was the other struggling reader in the group of eight. She was quiet in class, but joyful and interested in what was going on. Although she said little, she always worked hard to understand discussions and activities. However, she was easily discouraged and needed considerable individual attention in completing tasks and working through the many texts we read in class.

Tho was on grade level as a reader, despite her first language being Vietnamese. She was very quiet most of the time. Yet she was highly curious and seldom hesitated to ask questions when she needed assistance understanding a text or an activity. When she had questions, she was usually direct, to the point, incisive, and economical in her word use.

Before the study began, these eight were interviewed initially for approximately 30 minutes each, one by one in a quiet room away from the classroom. The interview questions were designed to obtain detailed demographic information about the students (e.g., age, birth date, parents' occupations), their ideas about history and what historians do, and their general thoughts about the subject. At a second interview session that followed the first by a day or two, these eight also engaged in a complex initial performance task in which they read two accounts of the shootings in Boston in

March of 1770 and examined three artists' depictions of the event. The students thought aloud as they read the documents and examined the images. Because they were novices at this type of task, before beginning they engaged in a practice exercise in which they read a small portion of history text and were coached in the activity of speaking out loud about what they were thinking as they read. Following the completion of the task, they were interviewed in more detail about the experience.

At the conclusion of the study, a second performance task was undertaken by the eight. At that point, the students read the four documents related to the battle at Lexington Green in 1775 and analyzed the two accompanying images I described in Chapter 1. The same think-aloud procedures were employed, as well as a similar postreading interview session. A final interview also was conducted that mirrored aspects of the initial interview with regard to students' views about history. My research assistant, Elizabeth Fasulo, and I conducted all the interviews and performance task think-aloud protocols, engaging four students a piece, one by one, in each of the initial and endpoint experiences. We met at length before each session to coordinate our understandings and practice how the tasks would be administered and interviews conducted.

These tasks and interviews were designed primarily to provide me with key information and data about the influence of the investigative approach I employed on the eight's capacity to learn to think historically as described by the theory of historical thinking underlying my pedagogical choices and practices. I describe the data collection methods and the procedures I used to analyze this data in more detail in Chapter 6 and Appendix A. I discuss the results of student experiences on the performance tasks and the changes from the initial to endpoint versions in Chapter 6.

The Other 15 Students

The class's remaining fifth-grade girls were Anika and Brittney, both African Americans and virtually inseparable friends; Chelsea, who was White (western European descent); Cindy, a Latina who was extraordinarily shy; Grecia, a Latina; Jessica, who was Asian American; Katie, who was White (parents were from Russia); and Vanessa, who was White (western European descent). The boys included Alex, who was White (eastern European descent); Anthony, who was a Latino; Javell, an African American who had been in a variety of schools in different parts of the world because his mother worked for the Foreign Service; Jonathon, an Asian American who was Jessica's cousin; Kedwin, a very quiet Latino whose parents had been born in Puerto Rico; Tim, who was White (western European descent); and Wayne, who was African American.

The Social Studies Curriculum

Like most social studies curricula based on the expanding communities model in the United States, fifth grade in this school district was reserved for giving students their first systematic, chronological exposure to American history. The treatment was designed in the standard survey sequence. Typical historical periodizations were used. Students would begin by studying Native Americans, move to the encounter with European countries, and then look more closely at English colonialism in North America. Following the colonization period, students would study about events surrounding the American Revolution and the Constitutional Period, briefly consider early 19th-century "Westward Expansion," and then finish the year by focusing on abolitionism and slavery. Teachers in the district reported that the latter topic often received short shrift due to time pressures, broad content coverage demands for such a survey course, and competition from other subjects, particularly mathematics and reading.

The units that became my charge were English colonization along the Atlantic seaboard, the American Revolution period, and "Westward Expansion." Because of the time it took to teach these novice students how to investigate the past in a manner that did some intellectual justice to my theory of historical thinking, I was able to deal only with the first two units. In early May, students began preparing for week-long state standardized tests that were followed by the school district's criterion-referenced testing program. Almost all regular attention to specified curriculum came to a halt in order to prepare for and take the tests. Only some mathematics and reading lessons were taught. In consultation with Proctor, we decided to end my ongoing, daily participation with the introduction of these tests. However, I did return a number of times after that to take care of loose ends, conclude a lesson and a discussion that had been postponed because of the standardized testing period, and collect data from my eight principal informants. The class also threw me a party, where we exchanged mutual expressions of gratitude for opportunities offered and accepted during the preceding 4 months.

3

History as an Interpretive Act: The Problem of Indeterminate Evidence Trails

Before describing our plunge through thin ice into the deep and some-times chilly waters of historical interpretation and the vicissitudes of deal-ing with the tensions that arise there, I want to reset the stage by return-ing briefly to the passage from historian Joan Wallach Scott that I quoted in Chapter 1. Here I add a bit more of what she had to say about the dif-ficult nature of doing history because of the deep interpretive stresses that follow its practice. I am particularly interested in her request that we be open about its tensions and stresses, because of what they portend for in-vestigating history in the classroom.

In a lengthy paper delivered at a conference in 1996 on "History and the Limits of Interpretation," Scott noted that history operates through an inextricable connection between reality and interpretation that in the end is denied, observing that the tension which arises from this denial is noth-ing new. Historians, she claims, have known about it for some time. She then states that the tension "inheres in the practice of history itself." She adds, "And I want to argue that there is no alternative to mentioning the tension—even in the face of severe political criticism. In fact acknowledg-ing it and working with it is a better strategy than denying its existence" (Scott, 1996, p. 1). In what follows, I frequently refer to the required-but-denied connection between reality and interpretation as history's "interpretive paradox."

Recent critiques of knowledge production in history have directed attention to this paradox by calling into question the ways in which the historical community has agreed to manage it. In response to these cri-tiques, some historians have appealed to a time-honored community norm in which an interpretation is understood as acceptable as long as it corre-sponds to the reality it purports to represent by sticking as close as pos-sible to the evidence at hand. Interpretive license is thus presumably controlled. However, because history operates on the powerful connection between reality and interpretation that is nonetheless denied, critics have stressed this denial by raising serious questions about the assumption that the two are completely "separable entities" (Scott, 1996, p. 1). If one gives up on the assumption of this separateness, as some critics of historical knowledge production I mentioned in Chapter 1 have done, the tension is magnified. The boundary between accepted interpretive practice and excessive interpretive license becomes strikingly fuzzy. Historical data no longer appear to "speak for themselves." Historian Robert Rosenstone once illustrated the blurred boundaries this way: "History is not a collection of details. It is an argument about what the details mean. The moment you start connecting facts into a meaningful story, you are indulging in certain forms of fiction" (quoted in Masur, 1999, p. 4). Onto this thin ice we skated in our initial lessons.

DEALING WITH INDETERMINATE EVIDENCE TRAILS IN ROOM 23

Making Sense of the Jamestown Starving Time, Winter, 1609–1610

One of the keys that I noted to learning to think historically called for in the research literature, implied in the *Standards* documents, and embedded in the pedagogical theory I was working from is understanding the nature of historical evidence. However, document and artifact trails—those shards and traces of the past left for us to study as we unravel what went before us—are often broken and incomplete, and therefore difficult to interpret. Historical investigators must scour whatever evidence there is and attempt to carefully *reconstruct* the historical context under study by building interpretations. By necessity, then, they must often imaginatively *construct* the missing pieces. Nonetheless, as my foregoing explanations should make clear, the community norm has been that investigators' imaginations are to be circumscribed by the parameters of the historical context and evidence at hand.

Remaining inside the parameters, as I also noted, is no small accomplishment for several reasons worth reviewing again here as a preface to my account of our inaugural investigative voyage. First, as Lowenthal (1985) observed, the past is a foreign country, difficult to penetrate from the position of our late-twentieth-century historical moorings. Reconstructing a sense of the historical context in a period under investigation is fraught with difficulties because it often remains virtually impossible for us "moderns" to get inside the experiences of those "ancients." Second, on any number of occasions the remaining evidence is so sparse and also

so open to interpretation that building adequate interpretations is problematic at best, raising issues about the limits of imaginative license and
the need to employ a form of conjectural logic (see Davis, 1988). And third,
any attempt to construct a history of events operates on a link between a
past reality and interpretations of that reality, an attempt that is simultaneously denied because we have yet to invent the technology to time-travel
to the place we wish to investigate. And even if we could, the past would
still be a foreign country, because we also have yet to invent a way to shed
our "modern" assumptions and sensibilities in order to make sense of others' worlds as they understood them. All of this inheres in the practice of
investigating history, to paraphrase Scott.

An exploration of the mystery of the Jamestown Starving Time offers an interesting opportunity to develop a type of historical thinking and
understanding that brings many of these key issues into sharp relief. The
evidence trail is thin and indeterminate. There has been much debate over
what happened and how to make sense of the available evidence. And
exploring what our forebears left behind provides a powerful opportunity
both to test the limits of the ability of investigators to creatively build an
interpretation from a form of conjectural logic (Davis, 1988), and simultaneously to use but constrain their imaginations to the historical context
and remaining evidence. The investigative approach I sought to employ
also promised to help students understand the subject matter's rule structure and the ways in which practitioners apply it (Bruner, 1960).

However, elementary students are taught early on to covet powerful
allegiances to texts' literal meanings. In the history classroom, students often become beguiled by a referential illusion (Barthes, 1986), the mirage
that "authorless" textbook histories actually demonstrate strict, direct correspondence to what "really happened" in the past, a process that creates
what Barthes (1968) calls the reality effect. Such reading experiences repeatedly reinforce what I will call here a fundamentalist epistemological
stance concerning historical knowledge. Students can seem quite puzzled,
for example, by the notion that investigators might reinterpret history from
time to time, in light of new evidence or different perspectives (see
VanSledright & Kelly, 1998). Their puzzlement about and general denial of
the possibility of revisionism leads them to believe that history stops with
the writing of the definitive textbook. I began teaching under the assumption that, to be successful, I would need to start dislodging this position.

I wanted my fifth-graders to slowly but surely learn to think like historical investigators: unseduced by a text's referential illusion, open to
questions, undaunted by indeterminate evidence trails, conscious of the
need to interpret and reinterpret, knowledgeable about and reasonably
secure in the understanding that exploring history could be a fickle and

temperamental enterprise. Perhaps most importantly, I wanted them to learn that giving up on a fundamentalist epistemology did not mean that "now anything goes." Rather, I wanted them to be able to appeal to the rules of the historical community to help arbitrate disputes about what the evidence tells us, as inconclusive as that still might be.

So, that is where we began. I was hoping that this type of initial learning opportunity would set the stage for the more in-depth investigative experiences that would follow. A close look at the Starving Time appeared to be a good way to begin. However, as with the larger study of the past and also much about teaching practice in general, this road seldom takes you directly to where you intend to go.

Conflicting Interpretations: Worms, Gluttony, Laziness, or . . . ?

By 1609, the Jamestown colony had grown from a handful of English immigrants to almost 500 residents. When spring 1610 arrived, approximately 450 of those Jamestown settlers were dead, most apparently having succumbed to starvation. The event remains a mystery because there appeared to be ample food available, making starvation unlikely. However, starve the settlers did.

To introduce the event, I began by orally reading the first few paragraphs of an account of the Starving Time from Hakim's (1993a) *Making Thirteen Colonies*. As Hakim does, I cast the events as a mystery, still open to interpretation by virtue of the limited amount of evidence from which to draw firm conclusions. Hakim relies heavily on the conjecture that the local Powhatan Indians withheld food and supplies from Jamestown, perhaps laying siege to the stockade for much of the winter of 1609–1610. This deprived the English inhabitants of food stored and found outside the stockade, precipitating the cycle of starvation. But she also notes that investigators are still puzzled about what occurred.

After reading the excerpt, I explained that we were going to try our hand at interpreting the Starving Time, testing Hakim's conjectures and, as necessary, coming up with our own. In short, we were going to become "detectives of history." To this end, I explained a step-by-step process for being what I called "good historical detectives," writing the steps on a large sheet of paper attached to the chalkboard. Figure 3.1 outlines the steps in this process and what I wrote verbatim on the board paper and asked students to copy into their social studies log books for future reference.

Although detectives are typically looking to "solve a case" by identifying *the* suspect, seldom is their work as unambiguous as it may appear in the media. That is, frequently multiple suspects emerge. Serious investigative work thus results when detectives pursue their case against a most

Questions Historical Detectives Ask To Solve the Mysteries of the Past

What happened here? How do I find out?

What evidence will tell me what happened?

DIG UP EVIDENCE

Where does the evidence come from?

How do I know where the evidence comes from?

CHECK SOURCES

How do I decide how trustworthy and reliable a piece of evidence is?

CHECK THE RELIABILITY of the SOURCES

How do I decide how important a piece of evidence is?

JUDGE the IMPORTANCE of EACH PIECE of EVIDENCE

How do I use all the evidence to build an idea in my head about what

happened?

BUILD AN IDEA of WHAT HAPPENED

How do I use the evidence and this idea in my head to make a case for

describing what happened?

MAKE AN ARGUMENT for WHAT HAPPENED

Figure 3.1. Facsimile of the Chalkboard Chart Used for Investigating the Starving Time

likely suspect by carefully interpreting evidence and constructing an argument about why a particular suspect is the perpetrator. In many ways, such work offers a close parallel to what historical investigative work is about—ambiguities, interpretations, arguments, and all. As I will note in Chapter 5, whether each of the 23 students understood what it means to be a "good historical detective" in the same metaphorical sense I did remains an open question. Using the detective metaphor was designed to shift the way students understood the study of history—from simply memorizing other people's facts to investigating, interpreting, and arguing about the situation themselves.

Students appeared intrigued by the prospect of solving the mystery. Using the grouped-desk arrangement in the room (in five clusters of four to five desks), I gave each group a set of additional documents to read and explore (see Appendix C). I described the nature of the documents, noting which were primary and which were secondary sources, explaining why they were considered as such, and then describing how "modern versions" of several of the primary sources also were provided to assist them in translating the Old English the Jamestown settlers had used. Students were asked to study the documents very carefully and follow the steps indicated on the paper attached to the chalkboard, writing out on a piece of notebook paper the last step where they were to make their argument about what they thought had happened based on the documentary evidence in front of them. I told them that, in about 15 minutes, I would ask a member of each group to report its argument. This was followed by momentary shuffling as groups passed out the documents in their groups.

A short period of silence ensued as students read the documents, continuing to rotate them among themselves. After about 10 minutes, a noisy debate began at each table as students discussed the documents and crafted arguments about events. At approximately the 20-minute mark, I interrupted the debates and began calling on group reporters. I laid some groundwork for this part of class by making it clear that once I called on a group speaker, he or she had the floor and I initially would limit counterarguments from other groups.

I began with Table 5, and Chelsea rose to speak for her table. She stated, "Worms ate the food." Several students almost immediately called out, "No way!" Coral, another Table 5 member, added, "We think the food froze or the food had worms." I responded, "One thought for you and then we'll move on. I didn't read anything in the clues [documents] I gave you about worms." Coral replied, "Well, we're just guessing because we don't know."

We then moved on to Table 4. Anika stood to speak for her table.

ANIKA: We think Mr. Percy ate it because he's the one who wrote all the letters. And because he was greedy. (*laughter from the class*.)

DR. VAN: [their nickname for me] What clues do you have to support that he ate the food?

KATIE: Because he wrote the letters.

ANIKA: Because when the people were eating their shoes, they didn't have any food to be eating because Percy had it all.

DR. VAN: You think Captain Percy was greedy and ate the food for himself? He hoarded the food?

GROUP: Yeah.

JEFFREY: (*interjecting from Table 1*) Table 1 thinks that we trust this document [the modern version of John Smith's comments on the Starving Time; see Appendix C, Excerpt 2] (*reading from the document*) " . . . we did not plan well, did not work hard, or have good government."

DR. VAN: (*in response to Jeffrey*) First, I want to say that you need to wait your turn. But now that you've thrown this out there, I want to ask you: So they got lazy and didn't organize themselves and the food was gone and they didn't know what to do to get more food, so they just sat around and starved? (*Table 1 students nod*) Interesting. Group 3? Ben.

BEN: But it could be that they were lazy, or that Percy ate all the food, or maybe they had a war with the Indians . . .

DR. VAN: So which do you think it is? Lazy, or Percy the glutton, or war with the Powhatans?

BEN: Well, one document [the Hakim account] says that the Indians fought them and starved them out and another says that they were lazy [John Smith's account].

DR. VAN: We have conflicting clues. One says the Powhatans were friendly and they brought corn. John Smith said that. He talks about that in one of the documents. Another document said there was an Indian war with the settlers that kept them from getting their food. So which was it?

BEN: We're not sure.

DR. VAN: Last one, Table 2? What's your position?

BRITTNEY: The Native Americans could have been thinking [that] they would get 10 times more food if they took what the settlers had, but maybe the settlers were just lazy . . .

DR. VAN: So what's your argument here—so what do you think happened?

BRITTNEY: (*with feigned bashfulness*) Okay, war.

DR. VAN: So they were starved to death by the Powhatans? Okay.

At this point we had to break for lunch. The following day we picked up where we left off.

"Well, So Maybe Percy Lied . . ."

I began by observing that we had constructed conflicting interpretations about what happened during the Starving Time. I wanted them to revisit the documents and carefully follow the step-by-step process I had laid out for them in the preceding class:

> When you try to solve the mysteries of history, you have to start looking at the evidence, checking the sources: Where does the evidence come from? When was it written? Is it reliable? Did someone make it up? Because, if you use that source for an answer, you might be missing something. You have to check your sources very carefully. What year was it? Was the author there? Did he or she see it go on? If they were there, they might have some idea. If they weren't there, how would they know? After you check your sources, you develop an idea in your head. Then you make an argument. Something like this: We think what happened in the Starving Time was . . . and then you say why and you cite the evidence.

My purpose was to get them to look more closely at the evidence at hand, so that they could point to it specifically in defense of the arguments they were putting forward. I also wanted them to begin assessing the validity, reliability, and significance of that evidence in order to judge one account against another. In effect, I was initiating the process of teaching them rules for interpretation and argumentation practiced in the discipline itself. Given their inexperience with this type of thinking and investigative practice, we had to start from somewhere. The somewhere I chose fit well with my reading of the literature and the reform documents, and fell within the parameters of the theoretical framework underwriting my practice. However, it did not address the interpretive paradox per se.

We revisited the different arguments advanced in the previous class (e.g., worms ate the food or it froze, laziness kept them from foraging for food, the Powhatans waged a campaign to starve out the settlers, or Percy was a glutton and had hoarded and then eaten all the food). I noted that only Jeffrey had held up and quoted from a piece of evidence to support his group's argument. We then talked about how to judge the trustworthiness of different accounts. I worked on making clear the distinction between primary and secondary sources, describing advantages and problems associated with each (see Figure 3.2). I wanted students to argue for the documents and excerpts they thought were most valid and against those they thought were not. Attempting to expose the interpretive machinery of historical practice and explore the need for what historian Davis (1988) calls conjectural logic, I took the opportunity to observe how this same thing happens among historians and those who write history books:

> Some of us have very different ideas. That's what happens. Often those historians who write the books, they disagree, too. They're not sure. Think of Table 5 as a group of historians. They have one idea, one interpretation of what happened. You, Table 4, have another; Table 3 has another, and Table 2 another. We have five different ideas of what happened here. These two groups seem to agree, so we really have four different interpretations of what happened.

Primary source: *A story told or written down (or photographed) by someone who was there.*

Some Possible Problems with Primary Sources

1. Author may not remember all the details
2. Author may see/hear/understand things differently (because of his or her point of view)
3. Author's ideas may be influenced by someone else who was there

Secondary source: *A story by someone who was not there but who read/heard about it from a primary source(s).*

Some Possible Problems with Secondary Sources

1. All of the problems with primary sources, plus . . .
2. Author may change the primary source's details
3. Author may put the story in his or her own words
4. Author may not understand what's going on

Figure 3.2. Facsimile of Chart Used with the Class on Primary and Secondary Sources

I then directed them back to the documents and essentially asked them to repeat the process they had conducted in the preceding class, but to do a more rigorous job of testing the evidence and then presenting what they validated to substantiate their argument.

After about 20 minutes of document study and very lively debate and discussion at each table (e.g., Coral shouted out at one point, "I got it! I got it!"), I called their attention back to the front to hear groups provide their reconstituted arguments. We began again with Table 5 and with Jamie, their new spokesperson.

JAMIE: In Document C-1 [see Appendix C] there's a quote that says George Percy said, "Thanks to God our deadly enemies saved us by bringing us great amounts of corn, fish and meat," and then another guy John Smith said he called the time the Starving Time, and that he gave the people food.

DR. VAN: So you think what?

JAMIE: George Percy ate all the food and was greedy.

CORAL: He took the food from everybody else.

ALEXANDRA: [another Table 5 member] He's talking about one thing, and John Smith's talking about another.

DR. VAN: I have a question. Which of those excerpts is written by John Smith?

JAMIE: "Excerpt 1."

DR. VAN: Actually, number one [Document C-1, Excerpt 1] was not written by John Smith because John Smith was gone.

ALEXANDRA: Oh, so it should be Percy. Overall, the reason we really think is that George Percy was really greedy. Captain Smith called it the Starving Time, but see George Percy said, "Thank God that we got food," but the captain said it was called the Starving Time, so Percy must have kept all the food to himself.

DR. VAN: He forced starvation because he wouldn't share?

ALEXANDRA: He [Smith] said, "What we suffered was too hard to talk about and too hard to believe. But the fault was our own."

DR. VAN: What does that mean, "the fault was our own"?

ALEXANDRA: [quoting Document C-2, Excerpt 2] "We starved because we did not plan well or have good government."

DR. VAN: But it doesn't say that Captain Percy hoarded the food; it says that maybe they were lazy.

JEFFREY: (*motioning wildly with his arms, then forcefully interjecting*) Yes, it said they had enough food to last a year . . .

ALEXANDRA: (*interrupting*) But he says that they got food from the
    Indians. So he must have kept the food to himself.

DR. VAN: Could Excerpt 1 maybe have been written earlier? Maybe
    right about the time John Smith left? And Excerpt 2 was
    written later?

CORAL: That means they would have more than enough food to last
    throughout the winter.

DR. VAN: Well, let's see what Table 4 thinks.

KATIE: We think exactly what they [Table 5] think. It's Percy,
    because he wrote the letter. Right here it says, "Percy's
    Account of the Voyage to Virginia and the Colonies First
    Days." So, maybe Percy lied. Maybe he said that no one's
    getting any food. If someone else would have written it,
    those people would have said, "Everyone's starving except
    Percy." But Percy wrote the letters, so he was just starving
    everyone. In the document it said that more people were
    coming and he probably didn't want to share with everyone
    coming.

DR. VAN: There's no evidence in these documents for this. You're
    speculating, right?

KATIE: Yeah.

DR. VAN: You have to say you're speculating like that, okay?

KATIE: (*insistently*) Okay, but he probably didn't want to share with
    so many people, so he was trying to get rid of the people who
    were already there by starving, and then he wouldn't have to
    share with them.

We then moved on to the other groups. Tables 2 and 3 quickly aligned
themselves with Katie's and Table 5's interpretation—that Percy was a
hoarder, took the food himself, deprived the others, and was therefore able
to remain alive and write accounts describing the starvation. Apparently
because he was ashamed or afraid of being labeled unjust and possibly later
tried for manslaughter, he lied about what happened there, making the
picture of settlement life seem rosier than it was. At their turn, Table 1
students—led by Jeffrey—promptly disagreed, noting that there was no
evidence Percy hoarded, that the other groups were confusing Smith's ex
post facto account (Document C-2, Excerpt 2) of the Starving Time with
Percy's a priori description of the initial good life at Jamestown and the
magnanimity of the Powhatans (Document C-2, Excerpt 1).

Given the documents at our disposal, it was likely that either poor
leadership in hunting and gathering food over the winter or a siege by

the Powhatans was a more palatable, evidence-based interpretation of the Starving Time. However, the die appeared to be cast. The popularity of "liar Percy," who hoarded food for himself, became the interpretive mantra of all but the four students at Table 1.[1] Since the evidence available to us in class—and even more thoroughly available to those who have scoured all the evidence traces—was largely inconclusive, we were left with competing interpretations in full view, an important lesson I wanted students to learn. But, on this issue of interpretation, I hastened to add that Table 1's reading appeared more rooted in the available evidence and therefore would be thought of as more plausible and defensible. Students in the other groups appeared undaunted by this, preferring the intrigue and mysteriousness of Percy, the rotund, food-hoarding liar. I chose not to press the point any further at this particular juncture, saving it for future lessons.

Attempting to understand events when evidence is inconclusive opened up the pedagogical landscape in a way that permitted me to demonstrate what I considered to be an important point—that historical inquirers can seldom if ever know for certain what "actually happened" back then. I wanted to use this opportunity to challenge the idea that what we know about the past is fixed and static, to contest the common epistemological position that what the textbook says is what is, thus exposing the referential illusion. I wanted to introduce the notion that knowing the past is a fundamentally interpretive enterprise, often replete with difficulties and unresolved and competing viewpoints. Although I am reasonably convinced that this occurred (by data on student's historical understandings I collected throughout the study and particularly at the end), I failed to anticipate arriving at the sort of solid majority interpretation of the Starving Time we did. This raised those knotty questions about the limits of interpretation in historical study and plunged us straight into the interpretive paradox.

---

[1] Although I have no data to directly confirm it, the overweight, liar-Percy interpretation may well derive from associational logic based on loose recollections of the Disney film *Pocahontas*. In it, then-Jamestown Governor John Ratcliffe is portrayed as a mean-spirited, overweight oaf, who happens to own a fictional dog named Percy. It is likely that some of the fifth-graders are confusing Ratcliffe (1608) with Starving Time Governor George Percy (1609–10) because of the presence of Ratcliffe's dog Percy in the film. I want to thank my doctoral student, Mark Stout, for calling this possibility to my attention. In Chapter 4, I note how this issue arose again later.

ANALYZING THE STARVING TIME LESSONS

The Thin Ice of Historical Interpretation

As an issue history teachers confront in the process of practicing history with their students, I think of the question of the limits of interpretation as a pedagogical dilemma (Lampert, 1985) rather than as a problem they can solve by doing this or that, for two reasons. First, in an effort to do intellectual justice to the subject matter of history, I think it crucial that even young students come to understand the limits on knowing the past with any resolute certainty. There is considerable support for this position, especially in the research and history teaching reform literature, and in some measure in the history *Standards*. This means that students would learn that it is impossible to see the past "as it actually occurred," that all that remains are traces and artifacts that must be interpreted. In this process, we become involved in bringing our own temporal positions to bear on the data in ways that require the imposition of a host of presentist assumptions not shared by our predecessors (see Lowenthal, 1985; Seixas, 1996; VanSledright, 2001). But once you go here, you wind up facing the tensions to which Scott (1996) refers—contested territory around conflicting viewpoints and understandings of evidence. Communities of inquirers therefore need some rules for what counts as more or less acceptable and valid interpretations.

In the community of historians, deference is usually paid to those interpretations that stay closest to and account for the available evidence, and use it to construct persuasive accounts. Yet cases in which evidence is extremely thin invite interpretive license and allow more freedom in the exercise of historical imagination, as inquirers attempt to construct a plausible understanding sans much evidence. In other words, the limits of interpretation are less obvious and easily discernible under these circumstances, as Davis's (1983) movement along these fuzzy boundaries in *The Return of Martin Guerre* attests. Although the liar-Percy interpretation appears less plausible than, say, a Powhatan siege or poor leadership given the evidence we had, it does not seem unreasonable. It surely invites an interpretation of intrigue, a theory most of my fifth-graders found acceptable. But is a majority interpretation here one that should be accepted? We had to traverse all this terrain when I chose to begin with the exercise on the Starving Time.

What makes this so pedagogically dilemma laden is precisely this matter of choice. I could have begun with an exercise in which interpretive issues came to the forefront but resolving them was less difficult because the evidence tended to clearly privilege one particular interpretation over others. However, this likely would have rendered my efforts at demonstrating the often inconclusive nature of historical inquiry and interpretation less immediately realizable, possibly derailing my goal of challenging fundamentalist epistemological stances fostered by the referential illusion common to many historical texts. As we saw, though, going to this place invited perhaps weakly grounded but wonderfully imaginative interpretations—such as liar Percy, the food hoarder—rather than more strongly, evidence-based argumentation. Despite my contrary intentions, was I teaching "anything goes," as long as the majority agreed?

Experienced history teachers will no doubt understand that managing this dilemma actually opens up an array of pedagogical possibilities. For example, walking out onto the thin ice of interpretive operations, as we did here, allows for the opportunity to raise and then teach about the issue of the limits of interpretation in the broader sense. It creates potentially powerful occasions to discuss evidence-use rules in historical inquiry. It also exposes the community's rules for adjudicating interpretations not only in historical study but also by extension to, say, disputes that occur on the playground at recess or in the hallway between classes. In this sense, falling through the thin ice simply provides a very rich moment in which to learn to swim, one that has wonderfully broad applications to the lives of students.

However, the water can be deep and cold. With novice historical investigators such as these fifth-graders, who have had little if any experience learning to swim here, dealing intelligently with the teaching–learning process requires considerable effort, sound knowledge of the subject matter, and extended time. As a result, those content-coverage mandates so many teachers labor under would most likely suffer. Few history teachers I have talked to—particularly those in overcrowded, high-need, low-resource urban schools—like the way these time, knowledge, and energy trade-offs sound. I explore this further in Chapter 7.

From Naive Trust to Widespread Suspicion?

The second reason that I view this as a dilemma to be managed has to do with what it may encourage in youngsters learning about history as a bounded subject matter for the first time. Is it appropriate for 10-year-olds to begin losing that sense of faith they have in the veracity of history textbooks, to be encouraged to abandon their sense of sublime trust in the authoritativeness of things they have been taught to think of as beyond question? And is what results—a form of intrigue-filled but overgeneralized suspicion in the case of many of the students here—acceptable in the name of cultivating their historically imaginative powers? What is the proper relationship between cultivating that imagination and educating an understanding of community rules that oblige evidence-based argumentation? These are tough questions, particularly in light of the fact that any group of fifth-graders will be comprised of students who are more or less ready to begin the process of challenging authoritative givens, and more or less ready to accept some arbitrated limits on their imaginative interpretations.

In a conversation I once had with Peter Lee, the British history education researcher who has done extensive work with children at a variety of ages, he remarked that he had talked with a number of students who, on being confronted with conflicting evidence and the potential for inconclusive interpretive moves, indicated that, well, perhaps people had just made things up and/or were simply lying. This jump from initial trust in the general veracity of accounts to concluding that people are prevaricating in one form or another raises again the question of what young children learn when you expose the referential illusion and reveal the inner interpretive machinery of doing history.

I observe this here because, as I ended my teaching experience and reviewed the data on student historical understandings—particularly that which I collected after I had finished teaching the students—I was struck by the frequency with which several students concluded that they could no longer trust most of the evidence they encountered (see Chapter 6). These students noted that the accounts they were reading (both primary and secondary) were constructed by people who might be or probably were lying and so what they had to say should be dismissed. This was not what I was attempting to teach, nor was I comfortable with students' prima facie drawing this conclusion. I had frequently tried during my teaching experience to dissuade students from concluding that people were simply lying. I stressed the idea that the point of view represented in a diary or a journal or in trial testimony needed to be understood in its historical context, that the way people remember and write down their memories is colored by their historical positions. I emphasized that all this needs to be carefully taken into account in making decisions about how to interpret and judge that evidence. Despite these repeated efforts, several students continued to prefer the idea that much of the evidence simply couldn't be trusted because people regularly and intentionally distorted the truth. This left them without much room to make interpretive decisions and construct persuasive arguments about the nature of events, staples of being good historical inquirers and thinkers, according to the theoretical framework I was employing.

Beneath the veneer of some students' moves from naive trust to widespread suspicion lies an understanding of the resilience of their epistemological positions. Herein also may lie the heart of this dilemma. On the surface, one could argue that my pedagogical practices during these Starving Time lessons were successful in dislodging a potentially stubborn faith in the unquestioned veracity of historical texts' representations of past reality. In other words, students rather swiftly learned to accept that history by its very nature is a thoroughly interpretive subject matter. Students' claims that you could not trust accounts because authors were lying was evidence for this. I had succeeded in shifting students' epistemological positions. They had embraced the idea that, to engage the past skillfully, you had to interpret accounts, authors, and the evidence, something that had been an important goal of the choices I was making in selecting these investigative exercises. That some pieces of evidence contained lies was only an outgrowth of the process of interpreting sources and documents.

However, to make the claim that one cannot trust the evidence because lying is constantly going on suggests that little in the way of a more profound epistemological shift had actually occurred. To believe that lying is an important feature of accounts and their authors is to invoke a criterion of truthfulness "out there," in reference to which the evidence frequently falls short. It is as though these students are saying, "If only they were to tell the truth, then we could get to what really happened." But because these authors chose to lie, the truth—which is "out there" waiting to be discovered—is for now beyond our reach. To raise the specter of lying is to simultaneously call upon the standard of truth. As such, the students who moved from trust to suspicion generally retained their epistemological stance—that the "real truth" could be had as long as we could get to the "right" evidence that conveyed it. This, in effect, was the job of historical investigators—to get to that unvarnished truth. Some of these fifth-graders appeared to miss the importance of point of view and its relationship to the historical context in which it is located. As such, the development of their ability to understand the historical agents they were studying was constrained.

Again, one needs to step out onto the interpretive thin ice and fall through; it appears to be crucial to the learning process. But learning to swim is a difficult and time-consuming task that is not always successful. Is a form of intellectual drowning, if I may use that metaphor here, acceptable with children this age? I believe this aspect of the dilemma is more difficult to manage than the aspect previously discussed. Managing the dilemma requires grit and endurance, efforts at identifying those students who appear to swing from one pole to another (from naive trust to widespread suspicion), repeated attention to the way their historical thinking evolves, and targeted efforts at challenging their assumptions and resilient epistemologies. But there is no guarantee of success, in spite of the potential intellectual legitimacy of taking this route. The past clearly is a foreign country (Lowenthal, 1985). Learning to interpret it skillfully and intelligently involves some peculiarly unnatural acts of thought by both students *and* their teachers (Wineburg, 2001).

From these initial lessons on the Starving Time, it appeared that my efforts to brace these forms of thought would meet with only qualified success. I thought much about this, pondering whether and how I would do better in managing this dilemma as I moved on. I imagined that where I was choosing to go could end only in a qualified result, making me question the wisdom of following this path. But I continued to be drawn to it nonetheless, because it tugged at my history teacher's sensibility with the weight of necessity. I felt supported in my move to explore history's interpretive machinery, and an encounter with the paradox that then confronts you, by Scott's (1996) declaration that "there is no alternative to mentioning the tension [it creates]—even in the face of severe political criticism. In fact acknowledging it and working with it is a better strategy than denying its existence" (p. 1). The tension dogged us throughout, in our investigations of five early English colonies in North America, which I take up next, and in our detective work on possible causes of the American Revolution, which I consider in Chapter 5. Knowing that that tension resides within the practice of doing history was some pedagogical comfort. It was a teaching dilemma I had to learn to manage effectively in order to attain my goals.

4

The Wiles of Evidence, Interpretation, and Reinscription: Investigating British Colonies in America

In early October, 1998, before this study began, I had stood in the office of the principal at Kendall Elementary School. I was there to negotiate my research study and my proposed participation as the history teacher in room 23 beginning the following January. The principal, with whom I had developed a close working relationship over the years of placing teaching interns in the building, listened attentively to my explanation. When I had finished, she smiled approvingly, gave her verbal consent to my plan, then looked me squarely in the eye and said, "But you will be following the school district social studies curriculum, right?" This was less a question than a directive. I indicated that, indeed, I would pay allegiance to the history curriculum scope and sequence called for in fifth grade. By the time I began teaching in January, it meant that my first unit would deal with British colonization along the Atlantic coast. The Jamestown Starving Time lesson sequence I described in the preceding chapter was my initial venture into this period in American history. But where to go from there?

During the first half of the 17th century, British colonization had spread to many locations up and down the North American Atlantic coast. Colonial charters were granted in Massachusetts, Maryland, Delaware, Virginia, the Carolinas, and other coastal points. By my calculations, we had roughly 3 weeks or so to cover this territory, not to mention studying the rather remarkable growth and change of those colonies during the 17th and 18th centuries. I needed to make difficult choices about which colonies to investigate because the schoolyear time frame did not permit extended study. We should be "up to the 'Westward Expansion' unit by mid May, if not before" Proctor reminded me.

HISTORICAL SIGNIFICANCE AS A PRESSING
PEDAGOGICAL DILEMMA

History teachers face this coverage issue all the time, necessitating tough choices about historical topics to be studied versus those to be short-changed. Like Proctor and other such teachers, I had my back pinned up against this curricular wall. However, to cast the issue this way is to partially mask an even more difficult issue I described in Chapter 1, that of historical significance. In order to pursue my goal of in-depth investigation, I could choose to explore the development of only a handful of British colonies and thus relegate others to the margins. However, in doing so I would be conveying a reasonably powerful message to my students that the colonies I had chosen were the ones that *really* mattered. I had no idea how to skirt this issue, which is why I think of it as a history teacher's dilemma. To accomplish my goals, I was convinced that I had to chose some and let the others go. I took some solace in believing that if I constructed a detailed and thoughtful rationale for my choices, I could defuse questions and criticism. I was also somehow comforted (it was a chilly comfort, though) to know that the school district curriculum specialists had chosen British (as opposed to say French or Spanish) colonization as the focus of study at this grade level. I was participating in this choice, yes; but I could allay some of my concerns by citing this set of parameters within which I had promised to work.

Nonetheless, I was continually troubled by this fundamentally Anglo-centric framework. One of my students, Javell, made the entire matter even more conspicuous a week after we began the unit. He asked point blank one day why we were not studying colonization in North Carolina, his birth state. Little did he realize, I think, how deeply his question went to the difficult and challenging domain of addressing the issue of historical significance (see Barton & Levstik, 1998; Seixas, 1994, 1996).

Jamestown, Williamsburg, Massachusetts Bay Colony, Maryland, and Quaker Pennsylvania settlements became the focus of our investigative efforts in this unit. I chose these five carefully, working from several criteria. The first goes almost without saying: I was bound by district curriculum policy to choose from British colonial outposts along the Atlantic seaboard in the area that later became the first 13 states of United States. Second, because my goal was to teach these fifth-graders to work with different types of historical evidence, learn to interpret and draw inferences from them, and then make evidenced-based arguments, I wanted them to do research in teams, each of which could focus their investigative efforts on one colony. With 23 students in the room, I reasoned that five groups of four to five students each would be suitable to address a set of questions I would provide them to guide their research endeavors. Later, I hoped, we would discuss what we had learned via different means. Third, the choice of which specific colonies to study was based on my understanding of American history as a discipline and a subject matter. In short, I wanted colonies that represented the three rather distinctive regions of eastern coastal North America—New England, Mid-Atlantic, and southern colonies—with their varying agricultural practices, politics, and industries.

However, in selecting Jamestown and Williamsburg, both closely linked Virginia colonies, I was ignoring other southern colonies such as the Carolinas and Georgia (as Javell pointed out). Again, I rationalized my choice regarding these two colonies on the basis of several criteria. First, I wanted students to do more with Jamestown than what we had done for the Starving Time activity. Second, I wanted students to understand a connection between the two colonies—that Jamestown's initial prominence was later supplanted by the pivotal English colony in Virginia, Williamsburg. And third, a number of students reported that they had visited Colonial Williamsburg, giving them some prior knowledge of the colony. I sought to take advantage of opportunities for students to utilize that knowledge.

Perhaps most importantly, the selection of these five colonial settlements was driven by the support offered through a set of materials, including primary and secondary documents, produced by the National Center for History in the Schools (NCHS) (see, e.g., Pearson, 1991, 1992; Pearson & Watkins, 1991), books and other print resources in Kendall's library, and a set of Internet sites I had culled together into a list, using search engines and key terms such as history primary sources, Jamestown history, Colonial Williamsburg, Plimouth Colony, Lord Baltimore, and William Penn. The NCHS materials and accompanying documents—many "translated" for students into contemporary English—provided us with rich resources for our investigative work, particularly in our efforts to understand primary sources. Having access to these particular curriculum materials tipped the final balance in favor of the five colonies I chose.

THE RESEARCH LOG, DOCUMENTS, AND MATERIALS

My pedagogical plan called for five independent research teams, each exploring a different British colony using a list of guiding questions, documents, books, and Internet addresses. This investigative process would occur daily over a period of about 2 weeks. The final week of the unit would be spent teaching each other what we had learned from our investigations and reinterpretations of the evidence.

My first task involved bringing together a variety of research materials, or assembling an "archive," if you will. I photocopied relevant documents from NCHS booklets I had purchased. I went to Kendall's library and collected a variety of children's books on the five colonies from a reasonably extensive set of holdings. I spent several hours on the Internet, identifying appropriate websites. I favored those that contained primary source materials. I printed a number of documents that I thought students would find reader-friendly. I would have preferred that students locate and choose these documents for study themselves, thus sharpening their strategies for using the Internet as a research tool. However, there was only one Internet-connected computer in the classroom that had to be shared among the 23 students. Kendall's computer lab was well equipped, but in high demand, and I had missed the window to sign up the class on a regular basis during the time I was teaching history. During the research period, pairs of students did take turns investigating documents on the sites, but there were serious time limits inherent in this arrangement. However, across the span of our daily research adventures, some students, without my prompting, scoured several Internet sites at home and brought to school documents they had printed. All the photocopied and printed materials I collected were organized into folders and placed into small boxes along with relevant books from Kendall's library—five boxes, one for each colony. These boxes effectively became the "evidence archive."

To focus the fifth-graders' investigative energies, I constructed a 15-page Research Log and printed one copy for each student. The length is deceptive; much of it was lined white space, reserved for writing down notes drawn from the evidence students encountered. The logs were tailored to each colony by variation in the cover page and some modifications to the types of questions contained in the log. The logs generally were organized around five thematic frames, or what otherwise can be called "big ideas" (Grant & VanSledright, 2001): (1) Who were the *people* who settled the colony you are researching? (2) How did they get along with the *Native Americans* they encountered? (3) *Where* did the colonists settle? (4) What was *life* like in the colony? (5) How did the colonists adapt and *change* over time? Each theme contained a number of more specific subquestions to further guide students' research efforts. A number of these subquestions asked students to construct evidence-based arguments about *why*, for example, a group of colonists chose to settle at a particular location, or *why* Native Americans and British colonists interacted in particular ways. After each thematic question and its subquestions, there was a section in which I asked that students write down the sources they had used, identify them as either primary or secondary, and then make judgments about which of these sources they found most reliable and why.

The assumptions guiding the development of the Research Log turned on my belief that the students needed considerable structure if the experience was to flow smoothly. Not having done this type of research before, working from such a wide array of materials, and exploring and assessing a host of primary sources, and then being asked to operate for an extended period in collaborative groups, necessitated clear guidelines for what I wanted them to accomplish. The Research Log was designed with this in mind. For example, with five thematically framed question clusters, a group with five students could spread them evenly across the team, with each member researching one cluster. A group with four students required one member to deal with two clusters, something I later—but not without difficulty—negotiated with those groups. Once they had finished researching the question clusters, the group as a whole would be responsible for integrating them into a final account of or story about that colony, complete with evidence citations.

COLONIAL DETECTIVE WORK

On a foggy morning in early February, following our excursion into the Starving Time, we began our broader colonial detective work. The first class was spent going over the myriad details involved in creating the classroom conditions in which the investigative process could commence. Initially, this entailed providing an overview of the research process, an introduction to the Research Log, and identification of the groups. Regarding the latter, I used the current seating arrangement (modified somewhat by Proctor the day before we began as part of her typical, periodic seat-change rotation) with the five desk clusters as research teams, assigning each team a colony. Because Jeffrey, who had been so energetic in his efforts to solve the Starving Time mystery, and because Coral, who had also been deeply engrossed by the mystery, had been seated in the same cluster, I assigned their group the Jamestown colony. I was very curious about what these two, as well as the others in the group, might do to further address the mystery if they would continue researching Jamestown.

These three introductory tasks consumed the entire hour. As we broke for lunch, several students rushed up and initiated a negotiation process over switching groups in order to join their friends. I politely but firmly turned them down, hunching that a single change would touch off a flurry of rearrangements that might only consume more time.

Another set of introductory tasks launched our second lesson. I called students' attention to the Research Logs and to the sections in which I had asked that they keep track of the sources they consulted during their investigations. I stressed that good historical detectives keep careful track of their footsteps through the evidence, jotting down their sources for the record. We then reviewed again the charts on which I had identified the investigative steps good detectives follow, as well as definitions and issues associated with primary and secondary sources (see Figures 3.1 and 3.2 in Chapter 3). I explicitly described how they could go about dealing with a source's reliability by noting such procedures as checking the date a document had been written or an image created, identifying who an author was, checking where the source came from, and seeing where an author had obtained his or her information, particularly if it was a secondary source.

About halfway through this class period, I paused to address questions. There were only two or three. One turned on the amount of time students would have to complete the research. Another involved concern about who would be responsible for which thematic section and how it would be decided. We took that up next. I asked that each group convene for 5 minutes and divvy up the thematic question clusters. They did so and then reported back to me. Two groups had difficulty and I arbitrated by assignment. In the two groups that contained only four students, I also assigned one student two thematic clusters about which he or she predictably complained. I spent several minutes explaining that those I chose were assigned two because of the relative speed with which they could accomplish both. I also noted that other research team members would be responsible for assisting once they had completed their sole section. A bit of grumbling continued subvocally, but the process appeared poised for inauguration.

On the shelves along the side of the room I had assembled the "archive" of materials, the five boxes containing books, documents, maps, and pictures, one for each colony. I sent a student from each research team to retrieve their group's materials. Once materials were transported to the tables, students were to commence their research by choosing from what was there. Within several minutes students had begun to pour through the materials. It was a noisy process; however, it was clear that about half the students had quickly begun to read and explore a book or a set of documents. Fifteen minutes later, we needed to break for lunch. I asked each of the students who had initially retrieved the materials to gather them up and return them to the shelves.

For the next seven class sessions, we essentially repeated this process. A student from each group would gather their archive from the shelves, return to their team, and investigations would commence and persist across the 50 or so minutes devoted to historical study. I spent much of my time traversing the classroom, checking in with various teams, assisting where necessary, and addressing questions. Several students, especially those who conceptualized the activity as one in which their task was to fill in the blanks in the Research Log with "correct answers," frequently followed me about the room, asking if what they had written was "right." I insisted that they needed to use a variety of sources and cross-check them one against another to establish what could be considered a justifiable response to the questions in their section. "That's what good historical detectives do," I again noted, pointing at the step-by-step process chart hanging from the classroom wall. I also insisted that they stop following me around the room. To an untrained eye and a naive ear, the classroom occasionally sounded noisy and sometimes appeared disorderly. However, things were being accomplished. Most of the students were busy at their investigative task—consulting sources, writing in the Research Log, negotiating the use of sources with their teammates, and sometimes asking them for assistance. My trips around the room confirmed that progress was occurring, however sluggishly.

As I watched the Research Logs take shape, however, I became concerned that students were not being particularly diligent about keeping track of their sources and responding to the question of reliability. Nor was much effort being made to consult more than one or two sources. At two different intervals during the 5 days we were engaged in research, I stopped the action and reinforced the idea that they needed to account for the sources they used in constructing their responses and that they needed to consult a variety of sources to test the strength of their arguments. I pointed out that we would be assembling these logs into five reports, one on each colony. Source identification would be required in those reports. Letter grades would be partly determined by the presence of such a record. I also collected the Logs at one point, wrote profuse comments in the margins of each student's, and "graded" progress using a check-plus, check, check-minus system. Doing these things helped increase the degree to which students attended to sources and the question of judging their validity and reliability. Much of my insistence was spurred by observing Jeffrey and Coral dig ever deeper into the evidence surrounding the Starving Time, keeping careful track of the sources they read and doing just about everything in their power to judge the reliability and validity of each. The example of Coral and Jeffrey suggested to me that such activity was not beyond these fifth-graders' grasp.

Still Solving the Mystery of the Starving Time

At several points, most notably when a few too many students had followed me around the room demanding to know if their answers were "correct," I had serious misgivings about the research activity I had chosen to undertake here. However, I was reminded of its power to teach critical historical thought by standing back and watching the efforts of Jeffrey and Coral, and later listening as the two of them debated classmates about the validity of evidence they had uncovered. These two appeared unwilling to rest until they had solved the unsolvable Starving Time mystery once and for all. Jeffrey, who could usually be easily distracted by the most innocuous things, remained almost completely focused on this effort for 3 consecutive days. Coral, less easily distracted, may have helped propel Jeffrey's compulsion. Nonetheless, for those several days the verve of these two coupled with a classroom debate they provoked became, at least in these moments, the epitome of success with respect to much of what I was trying to accomplish.

Four days into the research process, as I began class, I was greeted with Jeffrey's hand waving madly in my face. He and Coral believed that they had solved the Starving Time mystery. Based on reading more from John Smith's journal, they inferred that the Powhatans had most likely starved the settlers to death. However, the discussion quickly shifted to the trustworthiness of evidence. Here's how the first 10 minutes of that class evolved.

> JEFFREY: We found both primary and secondary sources on the Starving Time. The primary source was John Smith. He kept a journal while he was away. He said that the Indians refused to trade with the Jamestown people. The secondary source said that it was the colonists who refused to trade with the Indians. We think the secondary source is probably wrong. (*Coral nodding as Jeffrey speaks.*)
>
> TIM: I'm not sure that the secondary source is wrong. It could be that the primary source was wrong. They both could be wrong. How would you know?

Jeffrey tried to interrupt at each turn. I had to hold him back, but he kept standing up and attempting to interject comments. I called on Alexandra and told Jeffrey to wait.

> ALEXANDRA: I agree with Tim. How do you know the secondary source is wrong?
>
> JEFFREY: (*taking the floor with chin up and chest out*) We think the primary source is better because John Smith was at Jamestown. He would know what was going on. And besides the secondary source was like [that] Hakim book. It was like written in 1993, or something like that. The person who wrote it just read the primary source wrong; it's just that they think reading the primary sources . . .

TIM: (*interrupting this time*) Yeah, but . . .

JEFFREY: We'd rather go with someone who was there, like John Smith . . .

ALEX: I think it's good to have the primary source, but I agree with Tim that you can't tell for sure how the secondary source is wrong.

DR. VAN: One of the things I don't hear anybody saying is how you could try to figure this out. It's right on the list of things (*pointing to the chart on the back wall*) we wrote up on being good historical detectives. How could you check these sources?

THO: You could look at the dates.

DR. VAN: Yes, that's very important. But that probably helps you most figure out if it's a primary or secondary source. How would you figure out which source to go with?

ALEX: Well, you'd have to read them both carefully?

TIM: Compare each source almost word by word.

DR. VAN: Yes. But also, what about checking to see if there's a third or maybe even a fourth source? That way you could compare all of them, like Tim said. You could check them one against another to get a different picture of what went on, or to see how the details all line up. Now sometimes you can't find another source and you have to make a decision. It's hard to do, but sometimes you just have to decide the best interpretation based on what you have. And it might turn out that (*looking over at Table 1*) Jeffrey and Coral end up disagreeing. They have to each give their side of it, but back it up with strong evidence.

JEFFREY: (*as if to say his mind was made up*) Well, Coral and I agree on this . . .

DR. VAN: I know. I just mean it's possible that you might later disagree.

Many hands were waving about by this point. Alexandra was standing up on tip toes, hand raised, as though she was trying desperately to touch the ceiling. Reluctantly, I observed that we needed to change gears. I switched our focus with, "We need to get on with our research or we'll never get done. We'll talk about this more again." And so we would, at least once more at the end of the colonial research activity, and repeatedly when we considered similar investigative mysteries in developments leading up to the American Revolution. Though sometimes halting and tentative, and occasionally peppered with examples of analytical missteps with respect to the order in which documents had been written (for ex-

ample, see the initial discussion Chapter 3), these sorts of conversations
and the rather specialized discourse (primary and secondary sources, be-
lievability of sources) they invoked became the inspiration to press on with
this process when I doubted its efficacy.

Jeffrey's Shifting Analysis and Interpretation

Although at that point in the lesson I was mindful of the ticking clock that
pushed me to ask the class to return to their research activities, Jeffrey
and Coral continued their pointed investigation of the Starving Time. As
we wound down our colonial research endeavors a week later, the two
could still be heard debating the evidence and different interpretations.
In order to get a sense of how they were thinking about the sources they
were reading and using them to construct interpretations, I arranged to
interview them at the end of the unit. Elizabeth Fasulo, my research assistant, spoke with Jeffrey and I talked to Coral. The interviews lasted
approximately 20 minutes each, were conducted in separate rooms, and
were audiotaped.

It turned out that the interpretation they had pressed earlier in class
had been modified yet again by continued analysis of the evidence at
their disposal. The agreement Jeffrey felt so convinced they had achieved
that day in class had been eroded by further investigation. Jeffrey began his
interview by retracing several interpretive theories at some length. He recounted how several sources indicated the presence of enough food to last
that fateful winter. He noted John Smith's absence from Jamestown and
the control of the colony by Captain Percy. He added a menacing
Powhatan Indian tribe that had threatened to stop trading with the settlers. Then he referred again to a primary source's account that the lack
of good government had precipitated the starving process. Finally, he described the "glutton-Percy" interpretation (possibly referring to the
Disney film *Pocahontas* in the process). He noted what he remembered
to be Percy's rotundness.[1] He mentioned that Coral, who had not been
in his group before the recent seat changes, had argued that interpretation earlier. Here he seemed to be retelling the story of his initial foray
into the evidence and how he had gone against the majority interpretation by insisting that a better interpretation was lack of effective planning and government.

---

[1]Here again, we may be witnessing the association of the name Governor Percy
with Disney's portrayal of the overweight Governor Ratcliffe, who in the film
had owned a dog named Percy.

Questioned about his current stance and its relationship to having worked recently with Coral on interpreting the event, Jeffrey said, "No, we don't agree. I'm still trying [to change his mind]. I just said that they didn't have good government, good planning. Coral said that [that] was wrong." He added, "So we're trying to figure it out, 'cause the one [source] we really think is right is John Smith's. We think he's right. He got the letters from Percy . . . and Percy was the one who wrote the false letters." This prompted my research assistant to ask him if it was possible that Smith's account also could be distorted.

> JEFFREY: I don't think he would think something like, "Oh, the Powhatan Indians are stealing our food, like they're taking our food, 'cause they wanna war between 'em." But then there was another one [a primary source] by John Smith that said that, "We had a war and many of our man died." Then there was another one that said that same thing. That source said that like they didn't have good planning and government, so they started eating snakes and all this stuff. And a lot of their men died from starvation. See, the thing that really hit me that Coral said [was] that Percy ate all the food . . . a lot of men died but Percy lived.
>
> FASULO: So now you're thinking that Coral's right?
>
> JEFFREY: Yeah. A lot of men died, but Percy lived. So I'm thinking, yeah, he took the majority of the food.
>
> FASULO: But, he was big already before that?
>
> JEFFREY: Don't matter. You know, once you're big, you gotta get your calories, you know, your carbohydrates.

Even though Jeffrey and Coral had once apparently agreed that a Powhatan siege resulted in starvation for the settlers, by this point Jeffrey was being gradually persuaded to adopt the glutton-Percy mantra. He was probably influenced somewhat by remembering what he thought was his overweight characterization in the film *Pocahontas* and by the persuasiveness of Coral. Peter Afflerbach and I also encountered references to the film *Pocahontas* in an earlier study (Afflerbach & VanSledright, 2001). Fifth-graders in that study used the film as an arbiter in judging the veracity of two history texts we asked them to read. We referred to this practice of relying on a children's fictional film to assess the historical reliability and validity of other sources as the "Disney effect." In several ways, Jeffrey might have been doing the same thing here, in line with his classmates.

Within seconds of making the above pronouncement, though, Jeffrey was back to defending his "poor government and ineffective planning" argument, the one he had argued so powerfully in class approximately 3 weeks earlier. As he had initially, Jeffrey was encountering the wiles of historical evidence and the problems associated with making sound inferences and interpretations from it. As that evidence twisted and turned, appeared convincing and then receded in significance as other evidence competed with it, so, too, did Jeffrey's capacity to anchor it on one clear and convincing argument. Meanwhile, the same slippery encounter with conflicting evidence was occurring for Coral just down the hall.

Coral's Theory

Coral began by explaining his most recent experience with the evidence on the Starving Time:

> We had found the reading, I think a primary source, and it said that at first the Native Americans, the Powhatans, were on good terms with settlers of Jamestown. That was when they first arrived, and then we read another passage which said that the chief, he wouldn't even trade with them because they [the settlers] were like unpredictable. And they kept on going back and forth, back and forth. They would get mad at each other, and then they wouldn't give each other food or something. Like, we read one on one paper that said that they actually went to war. And then in another it said that they were they were all trading. I mean they were teaching each other how to hunt and things. It's just real hard to understand. And then Jeffery came up with something, because we couldn't tell who was telling the truth and who was lying, and we found out that something was a secondary source and we like just. . . . It's hard to really explain.

I acknowledged Coral's reticence and explained that I was interviewing him precisely because this event was so difficult to interpret and I was interested in his thinking process. I then asked him about the sources from which he was drawing inferences. He explained that he and Jeffrey had begun by concentrating on the primary sources because they believed that deferring to "people who were there" was a better analytical move. He noted that the sources went "back and forth—first the Indians were their friends and then they weren't."

He then began again, restating the ways in which he and Jeffrey had read the evidence. His approach to that evidence reflected its back-and-forth influence:

> Before John Smith left, he said [that] there was more than enough food to last them through the winter. And they got some corn from the Indians and we didn't really understand how that was. So, we came to the conclusion that like Percy was probably doing something, or somebody in the colony was doing something, to their food or taking it somewhere. It could have been the Native Americans, or somebody in their colony. My theory is that somebody in the colony was hiding it, was doing something with the food, or a Native American was.

I asked him on what basis he was making these claims. He argued that it was related to his sense of the evidence in the primary documents—that initially the colonists appeared to have enough food and had access to Indian corn via the trading process. But something strange had occurred, because suddenly the food disappeared and starvation began. Either the Powhatans or someone inside the colony (likely alluding to Percy) had attempted to deny food to many of the colonists.

At this point, I pushed him to stake out a position. He responded, "I'd probably go with the one that Percy wrote because it gave more detail, and in everything he wrote, he never talked once about himself starving. He always talked about everybody else." He paused and then added, "Like maybe just him and the Indians, and they were sharing food and things, or something like that." I asked him how confident he was of this interpretation. He hesitated to give it his full endorsement. I inquired about his hesitation. He replied, "Because people don't have enough information or they hear different stories and argue. And then one story gets argued to the point where people start believing that one, [even] when the other one could have been right." Finally, I queried him about how he chose what to believe in such cases. He answered:

> Well, mostly I like whatever has the most detail and what I mostly can understand, 'cause like with the Boston Massacre [referring to the initial performance task I asked my eight informants to undertake], I mean, I read a passage and it said that they were about six people dead or whatever. And in one picture I saw there was only like one person that was dead. So, that was like the least accurate. I'm checking one against the other.

No doubt Coral and Jeffrey were farther down the path toward reading sources carefully, and getting comfortable with inconclusive evidence and the difficulties of making convincing arguments from it, than were a number of the students in the class. To my chagrin, these others were still busy attempting to collect right answers to each question in the Research Log, moving quickly from one to the next without stopping much to take stock of a consulted source's nature or perspective.

Coral and Jeffrey, along with Alex, Alexandra, Ben, Katie, Tho, Tim, and several others, provided continuing rays of hope for what I was trying to accomplish. This was energizing. However, I also realized that the research tasks students were doing had somewhat lost the luster and intrigue of the Starving Time because students did not perceive that those tasks involved solving mysteries. In this sense, the excitement of the Starving Time lessons was over. In many students' minds, we had reverted to the dullness of collecting and reproducing other people's facts (Holt, 1990). In line with this, I also realized that those who were searching sources for such facts were doing so because that's what school had taught them to do, reinforcing their epistemological fundamentalism. My task was to teach them a different approach and attempt to re-create the element of mystery in historical investigation. Being an impatient sort, I had to remind myself of this frequently and redouble my efforts to work with those who needed more specific assistance in retaining the investigator's unceasing curiosity.

CONCLUDING THE COLONIAL RESEARCH WORK

We had been at the research process, using the sources and working with the Research Logs, for just over 2 weeks. At several points it felt as though we would never finish because it seemed to take students inordinate amounts of time to read, interpret, and then write responses into their Logs. I worried that this was an artifact of supplying them with too many sources, an idea I found difficult to imagine. To bring our colonial research to a close, I pondered a variety of approaches. The first was to use the notes in the Logs as a means of inviting the research teams to compile booklets about their colonies. These booklets could then be assembled into a larger volume, reproduced, and used for study purposes. But study for what? I needed a form of assessment as a means of checking on students' understandings of all five of the colonies researched and, I hoped, their growing awareness about the vicissitudes of practicing historical investigations. I mulled over several ideas, such as a paper-and-pencil test or oral research reports delivered to the class by each team. Continuing to fret about how long this investigation of the colonies was taking and wanting an alternative to a traditional test, I devised what I anticipated to be an efficiently administered "quiz show" exercise in which a research team would test its knowledge publicly against a set of questions I constructed from that team's Research Log. Before this quiz show could occur, however, we needed to compile booklets and they would have to be printed and distributed to each student.

Reinscribing History and Publishing the Results, "Just as Historians Do"

In mid-February, after I had collected and examined the partially completed Research Logs and then toured the room again to assess progress, I announced that we had to complete our colonial investigative work in one more class period. I then would be collecting and grading the Logs. I explained that, once I had graded them, my research assistant was going to digitize them and collate them into booklets, one for each colony. Then I would return the booklets—one copy for each research team member—and students would prepare presentations from them to be given orally to the rest of the class. As my above comments have indicated, I soon recanted on the latter idea.

These announcements set off a flurry of last-minute activity. Javell, Anthony, Vanessa, and Kedwin had fallen far behind the others, all for different reasons. I kept them in at lunch recess for two consecutive days in order to work with them on finishing up. Jeffrey and Katie had gotten into a nasty spat over their relative contributions to their team. On one of those two days, they also stayed in the classroom over lunch in order to work out the issue and complete their Logs, both under my supervision. By the end of the class period in which I had declared that I would collect the Logs, all but Kedwin had completed their efforts. Kedwin took his home overnight and came back the next day with his portion finished. I scored the Logs using a letter-grade system, as was Proctor's practice.

The next day, I returned the graded Logs to students, and then explained in detail the process of constructing a narrative paragraph or two using the responses to the questions in their section as the substantive material. On an overhead projector, I illustrated what I had in mind using fictitious Log entries for a colony I invented for the purpose. The students spent the remaining portion of that class and the next writing their paragraphs. Again, I circled the room, checking in with students, making suggestions, constructively critiquing their paragraphs, and offering assistance where needed. At the end of that second class, I collected the paragraphs. Several were still incomplete. I assured these students that there would be additional time to add more details because we still had to engage in the editing process.

Later that afternoon, I transferred all the paragraphs, collated by colony and order of themes, to Fasulo, who digitized them all into a single word-processing file. That night I printed the file, arranged the pages by colony, and produced photocopied booklets, one for each student by research-team assignment. The next day, we edited these first drafts. Proctor had spent a good deal of time that year teaching her students how to write, edit, rewrite, and create more polished documents. Most of the students had become quite adept at the process and completed it quickly. I told them that we did not have the luxury of repeated editing and rewriting activities because I was worried about time. I also said I was anxious to create a full book for each to receive and study because what I was seeing looked so good (a bit of hyperbole worked exceptionally well here).

Students did their editing directly on the pages of their first-draft booklets. I collected them at the end of class and had Fasulo incorporate the changes into the final version. I printed this last edition, collated it carefully into book form, added a cover sheet, and rushed off to print copies. The next day I presented students with their freshly bound "colonial history book," the fruits of several weeks of diligent investigative and reinscriptive efforts. On my drive to Kendall that day, it occurred to me that we could publish this book on the Internet. I thought I would run this idea past the students and Proctor.

With all of them listening attentively (a rarity), I solicited their reactions to the idea. A bit to my surprise, because several students had not done as extensive revisions as I had hoped, they were ecstatic. "We're going to be published? Wow, cool!" At that point, Proctor, who was at her desk at the back of the room, interjected that to do this was a great honor, that indeed they would be "published authors" by Internet rules, and "that's just what historians do with their work: They publish it once they're finished." Students beamed. On the cusp of raining on their parade, I noted a small problem—that I needed to get their parents' permission to do this. I intended to use only their first names on the website itself. Anticipating the possibility of a positive greeting to the idea, I had brought along permission forms. I asked that they take it home, have their parents look it over, grant permission if they desired, and return it to me as soon as possible.

A week later, I had permission from all but a small handful of parents. The reluctant ones said by way of their children that they were concerned about their child's being identified on the Internet and asked that pseudonyms be used. I agreed. Several days later, I was showing students their Five Colonies Research Book on the Internet using the computer and monitor in Room 23 (see http://www.wam.umd.edu/~bvansled/fivecolonies.html). Again, they were thrilled. The next day, Brittney explained to the entire class that her father had been so impressed that he had shown the site to everyone in his office—and then had printed copies and given them to whoever seemed interested.

Assessing Learning: "Dr. Van's Quiz Show"

Tests that assess recall of facts and details ostensibly learned during the study of a historical period remain reasonably popular among history teachers, primarily because they are efficient to administer and relatively easy to score. How effectively they actually assess what children know about history and, more importantly, can do with what they know is open to considerable debate, as I have noted. During my years as a history teacher, I became increasingly uncomfortable using recall-type assessments and moved in the direction of essays in which I would ask my students to take an interpretive position on a historical event and provide a supporting argument, drawing from evidence we had examined in class. In addition to the burden of grading these essays, I found that a number of students often had difficulty making good arguments and writing sound essays. I spent a significant amount of time attempting to teach them to do so, using precious class time to show how historians construct interpretive positions based on evidence. In this sense, I attempted to unmask the referential illusion (Barthes, 1986) and expose the interpretive machinery that creates the illusion. I was frequently chided by my colleagues about my inability to cover all the historical terrain I was mandated to by curriculum guidelines. "What are you doing in there anyway, playing games?" one colleague asked often.

As I approached the end of this colonies unit, I once again faced this pedagogical dilemma concerning assessment: how to test effectively—that is, to better understand what my students had learned in relation to my teaching goals—without using up too much scarce classroom time. Could I resort to employing essay writing among fifth-graders, some of whom were still struggling to compose coherent paragraphs, let alone full-blown essays? I reasoned that we could, but then wondered how long would this take, especially if much of it had to be done in class, where I could provide guided practice. What were other less time-intensive but still useful alternatives? Overestimating the value of every minute of the schoolday, even in elementary schools, is difficult. Real or imagined pressure caused me to feel serious pedagogical anxiety about addressing this assessment issue.

"Dr. Van's Quiz Show" was a compromise. I experienced it as an unsettling Faustian bargain. I could not only assess what students knew from doing research on their colony (the details of historical events) but could also get at the thinking behind what they knew (how they knew what they knew and supported it) by asking probing questions that followed up on initial responses. I could use a system in which a more detailed and supported response would net them additional points. I could structure the experience so that students would address questions as a research team, thus requiring cooperation with each other in an assessment setting. I was setting no precedent in using this form of cooperative assessment strategy. To a degree, I chose it because the strategy is employed occasionally in the state's testing program, which students would be taking in May. In part, this cooperative component was a form of pretest practice. The oral nature of the exercise also provided for open classroom review opportunities, in which research teams could learn about other colonies they had not researched. And I believed I could do all this in a way that consumed relatively little classroom time—and probably less time than oral presentations would take.

However, I was inviting the class to dance straight into that intense public competition that often breeds and then reinforces the types of attitudes and social distances (e.g., I'm a better human being than you are because I scored higher than you did) already present as early as third grade and manifestly evident in many fifth-grade preadolescents. Throughout the exercise, I fretted constantly about this. To suppress my anxiety, I told students I would practice zero tolerance for displays of one-upmanship. However, I knew that I could not control what they did outside my purview.

Room 23's more vocal students loved the idea of a quiz show. The quiet students, such as Cindy, Kedwin, Jessica, and Jonathon, said nothing. We went ahead.

The procedures were relatively simple. Drawing from each team's booklet, I compiled and then asked questions of that team. We went from team to team, one question at a time. A "round" consisted of one cycle in which each team had addressed one question. There was a 3-point scoring scale that I would arbitrate: zero for no response or an unreasonable interpretation, 1 for a response that was reasonable but lacked sufficient support based on evidence, and 2 for a reasonable and well-defended response. I would determine the number of rounds and figure out a mechanism for turning the final scores into letter grades. Once I asked a team a question, they had 1 minute to confer together to construct a response. Teams were allowed to consult their colonial booklets as they conferred. While a team was conferring, there was to be no talking among the other teams or points would be deducted from their score. One student would be chosen to respond for the team, although the respondent could change with the introduction of a new question.

As a concluding bonus round, students would be asked to each contribute one question. They could specify a particular colonial research team to receive the question, but I reserved the right to choose to which team the question was ultimately asked as a method of balancing the number of questions among the teams. The same conferring, no-talking, and scoring rules applied during the bonus round.

While Fasulo digitized the research booklets into a final book, incorporating the changes students had made, and I spent time at night preparing to upload the book to the Internet, we commenced Dr. Van's Quiz Show during the day in room 23. The first class period involved three rounds of questions, the second day, the same. The third day's class period provided time for the bonus round.

The first three rounds were devoted to questions I framed directly from details and interpretations students had amassed as they addressed the questions in their Logs. Essentially, oral responses reiterated the paragraphs students had composed. If a response did not contain references to sources from which details were derived or lacked sufficient support in my estimation, I would announce that the team was about to receive 1 point, then challenge the team to add supporting detail to produce a 2-point score. Teams struggled with this process during the first few rounds. Some were still attempting to learn a discourse for drawing from the evidence to defend their responses. I was pushing them to structure one for doing so in keeping with my goals. At several junctures, after a team was unable to augment their response in order to earn a 2-point score, I modeled what I had in mind.

Gradually students became more proficient. However, it was not unusual for a team to get hamstrung because members had not recorded sufficient support for their response either in their initial Log or in their paragraph. As a result, 1-point scores were common. Alex, Alexandra, Ben, Brittney, Coral, Katie, Tho, and Tim learned to finesse the process of providing evidentiary support even when it was lean in the booklet paragraph. For example, by quickly searching documents from the "evidence archive" they had researched (and, during the quiz show, still had access to) and finding something the team believed was relevant, one of these spokespersons would insert a sentence or two into a response such as, "We know the Quakers were against fighting, because in this primary source (*holding up a document by William Penn*), he talks about the Pennsylvania Quakers as pacifists." Even when I was reasonably sure that the student had not completely read the document and that it had not been cited in the Log or the booklet, I frequently gave credit for such efforts as a means of supporting their use of this form of discourse. However, I was dismayed that more responses did not contain the evidentiary and source support I was hoping they would learn from the colonial research process.

As we commenced the second set of rounds (4 through 6), I informed the class that I would begin to interject questions that dealt with their understanding of such things as primary and secondary sources and the problems they encountered working with them. I told them that I also thought it was legitimate to ask more directly about the specific sources they used in constructing responses to Research Log questions and in developing paragraphs for their colony booklets. I wanted them to know that I was holding them accountable for the type of strategic knowledge associated with practicing history, along with knowledge about the colonies they produced from engaging that strategic knowledge.

These comments were met with worried faces and several groans. Anika asked if students could use their social studies logs (the journals in which they had earlier recorded definitions of sources and their associated problems) to compose responses to my questions. I told her that I thought using the social studies logs would be good for the review process. With that we began round 4.

Research teams responded to questions about the often difficult work of understanding primary and secondary sources with considerable aplomb. They mentioned issues such as perspective, presence, and language that needed to be considered in making sense of a primary source and similar perspective issues that influenced the construction of secondary accounts. In response to a question about how one decides among conflicting sources, the research team led by Alexandra and Chelsea, who had studied the Pennsylvania Quakers, noted how historical detectives needed to search out as many sources as possible and then develop an interpretation based on the direction in which most of the sources pointed. Teams experienced little difficulty defining terms such as *primary* and *secondary sources*, even when I pushed them to put these terms in their own words (I refused to accept responses read verbatim from the social studies logs).

Overall, teams handled these types of questions more effectively than I had anticipated, showing some emergent understanding of the discourse of practicing history and processes involved in arriving at interpretations and reinscribing the colonial past. However, getting them to deploy this understanding routinely as they did their research remained another matter. Teams frequently muffed questions that required them to supply the actual sources they had consulted in addressing particular Research Log questions and identify which of these sources proved to be most useful and why. As I had noticed when I reviewed the Research Logs and read over their paragraph responses to the questions, often sources were missing or only one had been cited. Two teams noted that a sole source to a particular Log question had been a volume from the encyclopedia set in the classroom, a source not included as part of the archive I had assembled.

Over the course of the researching process, I had observed several students consulting such encyclopedia volumes. Upon querying them about this, these students said that the encyclopedias contained the truth and therefore were the best sources of information. Although I argued that the types of encyclopedia articles they were considering customarily were written by historians and were to be thought of as secondary sources, these students continued to give them much higher epistemological status. This stance was in evidence again in responses to source questions in the final rounds.

By the fifth grade, many students have learned that their task is to accumulate information—and as much of it as possible. Therefore, they are quick to adopt an information-quantity criterion in attending to activities that ask them to respond to questions (see Barton, 1997; VanSledright & Kelly, 1998). The approach they take involves going to the fountain of what they perceive to be trustworthy information—the encyclopedia or the textbook or the dictionary, depending on the task. Raising issues about the epistemological status of such sources seems to bounce off this rather hardened, school-reinforced approach. Once again, the quiz show demonstrated how much pedagogical work still lay ahead for me in helping a number of my students to become more sophisticated historical thinkers.

At the end of final round, scores for the groups were closely matched. The Jamestown and Pennsylvania Quaker teams were tied for the lead. The Williamsburg and Plimouth Colony teams were a close second. The Maryland team had slid into last place, having been assessed 3 penalty points for talking while another team was either responding to a question or conferring. For the concluding bonus round, I asked the students to take several minutes to think about all that they had learned from hearing the other research teams discuss what they had found. I then circulated 3-by-5 note cards on which I asked them to write a question for another team. They could identify the team specifically or come up with a more general question that any team might address. For almost 10 minutes, the only sounds in the room emanated from the heating-system blower and pencils and erasers on note cards.

At the 10-minute mark, I collected the cards and observed that I could choose the order in which I asked the bonus round questions and the team to which I directed them. I also reserved the right to rephrase a question to make it more comprehensible, but only as necessary. Other than that, the rules remained unchanged. The bonus round then commenced. We moved rapidly. Questions ranged from the almost self-evident (Did your colony keep growing by population?) to the somewhat arcane (Who were the leaders of the group your colony had a war with?). When I would announce a question and identify the author, that student's face would light up like Times Square at nightfall.

Twenty-two students wrote questions that day. One student was absent. At the end of the bonus round, each team had received and addressed four questions; two were left in my hand. I kept setting aside what I took to be the most difficult and arcane ones. These two in my hand were the ones that remained. After tabulating the scores, the Jamestown team had attained the sole lead. The Maryland team remained a low scorer, joined at this point by the Plimouth team (they had missed two bonus round questions). Then I asked students what we should do about the two remaining questions. Grade-savvy students that they were, they first wanted to know how the quiz show scores translated into letter grades. A quick calculation (assessing a ratio of opportunities to attain maximum score to actual score translated into a percentage and then into a grade using Proctor's 100-point scale) revealed that the lead team would receive an A, the two middle teams a B, and the two final teams a C. Tim raised his hand at this point and, in a magnanimous gesture, suggested that the two questions be given—one each—to the two last-place teams, giving them an opportunity to raise their scores enough to put them into the B range. As several less generous students cried out "No way!" and amid an undercurrent of grumbling, I smiled and put the suggestion to a vote. All but two students supported Tim's idea.

To our collective surprise, both teams managed their tough questions well enough to push their scores high enough to obtain a B. The Plimouth team received the question I noted above about a key war and a leader of a warring party, to which, after a flurry of consultations with each other, their notes, and Research Logs, they identified the Wampanoag and Metacom (or King Philip, as he was called by the colonists). The Plimouth and Maryland teams seemed pleased at their eleventh-hour performances, and the class applauded their efforts. So ended our excursion into colonial detective work and a review of what we had learned.

STILL ANTICIPATING A SHIFT IN EPISTEMOLOGIES

Spurred on by the assumption that young children's minds are quite elastic and malleable, I initially believed that it would be relatively easy to change their historical epistemologies. By carefully orchestrating a unit's activities around good historical investigative work, rolling back the epistemological blanket Barthes (1986) calls the referential illusion to expose the reality effect, and then showing off the interpretive machinery historical investigators ply in their trade as they examine primary sources, I imagined that I could get the fifth-graders to understand history as an interpretation of texts about the past. After all, the sources on which historians base their work are largely texts themselves. Even historical evidence such as film, photographs, and artists' images can be read as texts. Historical detectives read these texts, interpret them, amass the evidence around a defensible image of an event, and then use that image and everything else they have learned to reinscribe the past. This thoroughly interpretive, history-as-text epistemological stance appeared clearly self-evident and transparent to me. At the end of this unit, a number of my fifth graders still did not see it that way.

As I noted, children learn early in school that to be educated means acquiring what they call "information" (Barton, 1997; VanSledright & Frankes, 2000; VanSledright & Kelly, 1998). Learning history is indistinct from learning mathematics or science. To be a student means committing information—that is, scientific discoveries and gravitational laws, computational formulas, historical events and names—to memory and reproducing them on demand. Texts in which students find this "information" plainly convey their ideas reliably and validly. The texts vary only with regard to the information they contain. Texts and the words they contain, in effect, map directly onto the real world. The task of a text is to act as a conduit between the truth about the world and the reader. Schoolchildren are repeatedly invited to accept this arrangement without question. It's a neat and clean epistemological framework. The overt simplicity of it is perhaps its most seductive feature. Children and their teachers need not wrestle with the complexity of language, with the tenuous and shifting play of words that ostensibly stand for those real-world objects and persons they purportedly identify. The interpretive—and often contested—work in which human beings engage as they construct understandings of what words mean is hidden or masked.

The work we were doing in class challenged this tidy—but theoretically untenable—arrangement. It meant confronting the complexities inherent in making decisions about the significance of events and evidentiary sources, and assessing the quality of one person's information against that of others. Not all the fifth-graders were equally willing to engage in this type of experience, despite my frequent efforts to invite their attention to it.

Shifting an epistemological stance initially requires, it seems to me, an open acknowledgment about what your current stance looks like. In other words, with respect to historical study, you must take into account what I have described as your historical positionality (VanSledright, 1998, 2001). Historical positionality is about who you are. It is your own temporal bearings that you use to make sense of yourself in relation to the past and your imagined future. In many ways it is a worldview, formed from experience in school and out. As such, historical positionality is heavily context shaped and situated (see Bruner, 1996; Wertsch, 1998). A pivotal feature of it involves understanding how you know what you know and come to know it; that is, your epistemological stance. In attempting to construct an understanding of the past, for example, you impose that stance on new experiences making sense of historical events, sources, and authors' perspectives.

In room 23, many of my fifth-graders—those who went straight for the encyclopedia—were busy imposing onto the investigation process the simplistic, unexamined epistemological position I described above because it was all that they knew. "Go to *The* Source," they seemed to be saying. "Why reinvent the wheel?" I was surprised how deeply ingrained this particular position already appeared to be in children who were only 10.

It became exceedingly clear that if I were to realize my goal of helping these students become more proficient at historical investigative work, with all its complexities and judgments and interpretive processes intact, I needed to work more diligently at pointing out how texts such as encyclopedias had to be regarded as interpretations, subject to the same rules we applied to all such sources. Encyclopedia articles are written by authors who interpret the world based on other forms of evidence. More importantly, a text as a source, such as an encyclopedia article on Williamsburg, contains the perspective of its author, one that is imposed on past events based on that author's historical positionality. There is no way around this human imposition. There is no historical source that unequivocally rises to elevated epistemological status unless an illusion is in play (Barthes, 1986). Secondary sources in particular can ascend, but only with regard to their rigorous research, careful assessments of perspective and significance, and overall coherence. (Historical articles found in encyclopedias seldom satisfy these criteria.) And elevated sources can be and often are dethroned by new evidence and shifting tides in historiographical communities.

More difficult, unpredictable, and complex pedagogical terrain here. Thinking through all this as our colonial investigative work came to a close left my thoughts swirling as I considered all the decisions I felt pressing on me, with the study of events leading to the Revolutionary War looming ahead. Despite seeing rays of hope (Alex, Alexandra, Ben, Coral, Jeffrey, Katie, Tho, Tim), I realized that the fifth-graders' epistemological stances were not going to budge as quickly as I had anticipated. From a new set of possible routes I could choose, I narrowed things down (1) to a renewed commitment to question what I now redubbed the "encyclopedia epistemology" and (2) to a focus on perspective. Regarding the latter, I remained troubled by the way many students invoked the idea that certain eyewitnesses were "lying" because, as I discussed in the last chapter, to make a claim about lying is to simultaneously assume there is a capital-*T* truth to be found. It misses the point about the inescapable roles interpretation, perspective, and historical positionality play in assessing an account's significance, reliability, and validity. To invoke the lying/truth duality also undermines how these interpretive and perspectival forces influence understanding and writing (or rewriting) the past.

Armed with this decision to concentrate most specifically on the issue of perspective, I began mapping out the Revolution unit. My immediate goal focused on using the events leading up to the American Revolution to demonstrate the complex and recursive role a source's *and* a latter-day interpreter's perspective plays in making sense of history. Studying these events next in the fifth-grade curriculum sequence provided an added benefit in that this period is filled with striking examples of how political and economic perspectives, subtexts, and positions—in this case, on both sides of the Atlantic—shaped historical memory, as well as understandings of and writings about those events. Many opportunities to stress perspective and positionality appeared on the pedagogical horizon. Perhaps, I thought, compelling shifts in epistemological stances among my fifth-graders were within reach.

5

Source Perspective, Reliability, and Subtext: Investigating Causes of the American Revolution

Americans to whom I have spoken about the War for Independence frequently use wistful and romantic language when describing it. The American Revolution, as it is otherwise known, appears to reside in their memories as a largely bloodless struggle between a tyrannical British king and his puppet ministers and a freedom-hungry citizenry justly and inevitably entitled to their liberty. The list of American heroes associated with the struggle is long: John Adams, Abigail Adams, Samuel Adams, Crispus Attucks, Benjamin Franklin, Patrick Henry, Thomas Jefferson, Paul Revere, Martha and George Washington, Phyllis Wheatley, and on and on it goes. The battles and the bloodletting are generally forgotten, but mental images of a strong and stoic Washington crossing the Delaware and those brilliant "Founding Fathers" signing of the Declaration of Independence are quickly recounted.

The British generally do not share this shiny American view, nor do they celebrate those 18th-century Americans as heroes. During the 1770s, many saw traitors and treason, citizens of the Crown engaged in an unjustifiable rebellion that needed quelling. In discussing James Fenimore Cooper's *Leather-Stocking Tales*, D. H. Lawrence reportedly once claimed that Americans had murdered their way to democracy. A bit of hyperbole, no doubt, but the idea reveals a little of the residual partisanship that remained in the perspective of at least one Englishman more than a century later.

Many Americans typically do not see the birth of their independence as associated with murder. Rather they view it as signaling the opening act in the creation of the world's most powerful culture, a complex hybrid of peoples from all over the globe: America, the land of the free and the home of the brave. Historians have referred to this view as American exceptionalism, a widely shared conviction in the uniqueness of Americans, destined historically to be great and to lead the world to the splendor of liberty and democracy and the spoils of capitalism. This kind of upbeat view is part of what Michael Kammen (1997) calls the "heritage phenomenon" (p. 214), a celebration of selected memories of the past leavened with a considerable degree of historical amnesia (see also Kammen, 1991, Chapters 16, 18, 19; Lowenthal, 1998). Although Kammen notes that heritage is necessary and "comprised of those aspects of history . . . we cherish and affirm" (1997, p. 220), he also observes that "the unfortunate thing about this heritage boon is that it can lead, and has led, to commercialization, vulgarization, over-simplification, and tendentiously selective memories—which means both warping and whitewashing a fenced-off past" (1997, p. 221).

Americans' historical memories often pivot on what Wertsch (1998) calls a "freedom-quest narrative," a guiding mental construct that helps shape remembrance. It contributes in important ways to the heritage phenomenon and to notions of exceptionalism. Wertsch reanalyzed data from a study by O'Connor (1991) in which she asked 24 American college students to write a short essay explaining the origins of the United States. Of the 24, 23 constructed compellingly similar narratives in which they suggested that that origin involved the search for freedom from the various sorts of oppression Europeans (primarily the British) encountered in the 17th century. The 23 students explained that America was founded by these liberation-minded Europeans through the creation of a democracy in North America. In their separation from a tyrannical England and in their efforts to follow a line of unbridled progress over two ensuing centuries, Americans dissolved their Old World identity and were born again, unfettered and unconnected to Britain or Europe. Expressing the depth of their convictions about American exceptionalism, the students typically concluded that these freedom seekers produced the boldest and most successful political experiment and the strongest economic system and military muscle humankind had yet to see.

Wertsch (1998) was struck by the similarities among the essays and the power the freedom-quest narrative appeared to hold for the American (middle-class?) college students who wrote them. He argued that one can understand the narrative as a culture tool, a deeply appropriated cognitive structure composed of beliefs, values, and assumptions that permits those who carry it to employ it in understanding themselves and their place in the world. Wertsch maintains that the power of this narrative as a cultural tool—useful in defining American identities, however historically partial and mythical—should not be underestimated. Given its currency as a cultural tool, Bodnar (1992) would likely describe the freedom-quest narrative as "official history."

THE "HERITAGE PHENOMENON" AND
THE AMERICAN REVOLUTION

Where did these college students learn to think this way? How could they so easily defend acts of rebellion against one's country? How could they fail to note that while Americans were busy protesting British tax laws as a form of involuntary financial servitude and taxation without representation, they simultaneously engaged a culture of slavery on their own soil, a place where men and women were bought and sold as chattel? How could they not wonder about the paradox of Jefferson's phrase "all men are created equal," which was contained in a document that attempted to justify acts of separatist violence against British oppressors but apparently had no application to Jefferson's own slaves? And what of the ironies contained in 18th-century American views of women and treatment of Native Americans.

In part, as I remarked in Chapter 1, the answer lies in the sociopolitical use of history by those who would help us commemorate our past and inspire pride in it, those whom Lowenthal (1998) calls the heritage-keepers. In their work, both Kammen (1991, 1997) and Lowenthal provide a host of examples—from the work of historical preservation trusts to the National Park Service to mass culture celebrations covered by the media—in which the past is repeatedly whitewashed. Another part of the answer lies in the classroom. We need look no further than the average American history textbooks used in the fifth grade to understand how an exceptionalist, freedom-quest perspective gets shaped. The books tell the story much the way I have conveyed it in the foregoing. American patriots were right; the British were wrong. If the patriots had not revolted and thrown off an oppressive regime symbolized by a psychotic despot, the American birthright of liberty and democracy would only have been temporarily delayed.

The ironies and paradoxes of acts of rebellion against and triumph over perceived tyranny situated alongside American slavery and refusals to include women and the propertyless classes in the definition of liberty and democracy are frequently overlooked or downplayed. The books celebrate exercises in defining American exceptionalism, liberty, democracy, and the heroes who ostensibly brought them about. The American Revolution often serves as a shining example. To the extent that grade school teachers pursue such "official" narratives in their classrooms, the heritage phenomenon is reinforced. Children seldom get taught a *history* of the American Revolutionary period. Doing so would involve teaching them, at a minimum, to understand the struggle from both sides of the Atlantic.

Our historical investigations into colonial American history in room 23 revealed a number of examples of memory characterized by a whitewashed and fenced-off past (Kammen, 1997). Most of the students were partial to a decidedly U.S. way of looking at things. They were recipients of American exceptionalist thought and now were old enough and expert enough in mass culture and heritage phenomena to speak America's historical myths. Their study of and discourse about colonial development in British North America suggested that they thought it a natural outgrowth of freedom-loving Europeans striving for a better life on far-off shores. They seemed little troubled, for example, by the treatment Native Americans sometimes received at the hands of land- and wealth-pursuing Anglos.

Some, though, did exhibit signs of serious discomfort with colonial African slave trading and the growth of a slave economy in the New World. But when we discussed these matters in class, what they noted was bothering them was the actual nature of the experience for those who became enslaved. Many of the students had difficulty aligning those experiences with their post-civil-rights-era, presentist view of America, the home of ostensibly unfettered opportunity for all races. Most of the African American students in the class were no exception when it came to this understanding. Also, it was clear that the students generally did not understand the range of motives that fueled the British desire to colonize the New World. Their viewpoint was thoroughly contemporaneous American heritage, a product of a decade of encounters with those "official," attractive, and celebratory features of the American past that made them feel good to be citizens of the "the land of the free and the home of the brave." In this specific sense, my Latino/a and African American fifth-graders were little different than their Anglo and Asian American counterparts. This was puzzling to me, particularly in light of Epstein's (1998, 2000) work, in which she described how the Black students consistently chose different American heroes and seminal historical events than the White students in her studies.

My goal from the outset had been to teach American history, not heritage. I took my cues in part from Kammen's (1997) injunction:

> We must . . . recognize that the heritage phenomenon tends to be upbeat and affirmative in an unqualified way about the American past. Without minimizing what has been a truly remarkable saga of achievements, teachers should be sure to take into account the human and environmental "costs" of many of those achievements. We will not adequately prepare our students for the future if we do not communicate the history of failure as well as the history of success: the failure of rebels with and without a cause, the failure of the framers to resolve all the vexing political problems faced in 1787, the failure of subsequent reform movements to solve entirely the social ills they responded to, and so forth. . . . [I]t is essential that we teach historical habits of mind that will enable young people to cope with such matters as component parts of the civic culture. (pp. 223–224)

Standing in front of the class and looking into the faces of my 10- and 11-year-olds did little, though, to calm my sense of concern that perhaps by "young people," Kammen did not actually mean fifth-graders. I pressed on anyway.

By this point in my experience, I had become persuaded that one key to teaching history (as contrasted with heritage) was helping my students more deeply understand the complex role of point of view in historical study. This meant pressing them to look at the American Revolutionary era from a variety of perspectives. I also wanted them to begin learning about how their own perspectives on the American past are profoundly shaped by what I term their historical "positionalities" (VanSledright, 1998). By historical positionality, I mean those racial, ethnic, socioeconomic class, and gender factors that influence who and what we perceive ourselves to be and affect our understanding of a collective American past. Heritage perspectives and ideas about American exceptionalism conveyed in mass media products and sites for historical preservation, for example, are powerful agents of identity development here. But what pedagogical approach could I take toward accomplishing my goal?

There are a host of viewpoints one could consider in the Revolutionary era: Systematically attending to each one seemed to portend a mechanical, potentially disjointed treatment of the period. I sought to confront a broader Revolutionary era heritage whitewash—that American patriots were unequivocally justified in claiming their independence from and going to war against a tyrannical, oppressive British regime. With this idea in mind as well as concerns about how much time remained for me to consider such a topic before curricular demands pushed us to the next unit, I chose to use the era's events as parsimoniously as I could. In other words, we would not be considering a number of viewpoints and details. Here again, my choice involved tough decisions about issues of historical significance and their attendant messages to students. My pedagogical thinking and rationale (for better or worse) went something like the following.

As in any sociopolitical struggle, perspective becomes pivotal if a deeper understanding of what people were sacrificing their lives for is to be achieved. In the War for Independence and among those who held a stake in the conflict, perspectives proliferated—those of colonial patriots, colonial loyalists, African Americans both slave and free, Native Americans, the British Crown and loyal ministers, members of Parliament who supported the colonial patriots and those who thought of them as British traitors, and those who simply did not care one way or another. I judged that for a fifth-grader, exploring the conflict from at least the patriot's perspective *and* that of the British authorities would be a good start down the road toward developing a deeper sense of the role perspective and positionality play in historical investigation and in subsequent understandings of past events. I also worked from the assumption that that understanding could help challenge the unqualified heritage-based assumption that the actions of colonial patriots were unabashedly justified.

INVESTIGATING CAUSES OF THE WAR FOR INDEPENDENCE

In order to accomplish this, I chose to focus initially on possible causes of the conflict. By causes I do not mean what is frequently referred to as linear cause–effect relationships in historical study. Given the often thin evidence chains and the sometimes limited capacity we have for fully comprehending the intent of historical agents, I am generally suspicious of attempts to fix such links. In investigating possible causes of the Revolution, I was after multiple factors and catalysts that *may have contributed* to misunderstandings between the colonials and British leadership, ones that reflected diverging points of view on what a proper evolving relationship might be between Britain as a colonial power and its colonies. For example, I theorized that such an exploration would reveal, through analyses of primary and secondary documents, how separatist rhetoric and actions in the colonies fostered considerable alarm in England and subsequently led to strategies designed to counter both. But I also wished to present students with documentation on how the moves toward independence were not without antagonistic British policy antecedents.

I hoped this direction of study would play to my interest in exploring—near the end of the unit—the question of justifiable colonial revolt and requiring students to support their positions with evidence. As I implied earlier, I used this approach to problematize the heritage-fueled notion that American patriots unquestionably fought on the right side of the cause. I was fully mindful of other issues and historical developments such an approach would prevent us from investigating. Again, this was an all-too-forceful reminder of the choices history teachers must make, even within the confines of curriculum and testing policies that are relatively specific in terms of what they demand a teacher to address.

In order to make the transition from studying colonial development almost exclusively from a viewpoint of life in North America, I drew from a chapter titled "The Nasty Triangle" in Hakim's (1993b) *From Colonies to Country*. I began the first class of our investigation of the revolutionary period by conducting a guided reading of this chapter. In it, we encountered depictions of the way in which many colonists participated in and benefited—directly or indirectly—from a complex Atlantic Ocean trading system. This system brought raw goods from the colonies to England for manufacture, export, and profit, and slaves, spices, and the like to the New World from Africa and the West Indies, supporting the growing slave economy in the American southern colonies. Because the system involved highly lucrative but often deadly slave trading, Hakim used the term *nasty* in the title.

My goal in taking the fifth-graders through this chapter was, first, to provide some historical context. I wanted to demonstrate how thoroughly the colonies were complicit in this trading process and benefited by it. And second, I sought to begin the process of thinking about causes. For example, Hakim notes that colonists were prohibited by England from exporting finished goods. This was a means of preventing the colonists from reaping the full profits such trading practices brought England, a mercantilist policy that angered some colonial entrepreneurs and led to smuggling. These moves through the chapter also set the stage for exploring the Seven Years' War and the debt burden its outcome presented the victor, Great Britain.

Before we began reading, I used the timeline above the chalkboard to note how our investigations of colonial development led us up to about 1750. At about that point, the economic and political partnership between England and the colonies appeared to function like a well-tuned machine. I observed that by the mid-1770s, however, England and its North American colonies were engaged in a grave dispute that led to a bloody set of skirmishes in North America and eventually to the birth of the United States. "But," I asked, "what happened to the well-tuned machine? What provoked the war of words and then of guns?" I suggested that we needed to investigate this period to address these questions, not because it was a mystery in the same sense as the Starving Time but because people, particularly historians, often debate the answers to these questions. I wanted us to get in on the debate. Never shy about entering into a contest where they could express their opinions, the fifth-graders seemed much intrigued by the opportunity. I then noted that, in order to understand the arguments and viewpoints, we needed to look at the evidence, explore sources, and try to determine what the factors were that may have led to the War for Independence. Reading the chapter that class period would be our beginning effort in investigating possible causes.

We worked our way through a good share of the chapter on the first day. Hakim's (1993b) account moves from farming, codding, and shipbuilding in New England to planting and growing tobacco on southern plantations. It also makes other distinctions between the northern and southern colonies. I sketched the trade triangle in rather rough fashion on paper attached to the chalkboard board beneath the heading "What caused the American Revolution?" as a method of illustrating how it operated.

Eventually, the account took us to the slave narrative of Olaudah Equiano, who describes in vivid detail his capture and transatlantic voyage. His account is italicized and block indented in the Hakim text. After the second entry, broken up by two short paragraphs of interpretation and narrative tropes by Hakim (1993b), I stopped Jessica, who was then reading. I ask her what this cursive-looking text was and what it meant. She described it as written by someone who experienced it, without noting that it was a primary source. I interjected, "So, this is like a primary source?" She said, "Yes, I guess." Others were nodding and agreeing. Then I said, "So, this is a primary source within a secondary source," with inflection at the end of the statement as though I was really asking a question. Several nods occurred, and then Tho blurted out, "That's weird!" She appeared to think that secondary and primary sources could not occur together in the same document, possibly an artifact of seeing documents presented in separate and distinct fashion in her investigations into colonial development in the previous unit. Unfortunately, with her comment, we ran out of time in this class session. As a result, I was unable to further explore this idea with her then.

On the second day, after we had finished reading our way through the chapter, stopping to clarify language and discuss various points, I circulated a question guide that asked students to address several questions I had prepared. All but the last question were designed to focus their attention toward possible issues on which the colonists and English leaders might have had different perspectives (e.g., Why did the triangle trade begin and continue the way it did? Who benefited and how?). Students spent a good deal of the period working out responses to the questions, referring frequently to the chapter. Our discussion of these questions began at the conclusion of this period and took us through the next. The final question asked students to explain whether they thought Hakim's claims in the chapter were well defended with appropriate evidence.

In the third lesson, we began with this last question. Generally, responses were argumentative and sometimes quite astute. For example, several students dismissed the account outright for failure to cite sources. Ben argued that to test the validity of Hakim's (1993b) account, you would need to look at a series of sources, both primary and secondary, in order to compare them and "see what made sense" given what the accounts had said. The sentiment among others in class was much the same, although several students placed some emphasis on the importance of consulting primary sources in the process of judging the validity of Hakim's narrative.

By this point, a number of students were operating from the principle that the studying of multiple sources was crucial to building a defensible understanding of events. A couple of students maintained that

Hakim had violated copyright law by quoting Equiano without permission. I tried to settle this by noting an author's responsibility to cite the work of someone quoted and the need to ask permission to quote long passages. Seeking to respond to Tho's question in the first class, I asked her why she thought it strange to find primary source material (the Equiano diary) embedded in a secondary source. As I suspected, she was thinking it had to be either/or. I asked the class what we should think if an account contained both. Tho believed that this might make is seem more trustworthy, but it still should be read with suspicion. Others added that, in this case, it was necessary to check Hakim's sources. I said that I had and had found Equiano's account on the Internet, waving the account I had printed out. Tho said that maybe the Internet was not a very reliable place to get such an account. I tried to explain that I was being a good detective because I had checked Hakim's quotations against the source-identified text I had found on the Internet and they matched, word for word. Alex noted that, while we were discussing this, he had been examining the Hakim chapter and noticed that she had not cited any sources. He wondered if this indeed meant that she had violated copyright provisions. I mentioned that I thought it was possible and that we might continue to explore it. I also noted that Hakim had included a "Credits" section at the end of the book, where authors often indicate their permission to quote at length from sources. Despite this attempt at reassurance, skeptical Alex insisted that we be wary of Hakim's storytelling. Playing good historical investigator, he later discovered that Hakim had not cited the original source of the Equiano diary nor any other sources she had used (other than pictures), thus further raising his doubts about Hakim's historical accounting practices.

We concluded the class by switching back to an earlier question and to a puzzle I had with their responses concerning why the trade triangle had begun and continued. Many had observed that all the trade partners were benefiting splendidly by the arrangement. I asked, "Well why, if things were so wonderful, did the colonists start a war with England, a war that would threaten this mutually beneficial trade practice?" I had them go back to the text to investigate this and find possible clues there. Within several minutes, a handful of students reported locating several. After listening to their explanations, I wrote on the board: "The colonists were forbidden to ship all but finished goods out of the colonies, keeping them from making the money selling finished goods would bring" and "This sometimes resulted in the colonial smuggling that broke English law." I also mentioned that historians have reported that the English authorities knew that the colonists were smuggling but, because things generally seemed to be going so well, often simply looked the other way.

While by day we were discussing the trade triangle and divining possible causes for the American Revolution, at night I was building a collection of primary and secondary source materials. I hoped that this collection would take us deeper into understanding the diverging perspectives that would shape the contest between the colonies and Britain. I purchased the three-volume videotape series *The Revolutionary War* (Discovery Communications, 1996). I also purchased Ghere and Spreeman's (1998) *Causes of the American Revolution,* a set of lesson plans and primary source materials produced under the auspices of the National Center for History in the Schools (NCHS) and the Organization of American Historians (OAH). For the purpose of developing additional historical context, I continued to explore potentially interesting chapters in Hakim's (1993b) *From Colonies to Country,* the volume that succeeds *Making Thirteen Colonies* in the series. By *interesting,* I mean chapters that tended to be provocative either in their content or because they appeared to violate rules of good historical practice and investigation. I was working from the idea that poor history texts can be useful learning tools if students know how to read them critically.

Finally, I searched several historical document archives on the Internet and printed selected primary sources that dealt with British and colonial perspectives on the Stamp Act rebellion, the "Boston Tea Party," the shootings in Boston in March 1770 (what Samuel Adams called the "Boston Massacre"), and British and colonial accounts of the battle at Lexington Green. The materials in Ghere and Spreeman's (1998) booklet proved a treasure trove of useful documents, 20 to be exact, not all of which I ended up using.

As we finished our examination of the trade triangle, we had developed a list of three suspect causes. The first was a net advantage to England as a result of Atlantic trading practices and mercantilist economic policies, frustrating some colonial entrepreneurs. The second was smuggling by colonists that violated English law, despite the fact that it was generally overlooked by British authorities. And the third was the Seven Years' War that had left England deeply in debt, necessitating more exacting tax policies and engendering anger among the colonists.

In our effort to expand this list and build additional historical context, I introduced and showed the first 40 minutes of Volume 1 of the videotape series *The Revolutionary War* (Discovery Communications, 1996). From this videotape, we found possible additional evidence to support the three likely causes we had thus far identified and added seven more possible causes to the list during a discussion of the videotape. Although told from an undeniably pro-colonial perspective, the videotape, narrated by Charles Kuralt, provides a succinct narrative on the taxing policies initiated by British economic ministers in an effort to pay down the Seven

Years' War debt. It also outlines colonial resistance, implying that colonists were essentially justified in defying King George's decrees. Nonetheless, the videotape offered us a fairly compelling look at a number of issues that could be listed as possible causes (e.g., the Townshend Acts, the tax on tea, the Stamp Act). The videotape also provided us with a reasonably clear explanation of the famed "no taxation without representation" complaint colonial patriots registered with increasing stridency in the years preceding the Revolution. Additionally, the alleged "Boston Massacre" was treated in some detail, as was the British provision that prohibited colonists from moving westward beyond the Appalachians.

During our discussions of causes generated from the videotape, several students asked questions about the nature of some of the material that was contained in several voice-overs that were occasionally built into the film's script (e.g., an actor reading from an eyewitness account of the Boston shootings). Their curiosity turned on whether we should consider those actors' readings as primary sources, particularly since some were derived from eyewitness accounts or original texts (e.g., the Declaration of Independence). Thinking this a fertile area of inquiry, I turned the question back on the class. The consensus was that, even though an actor was reading, for example, from an original primary source, we still needed to consider it as such. However, Tim wondered out loud about how we could tell that they were actually reading directly from the source, not ad-libbing. Alex noted in response that we'd have to examine the original sources against the actor's reading.

At this stage, I conducted a formative assessment to determine how the discussion of possible causes was influencing students' thinking. To this end, I assigned them a brief essay. I asked that, before writing, they carefully study the 10 causes now lodged in their social studies log books. I asked that they think about the videotape we had watched and the account of the trade patterns and their consequences we had read in "The Nasty Triangle." The writing prompt asked students to produce a paragraph in which they were to choose three causes that they judged to be the most significant in leading up to the open conflict between England and the colonies. Responses were to be supported by evidence gleaned from our reading, the videotape, and our discussions. After the groans subsided and I addressed student questions (mostly about the length of the essay), they settled into the task. Studying causes and constructing an initial draft of the essay took the remainder of the hour. At the end of class, I explained that, in 2 days, I would be collecting and then grading the essays, and that they would have opportunities later to read what they had concluded to their classmates.

Later that same afternoon, snow began falling, rapidly enough for 8 inches to accumulate in quick order. In this area of the country, such rapid snowfalls bring many things to a halt, particularly schooling. School was canceled for the next 2 days. When students returned, their essays were due. For the first 10 minutes of class I asked them to apply finishing touches. The remaining class time was spent reading aloud, discussing, and arguing about the essays.

Much of the discussion and argument hinged on students taking issue with each other over their choices about most significant causes. If, say, Jonathon chose the "Boston Massacre," the Stamp Act, and the "Tea Party" as causes (which he did), others who favored the "Intolerable Acts" as an important cause (and a number did) debated him on his choices. For example, they argued for the importance of the "Intolerable Acts" in pushing colonial frustration and anger to heights that made the other British policy moves seem unimportant in retrospect. The tenor of the debate—always threatening to become too spirited—was controlled by my efforts to moderate it. Many students questioned their classmates based on the evidence they put forward, seizing on opportunities to politely interrogate essay claims that were weak in supporting argument. These students appeared to be growing steadily in their capacity to develop a language or discourse for engaging in this type of lively historical practice. Despite some success here, it seemed to me that much more still needed to be done.

After collecting and reading all the essays, it became apparent to me that the pro-colonial historical stance presented in the Hakim and videotape accounts played directly into students' heritage-charged pro-American historical positionalities foreshadowed in the previous unit. This occurred despite a number of attempts on my part to point out the partisan positions of both Hakim and the narrator and voice-over actors in the videotape. Virtually without exception, the essays contained arguments about significant causes that were tilted in favor of citing types of repression visited on the colonials by an intolerant British regime bent on dictating life in North America largely through unfair tax policies. As I looked ahead to the remainder of the unit, I realized I needed to step up my efforts to counter this type of one-sided perspective taking. However, before going there in earnest with an exercise distinctly designed to accomplish just that (see the "newspaper activity" below), I wanted to focus on expanding their understanding of the British king, King George.

Some recent scholarship hypothesizes that George may have suffered from a rare disease that could have made him seem mentally deranged a good deal of the time, particularly during the mid and late 1770s. From

our place in the twenty-first century in which the prescription of psycho-
tropic drugs designed to control mental states is commonplace, we can
speculate that his disease and resulting moodiness were often beyond his
and his doctor's ability to control because such drugs were not available.
Despite George's apparent lack of culpability for his shifting mental dispositions, he nonetheless was hardly a paragon of an intelligent, adept policy
maker. Yet we may now be in a position to be more historically sympa-
thetic and understanding of his state and its results. I wanted students to
know all this before their simplistic view of him as an irascible tyrant had
been fully cemented.

     To address this issue and build additional historical context, we turned
our attention again to Hakim's (1993b) treatment of King George, a narrative account that hints at his mental instability. Again, I pursued a guided
reading, this time of the chapter in *From Colonies to Country* titled "A Taxing King."[1] This exercise was hardly an unqualified success. It did not take
long for students to conclude, following Hakim's pro-colonial leanings, that
King George was a miscreant and could be dismissed as such. To offset this
reading, I repeatedly interjected questions about the Hakim's point of view
into our discussions of the text. I asked students to explain why they
thought the text was unsympathetic to King George. What might the
author's agenda be here? I noted the recent scholarship suggesting that
George may have been suffering from a debilitating mental disorder for
which his doctors had no treatment. I invited students to explain how this
possibility might influence the conclusions they drew from the reading.
Much of this effort met with resistance. Yet again, the chapter played directly into their pro-American, pro-colonial sentiments. King George was
a crackpot who mean-spiritedly waged a tax war against the colonial up-
starts. The colonists were entirely right and justified in fighting back and
freeing themselves from his tyrannical control. In effect, George was a bad
parent who needed to be resisted and countered, something that no doubt
tapped into some students' budding adolescent angst.

     In an attempt to focus their attention not only on causes of the Revo-
lution but also on how authors' viewpoints play out in a text as they attempt to re-create historical events, I developed an exercise in which I
asked students to respond to a set of questions about Hakim's treatment
of King George in this chapter. For example, I asked, "Why does Hakim
think King George made a lot of big mistakes?" and "Is it possible that King

---

[1] As an aside, Tim reacted to my announcement of this reading activity by referring back to our earlier discussions, saying, "Why do we have to read Hakim
again? All we do when we read her book is argue about how bad it is!"

George did what he did because he was angry at the colonists, because he thought *they* were misbehaving?" The latter question was designed to counter Hakim's somewhat one-sided treatment on the question of who was upset with whom. In effect, she portrays King George as the instigator of anger and frustration in North America, but does not indicate that King George, Parliament, and British ministers may have had cause to be deeply troubled by the colonists' recalcitrant actions, thus exacerbating and heightening the tensions.

When we discussed responses to my questions in class, I pressed students. The way they addressed the question in writing made it clear to me that they gave the possibility of British anger and frustration over "unruly subjects" little credence. I asked for elaboration, noting that the colonists were still British subjects and answerable to the Crown. "No," Jeffrey shouted out to a chorus of agreement, "they were free." I pushed him. "How do you know they were free?" Chelsea jumped in and said that they had signed the Declaration of Independence. I countered with, "So does that make them free in 1776? Or were they actually free only after they won the War for Independence?" Many students believed that they were free upon signing the Declaration. Again, I countered with, "Did they just *think* they were free from Britain? Does Hakim make it sound that way? Does signing a document make it so?" And on it went: I pressed the point-of-view issue, and they insisted on what their heritage-inspired positions told them was right. I came away from this experience with a newfound respect for the powerful partisanship David Lowenthal (1998) claims that heritage inspires. Because I was resolved to teach history rather than heritage, I felt compelled to produce an exercise that I believed would confront this influence more directly.

ASSESSING AUTHOR PERSPECTIVE AND SUBTEXT: THE NEWSPAPER ACTIVITY

Elsewhere (VanSledright & Afflerbach, 2000), I have raised the issue of the pedagogical wisdom of asking novice historical inquirers to make sense of primary source documents on a specific historical event before they demonstrate much prior knowledge of that event or show that they know how to read documents strategically (e.g., assessing the status of sources, reading and evaluating them intertextually, identifying author perspective). This is a knotty and complex problem in historical study. Since understanding the larger historical context in which an event occurred can be crucial to a careful, strategic reading of primary source documents, what is the best approach for building that context among novices? Does one begin with a narrative treatment, or two or three, and then proceed to dig more deeply by going back to the sources from which the narrative was derived? Or can a careful structuring and sequencing of the primary sources allow for the building of deep historical context surrounding an event?

In this unit as well as in my introductions of the Starving Time in the last unit, I had been operating on the hypothesis that first providing some narrative background (however brief) and then plunging into the primary sources was the more effective approach. However, as our experience with the videotape and the two Hakim accounts demonstrated, narratives contain powerful perspectives and subtexts in their own right. And they traffic deftly in the referential illusion. To the extent that they are so constructed, these narratives can predispose novice inquirers to adopt perspectives that align closely with their more generalized historical positionalities (e.g., proponents of all things American). Can encounters with primary sources drawn from conflicting perspectives on an event help to offset the adoption of a singular, one-sided perspective and teach novices to read all manner of historical texts more critically? Noting as I did in the last chapter how difficult it was to engage these students in rethinking their epistemological assumptions, I had my doubts. Nevertheless, the Newspaper Activity that we now would embark on was an effort to further press this issue.

The primary sources I had been collecting from the Internet and the ones I found in Ghere and Spreeman (1998) became the textual substance for this activity. I had accumulated approximately six or seven detailed primary sources on each of five different events that we had listed as potential causes of the American Revolution: (1) the Stamp Act, its origin and consequences; (2) the tea tax, its origin and results; (3) the Boston "Tea Party"; (4) the shootings in Boston in 1770; and (5) the battle at Lexington Green. These five events became the newspaper beats for pairs of students. I created four different newspapers for which students worked. Then I assigned student pairs to report on one event.

Because there were 23 students, we established 10 dyads and one triad, or 11 newspaper stories to be produced. One student in the group would act as an illustrator and the other (or others in the case of the triad) would act as a reporter(s), writing a newspaper account explaining the event as a cause. The primary source documents I supplied constituted the evidence from which reporters and illustrators could draw. I chose documents that represented various perspectives on, say, the Boston "Tea Party" or the shootings in Boston. For example, several eyewitness accounts (representing loyalist and patriot perspectives), British Captain Thomas Preston's account of the shootings, and other British soldiers' reports became the "evidence" for those working on the Boston Massacre. In effect reporters and illustrators, now with some prior knowledge of these events and a larger context within which to locate them, were asked to develop a story for their newspaper based on evidence gleaned from the primary sources.

The central element of the activity surfaced in the nature of the newspapers themselves, fictitious creations of mine but bearing some resemblance to actual late-18th-century types. There were four in total, and each had its own distinctive point of view. One London paper served as an "independent voice," charged to report stories in as unbiased a manner as possible, I explained to its reporters and illustrators. A second London paper was effectively an arm of King George, supportive of him and his policies. There were two Boston papers, I also explained, one a mouthpiece for the patriot cause and staunchly anti-Crown, and the other a loyalist paper, representing the position of those colonists loyal to the Crown, who felt besieged by the treasonable activity of the rebels all around them. I told students that the most important feature of this activity was that reporters and illustrators reflect the position and perspective of newspapers to which they were assigned, even if this meant that they had to produce an account contrary to their own beliefs and one that played a bit fast and loose with the evidence.

I selected and paired students carefully in two different ways. First, I looked for opportunities to put a more able and a less accomplished reader together, justifying this on the grounds that a number of the documents were difficult to read (I included modern translations wherever possible, some of which I translated myself, following the lead of the materials I had used in the previous unit) and that the better readers could assist the less able ones. Second, I put a number of the more outspoken "pro-American" students (based on their comments from earlier discussions) on the Boston loyalist newspaper or the London newspaper that supported King George. I believed this would challenge their one-sided perspective-taking practices. It came as no surprise that Anika, for example, immediately refused "to write for that stupid London newspaper that supports King George." With a slightly sarcastic tone to my voice, I told her that I was not allowing much choice in the matter and that, besides, I thought it would be good for her to see whether she actually could write well from a perspective she did not share. She grumbled for two class periods but eventually conceded, performing the task with some deftness.

Before we began the activity but after I had given each group the primary source evidence, I revisited the steps on Being Good Historical Detectives (see Chapter 3). I retrieved the chart from the back wall, where it had been hanging all along, and brought to the front of the room. I went over the steps, reinforcing their importance and explaining how what they

were being asked to do here again involved following these steps rigorously. I noted that historical investigators and newspaper reporters, along
with lawyers and private detectives, had a lot in common. However, I also
noted that in this case, although I was again asking them to be good investigators in reading the documents, I nevertheless wanted them, in the
end, to faithfully represent the position of their newspaper. I explained
that I was interested in having them see how, in doing so, history can be
twisted and turned to suit particular purposes.

The exercise turned out to be more complex and time-consuming than
I initially expected. It took us approximately 2 weeks, or about 10 class
periods, to complete. A number of students struggled to understand some
of the difficult primary sources. I spent a good deal of my time answering
questions and moving from group to group, querying students about their
understanding of the readings, modeling how to decode arcane language
in the texts, and assisting them in assessing the perspectives and possible
subtexts contained in the documents. As in the last unit, this frequently
involved showing them how to identify first who the author was and then
where the document came from (both acts of sourcing a text). Two illustrators almost immediately began drawing a picture of the event on their
beat without reading the documents. When I asked one how he managed
this feat, he told me that he already knew what happened because he saw
it on the videotape. He and I had a 15-minute discussion about the pro-
colonial perspective in the videotape and the fact that he was charged to
come up with a drawing of the Boston "Tea Party" from the perspective of
a newspaper that supported King George and deplored the dumping of
that tea in the harbor. How did he think two such different pictures might
look? As I turned to attend to another group, he was crumpling his first
drawing.

The exercise was difficult for another reason as well. It challenged
students to *simultaneously* conduct several complex interpretive maneu-
vers. First, they had to engage in the problematic text/context dialectic
that arose when they tried to determine the reliability of and perspectival
differences among the politically charged primary and secondary sources
they were reading. Second, they had to understand the sociopolitical
perspective of the newspapers to which they were assigned. Third, and
perhaps most importantly, they had to explicitly identify their own perspective on the conflict in order to understand the bearing it had on the
creation of their stories and illustrations vis-à-vis their newspaper's perspective. For students reporting for pro-British papers, the latter maneu-
ver was most challenging because they had to corral the desire to
impose their pro-colonial perspective on the evidence sources and their
newspaper's account.

Slowly, drawings and accounts began to emerge. I kept reminding students that a key to their success was my evaluation of the degree to which they faithfully represented their newspaper's point of view and used the evidence to support it, no matter how difficult that might be. In some cases, this necessitated partisan selectivity in how evidence was considered. At several different points, students such as Alexandra, Alex, Coral, Katie, and Tho questioned this approach, saying that, in their view, they would be distorting the overall evidence if they adopted in full the perspective of their newspaper. I reminded them that this was precisely what I wanted them to understand—how in this situation of escalating conflict, people filtered the evidence and used it for their own purposes. I asked if they knew what propaganda was. Several had heard the term and were able to provide a rough definition. This opened up another teaching opportunity as I explained how propaganda became a tool, for example, used by patriots to rally those colonists who seemed neutral in the struggle of opposing positions. I pointed out how the term *massacre* in the case of the "Boston Massacre" could be thought of as propagandizing, designed by patriots such as Sam Adams to distort evidence to achieve a particular purpose. Making sense of how this worked was pivotal to understanding the possible causes of the American Revolution, since initially about two-thirds of the colonists either remained loyal to England or declined to take sides.

Tho, for one, still remained troubled that, in crafting a newspaper story that distorted the evidence, she was violating the principles of being a good historical detective. I told her that I was glad she could make these distinctions because it allowed her to see the difference between historical constructions that carefully considered all the available evidence and attempted to account for it, and those designed to push a particular point of view with far less regard for that evidence. Later, I took this issue up with the entire class, using Tho's concern as a bridge. At about this point, it seemed to me that I was finally making some significant headway in teaching them how to read historical documents with an eye toward the perspective of the author and the influence this perspective had on what the author wrote. Privately, though, I worried that this lesson was being lost on a few too many. Again, I redoubled my resolve to push the ideas as often as I could, honing my sense of finding openings to reinforce them.

Students turned in a final draft and accompanying illustration to me at the end of the seventh class period spent on this activity. I studied them carefully and wrote a number of comments in the margins of both the stories and the illustrations. Mainly, I was attempting to get them to refine the edge of their articles to support the viewpoint of their newspaper, and then achieve better alignment with details in the picture. I suggested that illustrations could include captions—drawn from eyewitness evidence contained in their primary source documents—to support the storyline of the article and that they should contain a title below it, along with the artist's name, as they do in actual newspapers. I also made a number of comments about how to write a newspaper article. I clipped copies of short articles from the *Washington Post* and attached them to student drafts to illustrate this newspaper genre of writing (e.g., short sentences, one- or two-sentence paragraphs).

The next three class sessions were spent on completing final versions and illustrations in light of my comments. In class, I continued to stress the idea of correspondence between the viewpoints of the newspaper, the article, and the illustration. A couple of groups experienced protracted difficulties with this idea. For example, Wayne insisted on creating an illustration without reading the documents carefully and considering the perspective of his newspaper. Jamie, his partner, repeatedly pressed him to bring his illustration into correspondence by reading the documents with him. Eventually, after several revisions of his illustration, he achieved some success, later telling me that he now better understood how the Americans and British could view the events at Lexington very differently.

On the other hand, Ben took to the task quickly and astutely, asking me at one point if he could work from additional information from two other sources he had located on his own. Alex and Coral, uncomfortable with what they construed to be limited ideas provided by the sources I had supplied, requested a trip to the library to investigate additional material. Brittney and Alexandra demonstrated early that they understood the task of writing from the perspective of their respective newspapers, although they still appeared to be seduced by the epistemological idea that, if you examined enough sources, The Truth eventually would emerge, unmarked by their interpretations of those sources. I kept reminding them that, as we had often seen in our earlier investigations, historical detective work was similar to the difficult task of nailing Jell-o to a wall. Despite my intentions to the contrary, it may be that the choice of the "detective" metaphor and the "case-solving" concept it can imply catered to the resilient "encyclopedia epistemologies" of students such as Alexandra and Brittney.

Once final versions were complete, I circulated large poster paper and markers, and asked that students transfer their articles and illustrations to poster paper. I told them to think of these posters as front pages of their respective newspapers. I asked that they use the entire front page, increasing the size of their illustrations and writing their articles in columns the way they had seen them printed in the *Washington Post*. After these posters were finished, students took turns in groups presenting them to the class and answering questions from classmates about how they handled the writing and illustrating so that they were internally aligned and also matched their paper's perspective. Many of the questions were insightful. For groups assigned to the *Boston Globe* (loyalist perspective) and the *London Times* ("the voice of King George"), students asked reporters how they could write an article that supported a cause with which they did not agree. Alex and Coral (*Boston Globe*) claimed that they found it intriguing to tell and illustrate the story "from the other side."

Following this discussion, we hung the completed posters on the wall outside the classroom. That weekend, I digitized the front pages and posted them on the Internet (see www.wam.umd.edu/~bvansled/amrevo/newspapers.html). The students were delighted to now have been published twice.

EYEWITNESS TESTIMONY AND THE BOSTON "MASSACRE"

The newspaper activity had some success in leavening the students' unquestioned pro-colonial stance and challenging their heritage views on the War for Independence. It also focused their attention on the roles of perspective and subtext in reading primary sources and on the idea that historical investigators need to take differing perspectives into account. And third, it directed their gaze at how events in the past can be distorted for partisan purposes.

The fifth-graders began showing signs of a more well developed historical-thinking vocabulary and discourse, demonstrating that they could not only cite and discuss the evidence surrounding the Stamp Act or the "Tea Party," but could also explain the rationales they used in constructing an argument based on sensitivity to shifting perspectives found in that evidence. However, excited as I was to witness this sort of discourse in class, I wondered about how representational it was of their overall historical thinking and understanding. Were they talking about perspective and point of view merely because my structuring of the newspaper activity required it, or perhaps because they saw in it connections to ideas they had learned in language arts (e.g., understanding the point of view of an author or a character in a story)? Was this a distinct form of historical-thinking discourse they had learned, or something else? How deep did it go? What about students who appeared less facile with the vocabulary? With these questions and the doubts they inspired poking away at me, I resolved to press on them even harder.

The Ghere and Spreeman (1998) booklet contains an exercise that spells out how a group of students can reenact the trial of the soldiers accused of murder in the infamous Boston shooting incident of March 1770. The booklet contains the testimony of the witnesses called to the stand during the trial. This exercise seemed to me to provide another opportunity not only to read primary source material and draw inferences based on it—as we had been doing—but also to again pursue the issue of political subtext and perspective in such material.

The Boston incident offers another powerful example of the inherent difficulties in reaching surefire conclusions about what happened in the past. An occupying army sent to quell disturbances and enforce the Crown's policies (e.g., the Townshend Acts) raised tensions between colonial patriots and the British to even higher levels, particularly in Boston. In late February 1770, two Bostonians—one an 11-year-old boy— were shot to death by a British loyalist/customs informer after he was chased to his house by a rock-throwing band of anti-British rebels. He had attempted to protect the importing activities of two fellow loyalists, running squarely up against colonial patriots who were trying to enforce a trade embargo against Britain. At the funeral for the boy, Sam Adams helped raise anti-British emotion to a fevered pitch (Cummins & White, 1980; Ghere & Spreeman, 1998).

In early March 1770, historians tell us, soldiers and a group of Boston rope makers engaged in a running feud that began when a Redcoat attempted to get work in a Boston rope-making factory to supplement his poor military salary. He was ridiculed. Several fights erupted over a period of several days between soldiers and the rope makers and their supporters. Anti-British Bostonians took to roaming the streets in club-wielding bands. British regulars stiffened for confrontation. On March 5, outside a customs house, a group of Boston boys, later joined by adults, harassed British sentries posted there. Accusations were exchanged. The boys hurled ice chunks and snowballs. The disturbance escalated. A group of soldiers led by Captain Thomas Preston were dispatched, ostensibly to protect the customs house and the "King's money" it contained. In the midst of shouts and insults, a growing and menacing crowd, club-waving Bostonians, and abject confusion, the badly outnumbered soldiers fired their muskets into the crowd, killing five people. In the aftermath, justice was demanded. Who gave the order to fire was the question Bostonians wanted answered. Patriot sentiment quickly fell in against Captain Preston and his platoon. They were arrested and later tried by a jury chosen from neighboring towns. Eyewitness testimony revealed the degree to which partisan positions prevailed in filtering what those present saw. The fifth-graders were intrigued: What happened to those accused? In the midst of heads nodding support, Jeffrey predicted that they were convicted of murder and justifiably hung.

When conflict is readily apparent, as with the Boston incident, perspectives and opposing agendas seem propelled into the foreground, offering rich opportunities for studying and learning about how they work and how the historical investigator must operate in making sense of them. In some ways, here near the end of my experience with them, we were returning to the beginning, to yet another explicit confrontation with the interpretive paradox (see Chapter 3).

After a conversation with Proctor about when I planned to conclude the unit and turn the social studies portion of the teaching back to her, it became quickly apparent that we did not have the luxury of spending a week or more actually reenacting the trial complete with props, casting, line memorization, and the like. I implemented an alternative. We would imagine that we were there, taking turns reading the testimony aloud in class. When we had completed it, I would select four people—two "representative lawyers" for the prosecution and two for the defense—to make brief closing statements based on the testimony. I would take written petitions from students offering to act in these roles. The petitions would need to demonstrate qualifications for the task (e.g., ability to read evidence clearly, make arguments aligned with role). After closing statements the class would act as a jury and vote on the guilt or innocence of the eight accused British infantrymen and their captain, Thomas Preston. Finally, we would discuss the trial and the testimony, then tabulate our jury votes and compare them against the results of the original trial.

Before beginning, we reviewed what we had learned from the newspaper reports about the context of the incident and the incident itself, noting the differences of perspective on what had occurred. I purposely had not included specific material concerning the trial itself in the primary sources given to groups reporting on the Boston incident for their newspapers, saving it for this later pedagogical opportunity. We then began taking turns reading aloud the testimony (students worked from photocopies of it for the 29 witnesses called, including the soldiers and Captain Preston). The testimony of each witness begins with an explanation of who the person is and then describes what the person saw and experienced. Although I declared myself the judge and noted that I would tolerate no commentary on the testimony, it occasionally was difficult to stem the tide of grumbling and muttering and attempts to discredit certain eyewitnesses (soldiers, loyalists) who gave accounts contrary to the pro-American sentiments of some students.

Over several class periods, we read our way through all the testimony, then heard the four closing statements—again having to quell several attempts by Jeffrey, Jamie, and Anika to butt in and challenge the two who defended the soldiers. After the closing statements were completed, I opened it up to discussion before putting the question of the soldiers' fate to a jury vote.

Alex, Alexandra, Coral, Katie, Tim, and several others asked a number of interesting questions. The questions sought clarification on key events that led up to and involved the shootings. Coral and Tim both asked about the distance certain so-called eyewitnesses had been from the shootings. Who exactly were the Bostonians, as distinct from the soldiers, and how close were they to the front line? Alex then wondered about how the growing size of the crowd influenced the soldiers' sense of being overwhelmed. I noted that students needed to remember that not all Bostonians present were necessarily rebel patriots, that some were no doubt loyalists who would likely favor the troops. Brittney asked who was who. I suggested that they go back and reread the testimony and to check the eyewitnesses' perspectives and positions.

Coral asked a bundle of questions. He was attempting to sort through what the eyewitnesses were saying. At one point he commented, "Well, if it was so dark as some people said, someone could have easily impersonated Captain Preston's voice. Maybe someone yelled near the edge of the crowd and that's what the soldiers heard. So they fired." Jeffrey jumped on this comment: "Why would one of the Boston people do that? That would be stupid." I suggested that there were loyalists present who might have said this as a way of attempting to exact a sort of justice against their perception of the "crazy patriots causing trouble." Getting the soldiers to fire into the rebel crowd might serve that purpose. As though he realized how he might address his own question by shifting his perspective, Jeffrey immediately reiterated a version of my comment. Here and somewhat surprisingly, he demonstrated—despite an otherwise staunch pro-American leaning—his potential to understand the event more thoroughly by adopting another stance. Coral responded by again raising the possibility that someone in the crowd could have yelled "fire" and that, in all the confusion, the troops mistook this as an order from Preston to shoot.

Tim jumped in, defending the crowd, claiming that the soldiers were wrong. After saying this, he paused for a second or two and said, "But the more testimony I read, the more I begin to change my mind." He then offered a hypothesis that someone in the crowd who was heard to yell, "They dare not fire," was understood by the troops as an order from Preston to fire their muskets. In this sense, he supported Coral's conjecture.

Coral, turning to a set of analogies (ones he relied on often) that reflected one interpretation he was constructing in his head, tried to persuade the class that, "If it was dark as some of the testimony indicated, then it was hard for the troops to see what they were even shooting at.

They were scared and acting in self-defense." He asked Cindy to say "Don't fire." She did and he shouted out "Aaaahhhgg" as she said "Don't" to illustrate how easy it might have been to mistake what was called out in the jeering, chaotic crowd. He asked the class, "So, what did you hear?" Many said that they heard him yell out something and then heard Cindy say, "Fire."

Again Jeffrey jumped in, saying, "They all had different perspectives on the orders to fire their guns," referring to the soldiers and their testimony about their various understandings of when to fire. Then, challenging Coral's interpretation, he added sarcastically, "Except, weird, they all seemed to be in agreement about their orders to march back to their barracks!" Alexandra and Alex also interjected comments here. They raised questions and then offered their opinions. At different points, this discussion afforded me opportunities to say things such as: (1) Try to imagine this scene in your head . . . (2) Try putting yourself in the place of the soldiers for a minute . . . (3) Maybe the soldiers feared for their lives—wouldn't you in a situation like this? (4) Think about it: 40, 50, 60, then maybe 100-plus Bostonians are rushing up and surrounding the troops—they are way outnumbered! What would that feel like to you?

In the end, I passed out the jury ballots and students voted. Somewhat to my surprise, a majority rendered a guilty verdict against only two of the soldiers, Privates Montgomery and Killroy. These two, it turned out, were the only soldiers actually convicted of anything in 1770. Both were found guilty of manslaughter, branded on the hand, and then released. The others were acquitted. In keeping with their Massachusetts Colony predecessors, the majority of the student jury in room 23 paid close attention to the evidence and voted the same outcome. I announced the result of the 1770 trial and observed how interesting it was that most of them, on hearing the evidence, found for the same verdicts more than 200 years later.

With the few minutes remaining in class, we discussed how the results of the trial—only two convictions, with relatively light sentences meted out—may have been perceived among Boston patriots and acted as a possible factor leading up to the war. Several students noted that, no doubt, Sam Adams and company were infuriated, leading them to renewed anti-British activity. Katie observed, though, that King George was probably pleased. She also added that George probably wondered what was going to come next from these rebels, thus intensifying his desire to control them. I then noted that British leaders, anxious to retain colonies they understood to exist under British charter and thus British law, would think of themselves as justified in stepping up efforts to suppress rebellion across the Atlantic. Picking on Ben, I asked if he could see it from this perspective. He said that he could, but added that increased control most likely would not work, that too much had already occurred to pit the sides firmly against each other.

JUSTIFYING THE PATRIOT CAUSE, BUT . . .

We ended our discussions of the Boston trial on a Tuesday, at the end of April. Because the following Monday marked the beginning of approximately 2 weeks of mandatory state and school district high-states testing, the social studies portion of the curriculum was to be eliminated during that period. This testing juncture signaled the close of my experience as these students' American history teacher, something Proctor and I had agreed on several weeks earlier. I found it a frustrating moment. "I'm not done here yet," I thought. "I'm beginning to see progress, especially regarding the students' understanding of perspective and subtext in historical study. I need more time." Alas, a teacher's chronic refrain.

On Wednesday of that week before testing began, I introduced students to a final essay I would ask them to write. The essay invited opinion and argument on whether or not the colonists were justified in waging war against England as a means of securing their independence. Positions for or against—and I stressed that either was acceptable—would need to be supported with clear evidence drawn from our investigations into the factors that led up to the conflict. Essays argued well by citing specific evidence to support a position would receive higher grades. The due date for the essay was set for the Friday of the following week. Proctor observed that there would be opportunities during the assessment test-taking process for students to craft their essays in class under her supervision. I would return that Friday to collect them. Learning to write well and express ideas was something Proctor had spent considerable time on with the students in the months preceding the state tests. The tests were known for requiring the writing of short essays following particular prompts dealing with text excerpts students were asked to read. The essay I assigned fit into her approach well and served as good practice for the test, she said. I returned to collect the essays on the due date, and read and graded them that following weekend.

Most of the essays showed signs of careful craftsmanship and seemed to be the result of at least two drafts. I had hoped that at least a few essays would adopt the "colonies were wrong to revolt" position, but such was not to be. Paralleling the virtual unanimity in the essays O'Connor's (1991) college students wrote, all 23 essays were written in support of the colonists' declaration of independence and justified the outcome of the war that resulted. What was most impressive by my lights was the time many students took to supply supporting evidence. The degree of detail in so doing left something to be desired, but I appreciated the effort.

Jeffrey, forever the diehard supporter of the rebel cause, titled his short essay "The Righteous Right of the Colonists to Rebel." He wrote (and I produce it verbatim here):

> The America colonist had the right to break away from England.
> They had the right to break away because they wanted freedom.
> The King was crazy and cruel. He put unfair taxes on the colonist.
> He also [sent] his ruthless british lobsterbacks with there mindless
> captain to Boston. There all the cowards did was cause trouble.
> Finally, Crazy King George III wouldn't listen to the freedom loving
> colonist. From the evidence, we all know that the crazy, ruthless,
> no good king was mean to the colonist and that's why they rebel.

Other essays were less vitriolic, but for the most part no less supportive of the Americans' right to throw off their oppressors as they claimed their liberty. Javell, who usually balked at the simplest of writing assignments, settled in and wrote a two-page essay in which he cited details of the tea tax, the Stamp Act, and the "Boston Massacre" as events and policies provoking the rebellion. Alexandra's essay was notable for both its length (four pages) and for the way in which it attempted balance. It acknowledged how both sides were to blame for the conflict, how we needed to look at the situation from the east and west side of the Atlantic; yet, in the end, evidence justified colonial behavior. The issue of colonial rights and their perceived abrogation by British leaders appeared as a powerful theme in many essays, including Alexandra's.

Proctor, impressed with her students' writing, asked me to return following the testing period and invite each student read his or her essay to classmates. Following a number of these readings, several students— Alexandra, Brittney, Coral, Jeffrey, and Tim—queried authors on their position and evidence employed in support of it. I found this practice remarkable for two reasons. First, despite the fact that these students had themselves written essays defending the American revolt, they asked questions that showed their ability to see the conflict from different angles, sometimes pursuing arguments about possible solutions that would have avoided bloodshed. For example, Tim asked, "Why couldn't the colonists have turned away from British troops in America and gone over the Appalachians Mountains and claimed new land for themselves, independent of Britain?" Jeffrey, the stolid patriot supporter, began a challenge to one reader with the statement, "I'm not taking the British side, but . . . ,"—

and proceeded to defend the British position of attempting to quell insurrection by the likes of rebel Sam Adams on the grounds that Americans remained British subjects and, in such acts, broke British law.

Second, such comments and questions suggested to me that, even though the essays unequivocally supported American revolt, we had succeeded to a degree in our perspectival study of events to ameliorate blind faith in the justice of the rebel cause. Moreover, our experiences investigating the evidence itself demonstrated how moral judgments about the past must be tempered and informed by deep knowledge of historical context. Despite these types of successes, I took my leave of the class pondering their limitations and wondering how I could have done more to deepen and enhance their historical-thinking capacity.

6

Acquiring Procedures and a Discourse for Investigating the Past

Within 2 weeks of leaving my teaching duties, I asked my research assistant to interview Proctor about her reactions to what she had witnessed during the time that I taught history. I was hoping to get some useful commentary and criticism from a classroom expert who had observed much of what went on. One key question Proctor was asked dealt with whether or not she had any reservations about how her students experienced my teaching efforts. She responded by initially noting that not enough content had been covered and that the class was now behind where they should be in the district's social studies curriculum sequence. This was something I had worried about. However, Proctor then quickly observed that this was acceptable because, as she put it, "my students will never forget what they learned; they'll never forget what they were taught about analyzing and exploring history. The approach that he used helped my students learn American history in a new way, one that will stick with them. I've never seen them this excited about studying the past. Usually they forget this stuff right away. But not what they learned here. . . . I can easily live with that. Who couldn't?" I took this to be a kind endorsement of my effort. But what did she mean by learning history in a new way, one that would stick with her students? In this chapter, I explore that question.

In previous chapters I described in some detail our study of events in the British colonization of North America and of factors that played a role in the circumstances leading to the War for Independence. To understand what students learned about those events and factors, I engaged them in a number of formative assessments, such as the essays on the causes of the American Revolution and whether the Revolution was justified or not, the research booklet students created on investigations into the five colonies (which was later published on the Internet), and the newspaper stories and illustrations (also published on the Internet).

I also required them to maintain social studies logs in which they took notes on issues and events we discussed in class. I periodically examined and commented on the pages of these logs as a means of understanding how the students were making sense of the events we studied and investigative procedures we documented.

The emphasis placed on colonization and the American Revolution was intended to develop students' ideas about the general flow of events during the period in American history from 1607 to 1776, as mandated by the district curriculum. These events and their details served as the background, however, on which we foregrounded our historical investigative processes. Generally, the formative assessments indicated that students possessed an emerging sense of this period as one of swift sociocultural and economic expansion among British colonial outposts along the Atlantic seaboard, intensifying conflict with Native Americans and an ever growing reliance on slavery as expansion proceeded, and a developing impression of "independence" among some British colonists that later erupted into a full-scale war over who would control the colonies.

I rarely engaged students in summative forms of assessment. As a result, I make no unequivocal claims here that all the students in room 23 learned, for example, the typical chronological "story" of British colonization in America and about all the myriad events leading up to the American Revolution, the narrative frequently rendered in textbooks. Given my understanding of the rather dismal results that have emerged from an array of research studies (e.g., those noted in Chapter 1) on what youngsters— and, as some researchers also would add, most adults—remember about the details of such stories when they are taught as a grocery list to be recounted on tests, I was more interested in what my students learned about investigating and practicing history and constructing a discourse for doing so.

As I have explained, my primary goals involved teaching students to think historically, learning about and then demonstrating cognitive strategies for being good historical investigators, as they explored some of the historical traces and residues colonial ancestors left behind. I am in deep agreement with Lee and Ashby (2000) when they observe that "the acquisition of more powerful procedural . . . ideas (about, for example, *evidence* or *change*) is one way—perhaps the best—of giving sense to the notion of [growth in learning] history" (p. 200; emphasis in original). But make no mistake; I also was deeply concerned that students learn about the American past as well. To accomplish this learning, I worked from the assumption that by *investigating the past* themselves—interpreting it and building their own arguments about what had occurred—they would more readily *remember the events* we studied. As a consequence, I developed assessment tasks that would shed light on their thinking and interpretation-building capabilities, given particular historical contexts. In short, the focus of my research documentation regarding student learning hinged on assessing *what they could do with what they knew*, rather than merely on their capacity to recall bits and pieces of the past. In what follows, I concentrate on the outcome of that principal goal.

Assessing what the fifth-graders could do with what they knew necessitated the construction and administration of what I called in Chapter 2 performance tasks. To review, I created two of them. I administered the first before I began teaching the students and the second after I had finished teaching them. Both performance tasks involved reading, analyzing, interpreting, and drawing inferences from a set of primary and secondary sources, the approach historians use to make sense of the past. The initial task dealt with the shootings in Boston and the second with the opening battle of the American Revolution at Lexington Green. Because the tasks require that students talk aloud (i.e., verbal-report protocols) about what they are thinking as they read and interpret the documents, they are time-consuming to administer and generate voluminous transcript data that must be carefully scrutinized. As a result, it was too onerous to ask that all 23 students engage in the two tasks. Instead, with the help of Proctor, we selected the eight students to serve as representative primary informants for the class as a whole: Alexandra, Ben, Candy, Coral, Jamie, Jeffrey, Kendra, and Tho.

Beyond providing data that could serve as a litmus test of my teaching efforts—and to the extent that they were so aligned, with the history reform recommendations—the results and analysis of the performance tasks can shed light on novice–expert historical-thinking practices. From studies on how expert historians read, analyze, and interpret historical documents (Leinhardt & Young, 1996; Wineburg, 1991, 1998), we have learned much about the nature of such expertise. However, these studies are silent about novice historical inquirers such as the fifth-graders in Room 23. As a result, we know little about how these American youngsters read, analyze, and assess similar documents. Therefore, we also know little about the specific steps we might take in moving such students down the road toward the more expert forms of historical thinking called for in history education reform recommendations. My pedagogical approach, for example, was rooted in only one theory for doing so.

British researchers on the CHATA Project (Concepts of History and Teaching Approaches; see Lee & Ashby, 2000; Lee, Ashby, & Dickinson, 1996a, 1996b) have done systematic research with a variety of students, some the same age as the ones with whom I worked. Their research has been longitudinal in nature. For approximately a decade now, they have studied primary through secondary children's "progress" in learning to think historically, much as I have described throughout this book. Results to date have been organized into several conceptual strands. For example, one represents changes in students' ideas about causal structure and rational understanding in history. The results indicate that (1) at any age, students' ideas about causality and rationality in historical explanations vary widely and may be more or less cognitively advanced (i.e., young students can display more sophisticated understandings of such concepts than older students); (2) individual students' ideas about the large idea of historical explanation do not necessarily "progress" at the same rate; (3) spurts in progression in different conceptual areas, such as causal and rational explanations, can occur at different ages and grade levels; and (4) the slowest "progression" in historical thinking was observed among students in schools without a distinct history curriculum.

In a second strand, understanding the nature of historical accounts, some British students were observed moving from the view that the past and history were the same to the more complex view that historical accounts were constructed by authors whose own positions influenced their writing. This process, the more cognitively sophisticated students noted, explained the differences among accounts and therefore the fact that it was "the nature of accounts to differ" (Lee & Ashby, 2000, pp. 212–213). Progression in these CHATA studies tends to be age-related; yet the researchers point out that attaining a certain age does not necessarily result in progression in particular ideas.

It is important to understand that progression in historical thinking among students in British schools is influenced by history teachers who have been taught, for example, to offer children opportunities to read and analyze historical documents—in keeping with their discipline-based national history curriculum—much earlier than is the case in the United States. Consequently, CHATA researchers' descriptions of progression must be applied with considerable caution to students, such as those in room 23, who have not had such opportunities and where research on how those opportunities link specifically to progression has yet to be done (Lee, 1998, p. 216). The performance task data generated by the eight students in this study were analyzed with all this in mind.

In several ways, my analysis is primarily an attempt to construct an emerging theory about how young novices in U.S. schools read historical documents and how they can learn to read them more deeply and competently once given a vocabulary and a set of strategies to do so. In this sense, the results participate in a conversation about where such novices begin, and can be moved initially, with regard to academic development in the domain of history (Alexander, 2000).

UNDERSTANDING THE PERFORMANCE TASK RESULTS

The performance tasks (i.e., think-aloud protocols that produce verbal reports) generate examples of what students do as readers of history texts, which are often referred to as "sources" by historians. This approach is largely an indirect way of assessing historical thinking. Asking students to tell you directly how they would read, analyze, and evaluate historical documents in an interview setting does not necessarily correspond to what students do when actually confronted with the task. In other words, what students this age say they do when they read and what they then actually do can be two different things. Although I did interview students concerning what they believed generally about analyzing and evaluating historical documents, I also wanted to see specific performances as a means of qualifying their responses with additional data. In my judgment, performance tasks that include verbal reporting are some of the best assessment tools currently at our disposal for understanding what children can do with what they know.

Analyzing the results of the performance tasks is a complex undertaking. Engagements in the task generate recordable verbal reports that contain at least two features of students' active cognition: (1) their capacity to use both general reading strategies (e.g., monitoring comprehension) and expert heuristics (e.g., cross-checking texts against each other) to build an interpretation of an event, and (2) the actual interpretation or understanding the students construct concerning the event about which they read. Indeed, I was interested in students' actual interpretations of the Boston "Massacre" and the battle at Lexington. However, because my pedagogical goals focused first on teaching procedures for engaging and constructing evidence-based interpretations, I concentrated my analysis on the development of the eight students' strategic-reading, analytic, and interpretation-building capabilities, particularly with regard to their use of the expert strategies and heuristics. As a result, I went through several stages of developing and refining a system that I could use to understand the degree to which the task data would speak to the procedural historical-thinking goals I was primarily pursuing.

When I arrived in the classroom, many of my fifth-graders could hardly be classified as expert readers, of history or much of anything else. A few of them struggled to read in general. And like many other U.S. students, mine lacked exposure to the primary source documents and the investigative learning opportunities afforded many British children. Under these circumstances, the procedural heuristics derived from work on how expert historians read cannot be easily applied to such young novices, except to note they are seldom used. The question is, if novices such as the eight readers representing my fifth-grade class are not reading history texts and documents like expert historians, what are they doing when they encounter sources? And further, what process indicates how they move from where they are as novices to a place where they read more like the experts? Here I present such a process. It describes how my eight readers encountered, read, analyzed, evaluated, and constructed interpretations first of the Boston "Massacre," and then, much later, of the battle at Lexington. For those interested in how I developed the model that resulted, see a detailed account in Appendix A.

Approaches to Document Analysis in the Performance Tasks

With the exception of Candy and Kendra, who occasionally had difficulty decoding words (Candy more so), all my readers were reasonably skilled meaning makers when it came to encountering texts in general. By this I mean that they could deploy a series of comprehension and monitoring strategies (e.g., summarizing what was just read, predicting what was coming next, drawing from prior knowledge) described by Pressley and Afflerbach (1995) as crucial to what good readers do to construct meaning from text. Being strategic in this way also enabled most of my readers to judge a text with regard to whether or not it made sense, whether or not the characters were believable, how they felt about the action, and the like (again, this was less pronounced for Candy and Kendra, the two less accomplished readers in the group of eight). Pressley and Afflerbach maintain that being able to make such judgments also is a hallmark characteristic of good readers. Their characterization of good reading defines it from a general and global perspective. However, it says little about the highly specialized reading strategies expert historical investigators employ.

Fundamentally, I wanted my students to become historical investigators who could build defensible, evidence-based interpretations of the past themselves. The historical reading and thinking processes that allow for building such interpretations involve the analyses and *evaluative comparisons* of multiple sources of evidence (e.g., texts or documents such as diary accounts, letters, books, images, and artifacts). The evidence must be analyzed with respect to how it coheres (or not). The evidence must be analyzed to determine its power in corroborating and supporting claims made as interpretations of an event. These analytic processes and crucial evaluative comparisons help investigators judge historical agents' perspectives, understand the status of accounts, and establish historical context as an interpretation is systematically refined (e.g., Lee & Ashby, 2000; Leinhardt & Young, 1996; Wineburg, 1991; 1998). Therefore, to make sense of the past, historical investigators move beyond relying solely on the types of comprehension and monitoring strategies and *intra*textual evaluations described by Pressley and Afflerbach (1995); they also must engage in what might be called critical *inter*textual analytic and evaluation strategies, those described by the research just noted on what expertise in historical thinking and investigation looks like.

Procedures for Reading Documents and Sources in the History Domain

One can think of such approaches to reading historical texts—strategic comprehension monitoring, intratextual evaluating, building event knowledge in order to construct an initial interpretation, and then refining that interpretation through intertextual evaluations—as levels on a continuum. At one end are the more general and less domain-expert approaches, and at the other end are the specialized and more domain-expert approaches. Movement for novices is from being less to becoming more astute as a historical investigator who can analyze multiple sources of historical evidence framing a particular event to construct a defensible interpretation. Figure 6.1 depicts how these approaches to reading and analyzing historical evidence fall on that continuum. The key distinction between the general approach (the two levels on the left) and the more historically-specific approach (the two levels on the right) is in the degree to which a reader relies on *intra*textual analyses (levels 1 and 2) or can also utilize the critical *inter*textual analyses (levels 3 and 4) that enable a more full understanding of the past through the construction of evidence-based interpretations. The two performance tasks were designed to be sensitive enough to measure these differences in the initial and the endpoint administrations.

To illustrate how movement on the continuum could occur for a reasonably good reader who engaged in the performance tasks, consider the following generalized example. Upon confronting a set of documents about a particular historical event, a young investigator who has little prior knowledge about that event (not uncommon among novice fifth-graders in American schools and certainly the case for my eight students) begins reading by employing comprehension and monitoring strategies (e.g., rereads, notes presence or absence of prior knowledge, summarizes) to make sense of an initial source. This is reading at level 1 (monitoring comprehension). If successful at making sense here, he may register evaluations of that text or image (e.g., "This person in the story is crazy!" "This is so beautiful!"). Making meaning (comprehension) enables the types of *intra*textual evaluations that characterize reading at level 2 (evaluating intratextually). However, meaning making and evaluating ideas and ac-

General reading practice | | | *History-specific strategic expertise*

LEVEL 1	LEVEL 2	LEVEL 3	LEVEL 4
Process: Using Comprehension Monitoring	*Process: Making Judgments and Evaluations*	*Process: Drawing from Accreting Event Knowledge*	*Process: Testing and Refining of Interpretation*
• Reader checks details, rereads, summarizes, and/or predicts developments in the source	• Reader judges aspects of a source by indicating whether its various elements make sense, internally cohere, are palatable	• Reader acknowledges growing event knowledge	• Reader makes intertextual evaluations of the sources' validity, reliability, subtext, and agent intentions as a means of constructing a refined, evidence-based interpretation of the event
• Reader can then make initial sense of source	• Strategy: Intratextual evaluations	• Identifies the authors in sources and corroborates details across sources	
• Strategy: Intratextual analyses		• Uses growing knowledge from the multiple sources to construct an initial interpretation of the event	• Strategy: Intertextually critical evaluations
		• Strategy: Intertextual analyses	

Figure 6.1. Movement along continuum of strategic levels in students' analyses of historical sources. For the coding categories that demarcate each level, see Figure A.1.

tions of this general type do not constitute historical thinking, nor do they necessarily lead to domain-specific growth. The investigator must (be taught to) progress in the following way.

As the inquirer encounters more evidence about the event via a second or third text or image, his knowledge of the event grows and he begins constructing a tentative interpretation. Here he draws from his accreting event knowledge, and in the case of primary source documents, from an emerging understanding of the historical context in which the words were uttered and action performed. To better understand this context vis-à-vis the author's description of it, he notes who the author is and when the account was written (or drawn or painted). He then cross-checks the account against previous documents and corroborates specific details. This is reading *inter*textually at level 3 (building historical event knowledge). Finally, if successful at the previous three levels, he begins to evaluate the evidence intertextually with respect to the reliability of the agent or author, the larger historical context, and the different perspectives in play. Doing so allows him to systematically refine his interpretation of the event. This is reading at level 4 (intertextual evaluation).

For novice investigators who know very little about particular historical events, cognitive growth that enables learning about such events is signaled by movement from reading which is strategically general and analytically *intra*textual to that which is discipline- and subject-specific, critical, and *inter*textually analytical. This growth can occur if classroom opportunities provide for learning the necessary vocabulary, procedures, and heuristics. Short of those opportunities, novices fail to learn to read critically as outlined by levels 3 and 4. They therefore fail to learn to think historically. Since one of my central interests in this study involved teaching the fifth-graders to move across the continuum, noting the differences between students' initial and endpoint source-analysis levels on the performance tasks offered a salient means of assessing the efficacy of my investigative teaching approach.

HISTORICAL INVESTIGATION THROUGH CRITICAL READING

Before describing how students read and analyzed the documents and images during the first performance task dealing with the shootings in Boston, I briefly lay out their understanding of history as a subject matter and discipline. This provides a backdrop for making sense of the way in which they approached that initial January task. How the fifth-graders conceptualized the subject matter provides clues to how they were predisposed to reading and analyzing the historical documents as sources.

Students' ideas were derived from interviews we conducted before the performance task was undertaken. In addition to collecting detailed demographic information from the eight, we asked them questions such as: What do you think history is? Do you have your own history? Do you know what historians do? If so, please explain. Often historians disagree about what happened in the past, and when they do, how do you think they finally decide what to write down? I summarize the eight students' views here.

Initial Understandings of History

Generally speaking, the eight viewed history as "what happened before what's happening right now" (Ben's description). Five of the eight added that for it to be history, though, it had to be important, or about famous people and events. Therefore, when we asked them if they thought they had their own history, these five said no, because they had not done anything "big" or important yet. This idea, likely communicated via mass media depictions and previous experiences studying history in school, runs counter to the "new social history" now characterizing historiographic movement in the discipline. Social historians view history from the bottom up, arguing that those people and events previously thought to be unimportant are worth understanding for their broad and sometimes powerful influence on historical change. Regarding what historians do, five of the eight said they had no idea. Coral and Jeffrey both speculated that historians study history and "big events." Ben, also speculating, thought that historians wrote textbooks and kept records of past occurrences.

In an effort to get a sense of their historical epistemologies (i.e., beliefs about where historical knowledge comes from and how we know what we know), we asked them to talk about how they thought historians might arbitrate disputes among themselves about what occurred in the past and what it might mean. As has been documented in other studies that have explored this issue with novices, the eight suggested such things as (1) appealing to a majority vote to settle the dispute, (2) including a variety of contrary viewpoints in writing about the issue ("combining different stories," as Kendra noted) even though this might make the ensuing account incoherent, and (3) going to an indisputable source such as an encyclopedia (or an ancestor who "was there") to settle the controversy. The first and last responses were the most prevalent. Only Jeffrey appealed to the idea—and tentatively so—that historians would need to exhaust the evidence sources and then, in the end, go with what they believed, despite lack of agreement with others. It was difficult to tell from Jeffrey's response the degree to which he thought a historian's "belief" needed to be linked to the evidence.

The Initial Performance Task: Interpreting the "Boston Massacre"

As with interpreting and understanding the mystery of the Jamestown Starving Time (outlined in Chapter 3), the shooting of Boston citizens by British army sentries in March 1770 presents similar formidable interpretive challenges. Accounts of the incident conflict, even among eyewitnesses with front-row seats. Where there is a crowd, there is noise and often considerable movement. Add a serious, running conflict among those gathered and there is potential for mayhem. Mayhem often results in chaos, and chaos is difficult to comprehend. Because of a strained relationship between the colonies and England in 1770, political allegiance and partisan subtext underlie much of what people saw, remembered, and testified about the event. American rebels, who by 1770 had become engaged in a vitriolic propaganda war with England, saw the death of the five Boston citizens as a perfect excuse to claim "massacre" and further incite Americans to acts of rebellion against the Crown. British leaders were appalled at the actions of Boston citizens and galled by the propaganda war colonial patriots waged in its wake. In reading about this incident in the initial performance task, students were challenged to sort all this out.

The performance task involved first the reading of two conflicting documents concerning the shootings (see Appendix B). The first was Hakim's (1993b) rendition of the event. She adds invented dialogue and concludes with the judgment that both sides were wrong in their actions, but she does not address the question about how it was that the soldiers came to discharge their muskets. The second account was a primary source, Captain Thomas Preston's testimony about the skirmish. It was the longer and more difficult of the two texts. However, it is revealing for its British perspective on how escalating tensions in Boston set the stage for the tragic event and for how Preston explains his view on the discharge of weapons by his troops.

The eight informants were given the documents one by one and asked to think out loud as they read, each in turn. Students did this individually, accompanied only by either myself or my research assistant. Just before they began reading the first Boston "Massacre" document, students were told that they would be reading two texts and looking at three pictures that dealt with shootings in Boston, Massachusetts, prior to the American Revolutionary War. Their purpose was to construct an interpretation of what happened, who did they shooting, and why. The eight also had opportunities to practice reading and thinking out loud on an unrelated text before they began the actual performance task.

We had the students read and think out loud without much interruption except to ask when necessary: What are you thinking now? This was referred to as the "online" portion of the task. Following their reading of the two written documents, we interrupted the online portion to ask several questions, such as: Which document did you like the most and why? Did you notice any differences between the two? Who were the authors of the two documents? What difference does it make where the author's information comes from? Which document did you think told the story most accurately? Such follow-up questioning processes were referred to as "retrospective interviews."

After the document-reading procedure was completed, each of the eight were told that they would now be shown three images of that shooting to further assist them in making sense of the event and addressing the questions we asked (see Appendix B, Figures B. 1, B. 2, and B. 3). We asked them to talk out loud (i.e., online) about what they were thinking as they looked at the images. The purpose of using the images was to aid the process of constructing an understanding of events by the presentation of additional evidence (although conflicting depictions) and to further elicit how they were thinking about different types of evidence and using it to construct an interpretation. I also thought it might be helpful for the students who were reading below grade level to have an opportunity to "see" renderings of the event as well as read about it.

We let them work their way through the images, encouraging them only as necessary to speak up with prompts such as "What are you thinking now?" After they had completed the image examinations, we followed up with retrospective interviews, using questions such as: Can you order the images from most accurate to least accurate? Why is image X more accurate to you than the other images? Do you notice any differences in the images? The images all describe the same Boston shootings, so why are there differences? Where do the images come from, do you think? How do they compare to the documents?

The online vocalizations of the eight students on all the Boston "Massacre" sources were filled with examples of efforts to use comprehension-monitoring strategies (level 1 on the continuum in Figure 6.1), more so with regard to the written documents. They all reported knowing little about the Boston shootings, although several noted that they had heard the term "Boston Massacre." Without much prior knowledge, the demands of constructing meaning from the documents remained steep. As a result, the vocalizations were dominated by evidence of repeated efforts to summarize, reread, and question the documents (level 1: monitoring). Document 2 was especially demanding from a meaning-construction perspective, with its eyewitness testimony and 18th-century language. Intratextual evaluations (level 2) were also limited and displayed frequently only by the more accomplished readers (Alexandra and Coral, and occasionally Jamie and Jeffrey). As a possible gender-influenced reaction, Coral and Jeffrey were particularly quick to make evaluations of the violent actions of the Bostonians and British soldiers, judging the actions of each intratextually (level 2) but not intertextually (levels 3 and 4). However, as they read more about the incident and then examined the images, intratextual evaluations tapered off, perhaps a consequence of becoming perplexed by conflicting versions of the event. However, they did not articulate this online. Only Jamie's intratextual evaluations (level 2) increased markedly.

As the eight worked through the three images, spontaneous vocalizations that involved *inter*textual comparisons increased slightly. However, they were almost exclusively limited to occasional registrations of accreting event knowledge (level 3: building event knowledge—corroborating details across accounts as initial interpretations of why shots were fired were constructed). Initially, the images tended to muddy efforts to address the question: What happened here? Students spent a good share of their time describing and summarizing details they saw in the images, as though the images were not related to the documents they had just read. Candy, the Spanish-speaking immigrant from Peru, had significant difficulty making sense of both the texts and images, verbalizing some monitoring-strategy use, but most often getting stuck trying to sort out actions and details in the images or decode words in the documents. As she attempted to understand the images, she did utilize some growing event knowledge, occasionally corroborating details she had gleaned from the documents (level 3). However, she engaged in no evaluations, intra- or intertextual, apparently moving from reading at level 1 to reading at level 3, and then back again.

Kendra, the other less accomplished reader, also struggled with the images. She made only 4 intertextual vocalizations in a total of 13 online vocalizations. A vocalization was defined as a simple sentence unit in the transcript. In other words, to say that Kendra offered 4 intertextual comments is to say she spoke 4 distinguishable sentence units coded as efforts to build an interpretation of the event by corroborating details across images and documents. Only Ben (1 vocalization) and Coral (2 vocalizations) offered online judgments of the comparative validity and reliability of the images with respect to the documents as a means of refining their interpretations of the event (level 4).

The eight came away virtually as puzzled about what had happened in Boston after the task as they were without much knowledge of it before beginning. Part of this can be understood as an outgrowth of the event itself, where what we can say for certain about it is hampered by conflicting evidence and viewpoints. However, despite relying very heavily on general comprehension-monitoring strategies during the task, the students, with the exception of Candy, offered a number of nascent ideas afterward for comparing and contrasting the documents and images (i.e., level 3, using corroboration of evidence to build event knowledge) as they attempted to construct initial interpretations that explained the event.

When asked retrospectively about why the documents' renditions of the event varied, Alexandra, Coral, and Jeffrey noted that the point of view of the author could have contributed to this. When pressed to explain, they talked about learning in language arts that an author's point of view was important in understanding and writing stories. Ben, Jamie, and Kendra also made similar reference to point of view but had difficulty elaborating on the idea, other than to note that, in the images, it was the literal "angle of view" of the artist that accounted for the differences. In noting this, they appeared to presume that the artists were there as the event unfolded, as though the images were more akin to photographs. Candy and Tho did not mention point of view, but instead indicated differences in the level of detail included in both documents and images, without reference to choices an author/artist might make about including more or less detail.

Regarding a question about deciding which documents and images were most accurate, Alexandra and Jamie framed their responses in terms of "being there." In other words, in their view the ultimate way to establish the accuracy of an account was to know whether it came from someone who was there. Having said this, though, they made no attempt to go back and check the origins of the documents or images lying on the table to determine whether any of the authors or artists had been there (this would not have been possible with the images because they did not include artists' names or original dates). Ben thought that accuracy was tied to a balanced perspective achieved by the author or artist. He explained this in terms of what could be construed as a form of objectivity and/or detachment, something he alluded to learning in language arts. Candy, Kendra, and Tho took the position that accuracy was based on inclusion of detail and author's writing style with regard to the documents. As Kendra put it, "I think the first text is the most accurate because it has the most details and is easiest to read."

To get a broad sense of how students moved back and forth across the continuum of general reading to history-specific critical analyses as they proceeded through this initial performance task, I counted the frequencies of their vocalizations (a simple sentence unit) that represented the different levels, 1 through 4. Those frequencies are shown in Table 6.1 by level. Of all vocalizations on this task, 83% were of the general, intratextual reading and analysis type (levels 1 and 2), with 61% of them at level 1 only. Only 17% of the vocalizations across the sources represented the critical history-specific analytic type characterized by levels 3 and 4.

Table 6.1. Initial Performance Task Results (January): Student Vocalization Frequencies by Source and Analytic Level

Number of Vocalizations[a]

Student	Document 1 Analytic Level				Document 2 Analytic Level				Image 1 Analytic Level				Image 2 Analytic Level				Image 3 Analytic Level			
	1	2	3	4	1	2	3	4	1	2	3	4	1	2	3	4	1	2	3	4
Alexandra	7	6	0	0	10	7	0	0	2	1	4	0	2	0	4	0	3	0	7	0
Ben	7	3	0	0	15	1	0	0	3	1	0	0	5	2	4	1	1	2	5	0
Candy	15	1	0	0	21	2	0	0	11	0	3	0	4	0	2	0	6	0	6	0
Coral	6	9	0	0	11	4	1	0	3	0	3	0	1	0	0	1	2	0	3	2
Jamie	9	7	0	0	9	12	0	0	4	0	2	0	3	0	0	0	3	2	2	0
Jeffrey	11	13	0	0	11	10	3	0	1	1	2	0	1	2	2	0	0	0	2	0
Kendra	6	2	0	0	19	1	0	0	4	0	3	0	3	0	0	0	1	1	1	0
Tho	8	0	0	0	15	0	0	0	2	1	3	0	1	1	0	0	1	0	4	0
Total	69	41	0	0	121[b]	37	4	0	30	4	20	0	20	5	12	2	17	5	30	2

Total, all vocalizations: 419
Total, levels 1 and 2 combined: 349 vocalizations, 83% of total
Total, levels 3 and 4 combined: 70 vocalizations, 17% of total

[a] One "vocalization" is considered a simple sentence unit in the transcript produced from a think-aloud protocol.
[b] The large frequency count at analytic level 1 for this primary source document (Captain Preston's Testimony) reflects both the high text-processing demands it makes on novice readers and its longer length relative to the first document in this task.

One would expect to see heavy reliance on comprehension and monitoring strategies (level 1) when inquirers have limited prior knowledge of an event being described in a document or depicted in an image, and when particular documents involve heavy text-processing demands (e.g., the Captain Preston account). Furthermore, for novice inquirers who have not been taught how to read historical sources intertextually—comparing accounts, corroborating details, assessing author/artist perspectives, and the like—it would not be surprising that even the most accomplished readers would still rely mostly on general reading strategies (levels 1 and 2), with some attempts to corroborate details (level 3) only as they went deeper into the accounts and were able to use their growing event knowledge to construct initial interpretations. It would be unusual to see the types of intertextual evaluations (level 4) that permit investigators to refine their interpretations.

Most promising, though, from the online vocalizations in this initial task and especially from the retrospective comments the eight offered was evidence that most of the students had a nascent understanding of point of view, which possibly could be linked to the way an account might be assessed in terms of its reliability. Also important was evidence that comparing and contrasting texts and images as a means of accreting event knowledge and using it to construct evidence-based interpretations was not beyond their capacity. In others words, these 10- and 11-year-olds generally seemed poised to become historical investigators in their own right, ready to move beyond a reliance on reading at levels 1 and 2 on to levels 3 and possibly 4 as they encountered multiple forms of evidence in investigations we would conduct in class in the 4-plus months that would intervene between this initial task and the endpoint one.

An Endpoint Performance Task:
Interpreting the Battle at Lexington Green

For the second performance task, conducted almost 5 months later in May, the same verbal-report procedures were employed. This time, we used four texts and two images that dealt with the battle at Lexington Green (see Appendix B). The first document contained a verbatim recounting of the incident by a group of Massachusetts minutemen who were present at the skirmish. They testified to the events under oath at a hearing following the incident. The second document was British Ensign Jeremy Lister's account of the event written 7 years after its occurrence. The third and fourth documents were brief newspaper accounts of the event, one from a Massachusetts newspaper and the other from a London paper. The artists' images represented the event from different angles and, when compared, contained conflicting details and perspectives.

The purpose of changing the focal event was to obtain some degree of parallelism in the way the procedure was administered. That is, students reported having heard of the Boston "Massacre" and a couple remembered having seen a picture of it before they engaged in the first performance task. However, the prior knowledge they had to draw on in analyzing the sources was limited. In our study of the causes of the American Revolution in class, we had noted in a general sense the shots fired at Lexington as one of many possible causes of the American Revolution. Only Ben and Jamie had looked more deeply into the details and read a couple of sources, none of which were used for this performance task. As with the Boston "Massacre," the Lexington event contained a similar riddle element: Who gave the order to fire weapons? Therefore, primarily because the answer to the question was inconclusive, and because students' prior event knowledge was again relatively limited, it seemed a reasonable event to pair with the first task. The goal was to attempt to equalize the degree to which the eight students could rely on their event knowledge to read, compare, contrast, and corroborate the texts and images of the battle at Lexington. If the lack of prior knowledge about a particular historical event were rendered in as similar terms as possible from initial to endpoint task, then in understanding students' readings and analyses, concentration could be placed on the specific processes (e.g., corroboration, judging of perspective) they relied on. In part, this demand was met. However, the eight did know that this was termed the first battle of the Revolution, and Ben and Jamie held a bit of an edge with regard to possessing more knowledge about it as they began the task.

During the endpoint performance, all eight students appeared more adept at analyzing the documents and images using the specific types of critical and intertextual historical reading and thinking practices characterized by levels 3 and 4. Frequency counts of such critical, intertextual vocalizations went from 17% of the total in the initial task to 41% in the endpoint task, a more than twofold increase. Although students still relied on a number of comprehension strategies to derive meaning from the documents and images, as they moved from document to document and then to the images, they quickly began constructing detailed interpretations of the battle at Lexington. As a result, the general, intratextual reading strategies (levels 1 and 2) were quickly displaced by the more historically specialized, intertextual analyses (levels 3 and 4) designed to systematically identify the sources of the evidence in front of them, corroborate details from one source to another, and judge those sources with respect to their validity, reliability, and point of view. Several students were particularly astute about judging an artist's and/or an author's perspective as a method of gauging the political subtext of the document or image and using it to assess whether they trusted it as reliable for building a defensible interpretation of the events at Lexington.

Students tended to pair documents and images as they analyzed them (Documents 1 and 2, Documents 3 and 4, and the two images, respectively). In part, this may have been a possible artifact of the way they were grouped during the tasks, but it also may have been that most students assessed them this way because they were identifying the first two as primary source texts, the second pair as secondary sources, and the third as nontext pictures all to be grouped accordingly by source and type. In either case, it meant that the first piece of evidence about the battle in the pair produced a series of general comprehension and monitoring efforts and intratextual evaluations (levels 1 and 2) that were followed by a significant increase in the degree to which most of the students then intertextually cross-checked and evaluated (levels 3 and 4) the second piece in the pair against the first, paralleling how historians read. In the initial performance task in January, there was some of the same sort of clustering going on. However, students generally missed the idea that the documents and images could be grouped and assessed one against another as a means of interpreting the Boston shootings. Only after they were prompted by questions in the retrospective interviews about examining the evidence this way did several respond by doing so. Much more spontaneous history-specific intertextual evaluation (level 4) occurred in what appeared to be intentional pairing of images and documents in this endpoint task.

Responses to the retrospective questions following the endpoint task showed a marked increase in the degree to which students talked about author perspective and possible political subtexts (e.g., Ensign Lister, clearly a British sympathizer because of his army affiliation, might well be distorting his narrative to avoid being blamed for firing the ill-fated shots that started the war). Such talk was almost completely absent in the January retrospective interviews. This process sometimes revealed the degree to which students, Jeffrey particularly, were influenced by their own unexamined assumptions. Students sometimes quickly imposed their American allegiances and similar heritage-inspired historical positionalities on the their assessments of subtexts (see VanSledright, 1998, 2001). The process of imposing such unchecked judgments on evidence was something I had worked hard to constrain by insisting that students be able to provide ample support for their assessments (see Chapter 5). Although much of this reticence occurred, several students were extremely quick to impose judgments that were rooted in nothing more than superficial rationales such as "it's what I think." This area of teaching historical thinking to young, eager students clearly will need more attention in future studies.

The Eight Readers and the Six Lexington Battle Sources

In Chapter 1, I described Alexandra's reading of the Lexington battle sources. Here I provide additional details about her reading and analytic movement through the documents. Alexandra, one of the better readers in the class and certainly a colonial patriot partisan, had little difficulty navigating the documents and images. Her analysis of the testimony of the 34 minutemen was characterized by descriptions of what she thought the source was indicating about the action (level 1: monitoring). She summarized frequently, but by the end of this first source she was making a number of intratextual judgments about the actions of the British (level 2: evaluating intratextually). She then read the title of the Lister narrative and noted that it had been recalled and written down 7 years after the minutemen's testimony she had just read. Here she was carefully assessing the status of the account as a means of corroborating it against the minutemen testimony (level 3: building event knowledge). Her assessment raised her suspicions about Lister's reliability (level 4: intertextual evaluation): "He [Lister] could have made this up . . . to save his own skin, so he wouldn't have to go to jail. . . . I don't believe any of them yet!" In reading, commenting online, and analyzing the *Salem Gazette* and *London Gazette* newspaper accounts, she checked details between the two to further corroborate an initial interpretation she was building (level 3). As Alexandra attempted to refine that interpretation, she also was quick to comment on the sources as a means of identifying their origins and thus their perspectives and political subtexts (level 4).

Prior to seeing the two artists' depictions of the battle, she indicated being unsure who had fired first at Lexington Green, demanding "more evidence" before deciding. That evidence came in the form of the two images. As she moved to examine them, she was careful to check the captions first. After looking at the artist's rendition in Image 1, she complained, "I've had evidence from primary sources and now I get a picture? And I don't even know if it's a secondary or primary source. If it's a secondary source, it could be lying. Well, they [historians drawing conclusions based on primary sources] don't even know if the British actually shot. I'm not taking the British side, but . . ." After repeatedly assessing the validity of Image 2 with respect to Image 1, Alexandra concluded, "I just think the same of both of them. They don't help! I can't decide [on who fired first]." Then, as I noted in Chapter 1, she announced forcefully, "I just don't see how historians can do this!"

Ben, a better reader than I think his school district criterion-referenced test scores indicated, began his online reading and analysis of the minutemen testimony by questioning British tax policy and how that led up to the armed confrontation at Lexington. Here he displayed an understanding gleaned from his beat during the Newspaper Activity. He also was quick to judge this account as a primary source. Halfway through, he declared, "So this is the point of view of the colonists, a primary source." He then went to the second document, summarizing its details as he read. Upon reading the final lines and the attribution to Ensign Lister in 1782, he spontaneously offered his assessment of the first pair of accounts: "This person's point of view [in Document 2] was the British. Now, I think you got somebody who thinks the colonists shot first and somebody who swears on the truth that the Redcoats shot first. I think these two are just trying to defend their own side, so that they could win the war; like if I was a British, I would try—like if I knew that we shot first—I would just say that they did it 'cause we wanted to win the war." After examining the two newspaper documents, he reiterated essentially this same position. Then, following a momentary pause, he switched his perspective on the *London Gazette* account, observing, "I think a loyalist shot first, or somebody on nobody's side." Later in the retrospective interview, when asked what he meant by his observation, he said that it was possible to conclude that someone, such as a loyalist, who wanted to see a war in which the superior British army would crush the patriots, may have been hiding in one of the houses surrounding Lexington Green and fired a shot that caused a British response and initiated the battle.

He followed a similar process in his online analysis of the two images, describing details and reading captions aloud, which signaled his method of checking sources (he identified both as secondary accounts). He then judged the second image to be clearer but less accurate because its arrangement of troops, buildings, and other objects did not align with the initial interpretation he had constructed following his analysis of the previous sources. Here he demonstrated his capacity to evaluate these additional sources as a means of refining his interpretation. During the retrospective interview, he repeatedly championed his theory that a colonial loyalist had fired the first shot.

Candy, who had made some gains in her capacity to exercise comprehension and monitoring strategies in making meaning from text across the semester, relied on them very heavily throughout her analysis of the documents and images. Only after finishing up on the last image did she say anything online about corroborating evidence in an effort to develop an initial interpretation of the battle. At no point did she engage in level 4 validity, reliability, or perspective assessments. She was the only student who did not. This was not entirely surprising. Candy was still having difficulties decoding certain words, and the task documents contained some language and syntax she was unfamiliar with, despite having encountered similarities in sources throughout the preceding months. Eighty-three percent of her online comments were at general-reading levels 1 and 2, with the majority being at level 1 (see the frequency count for Candy in Table 6.2).

In the retrospective interview, Candy did demonstrate some awareness of how it is that accounts vary. In response to a question about why the authors and artists framed the battle in different ways, she said, "They found many different stories in their research, because they must have found it in different places, or else they must have not wanted to put in certain words." But she concluded that an investigator decides on the validity and reliability of accounts and images based primarily on the number of details and information they include. These criteria are more commonly invoked by fifth-graders who have not been taught to analyze evidence as we did in class (see VanSledright & Kelly, 1998) and by second-graders, the youngest students in the CHATA research (Lee & Ashby, 2000).

Coral said that doing these performance tasks made him nervous. Likely as a result, he tended to say little in his online analyses, despite being a very skilled reader. His comments were mostly confined to monitoring strategies (level 1) and intratextual evaluations (level 2) until he had completed reading all four written documents, and then again after examining both images. At each of those points, he offered concise assessments of the validity and reliability of the various sources and clear judgments of political perspectives in the evidence in front of him. Watching him read and listening carefully to the little he did say, one could almost witness his mind busy at work—quickly reading the documents, summarizing them, holding his intertextual judgments at bay while he entertained various interpretations—synapses firing madly all the while.

Once having arrived at an interpretation he was initially comfortable with, Coral was quick to make intertextual judgments to refine it. For example, as he finished the *London Gazette* account of the battle, he paused and then noted, "I guess these all come from different points of views. The newspaper [*London Gazette*] has taken both points of view into fact. One point of view talked about how British soldiers killed all the men, and then the British point of view, they're saying that they've wounded one of their men and one of the horses got shot. Maybe they're all trying to cover something up, like they don't wanna get the blame, so they make their own story up." His efforts to corroborate details and rely on the primary sources as arbiters in judging the accuracy of images were also quite direct: "Picture 2 is more realistic. In Picture 1, they show people just lying on the ground. They don't show any people dead; they only show like one per-

Table 6.2. Endpoint Performance Task Results (May): Student Vocalization Frequencies by Source and Analytic Level

Number of Vocalizations[a]

Student	Document 1 Analytic Level				Document 2 Analytic Level				Document 3 Analytic Level				Document 4 Analytic Level				Image 1 Analytic Level				Image 2 Analytic Level			
	1	2	3	4	1	2	3	4	1	2	3	4	1	2	3	4	1	2	3	4	1	2	3	4
Alexandra	5	6	1	0	2	0	5	4	5	2	4	4	5	3	3	3	3	1	2	1	2	0	5	6
Ben	3	1	5[b]	1	3	0	0	4	3	0	2	1	4	0	4	3	2	0	2	1	0	0	1	2
Candy	7	1	0	0	5	1	0	0	5	1	0	0	4	1	1	0	3	0	1	0	1	0	3	0
Coral	2	3	1	0	4	0	3	0	3	0	0	0	1	1	2	3	2	0	0	0	2	0	2	2
Jamie	3	3	1	0	3	2	2	5	1	2	2	0	3	2	2	0	2	0	4	0	1	0	5	1
Jeffrey	7	4	0	0	1	1	5	5	1	3	2	1	0	2	3	1	3	3	0	0	1	1	1	3
Kendra	9	1	1	0	6	2	0	0	6	0	0	0	3	0	3	0	4	1	1	0	3	1	4	2
Tho	2	6	1	0	4	1	4	0	2	0	2	0	2	0	2	3	1	2	0	0	2	0	2	0
Total	38	25	10	1	28	7	19	18	26	8	9	3	22	9	20	13	20	7	10	2	12	2	23	16

Total, all vocalizations: 348
Total, all levels 1 and 2 combined: 204 vocalizations, 59% of total
Total, levels 3 and 4 combined: 144 vocalizations, 41% of total

[a] One "vocalization" is considered a simple sentence unit in the transcript produced from a think-aloud protocol.
[b] Ben's capacity to articulate significant, accreted event knowledge while reading this first document may reflect prior knowledge he had at his disposal from covering the Lexington battle on his "beat" for the Newspaper Activity described in Chapter 5.

son that's dead. And in one document I read, it says there were about seven people that died, and if you count the British soldiers, there's about eight." Asked following his online analysis whether he now knew who fired first at Lexington, he said that he still was not sure, and that was acceptable because it was how things often are in studying history. He did inject that it ended up being a matter of perspective in such cases, and that you base your interpretations on your understanding of the evidence and the sentiments such evaluations of it produce.

Jamie analyzed the accounts and images much the way Ben did, suggesting that he, too, was a better reader than his test scores would have predicted. His similarity to Ben may have been associated with his investigation of the Lexington battle for the Newspaper Activity. He tended to offer a number of comments that indicated his efforts to corroborate the details in the accounts with event knowledge gleaned from examining other sources while doing research on his beat.

Jamie was very proficient at identifying whether the sources were primary or secondary in nature. After reading the first paragraph of the minutemen testimony, he said, "This person that's telling this story was like there." He took the same tack with each successive account. As did most of the others, he judged accounts and images in pairs. Upon finishing the Lister narrative, he stated, "They both have different stories. They [the colonists] say they never fired. The British say the colonists fired first, and they fired back. The colonists never said they scattered and they never said about being behind a wall or anything. They [colonists] claimed that the British fired first, that they didn't fire at all—they didn't do anything. Two different stories, two different sides: He's [Lister] for the British; he's (*pointing at the first document*) for the Americans, (*adding sarcastically*) Don't you think they'd wanna tell the good part about their side?" This level of analysis characterized Jamie's approach to the documents and images. He elaborated on his approach in the retrospective interview, noting, like Coral and Alexandra, that fully understanding the Lexington battle may be impossible and that it boils down to having to look at it from at least two different viewpoints.

Jeffrey was one of the most loquacious students—in online performance tasks, in interviews, and, as we have seen, in class. He simply had a lot to say and liked to hear himself talk. He also was far more skilled at historically analyzing the documents, and reading in general, than his reading test scores would have suggested. Like most of the others, he analyzed the documents and images in pairs, reserving most of his intertextual analyses until he had read a section or two of the second document in the pair, or had examined and described both images.

Jeffrey was also by far the most judgmental, throwing in a number of intratextual evaluations of the actions or assertions of characters in an account. Halfway through the minutemen testimony, he displayed his class-room-honed, pro-colonial position by abruptly calling the British cowards, because the minutemen claimed they were shot in the back. He kept at this sort of judgment throughout. This propensity to judge served to sharpen his critical edge as he moved across the documents and images. He fluidly traversed the reading levels and types of analyses on the continuum (see Figure 6.1). At the midpoint in Lister's narrative, for example, he stopped to offer this assessment: "So, now it's the other way around. Because the first document said that the British fired. But in the second document here he's saying that the colonists fired. I don't believe the British in Document 2; it says the Ninth British Army in Document 2. I don't trust them. I know that the colonists did some crazy things before the Revolutionary War, but I still think that the British [Army] had no sense at all coming to the colonies. So I think they're just lying . . . I bet you the person in Document 2 never'd have brung that up if that person in Document 1 didn't bring it up." After finishing the Lister account and carefully calculating that it was written 7 years after the event, he sarcastically added, "So he wrote that, right? A primary source. I could understand it if he tries—the key word is *tries*—to remember what happened at Lexington Green, but no way." His analysis of the two newspaper accounts followed the same analytic pattern.

By that point, his pro-colonial sentiment appeared to be getting in the way of his capacity to refine his interpretation by evaluating new evidence based on its various viewpoints, as we had stressed in class. However, when he finished assessing the two images, he drew the conclusion that the second was probably more accurate than the first. In making this assessment, he acknowledged that he was opening the door to the possibility of an alternative interpretation, that it could have been scared colonists who fired first—but accidentally, he hastened to add. In the retrospective interview, he talked at length about understanding that different perspectives are involved in interpreting the battle. He grouped the minutemen testimony and the *Salem Gazette* account together and did the same for the Lister narrative and the *London Gazette* article. Then he noted, "The British [guy], he [Lister] seems to be, he's just trying to defend himself . . . he's just trying to save himself. But the colonists did that, too. They had different perspectives on what was going on. Different people, so they might have different stories to save their people." To further rationalize his suspicion about the British, he later invoked his knowledge of the Boston "Massacre," having researched it for his Newspaper Activity. He underscored his distrust of the British based on their actions in Boston: "I just don't like them. I'm sorry. I don't like what they did to the Americans. I don't like what King George did. I don't like Captain Preston's lying. I just don't like it."

This position was also his in-class mantra, which he was fond of declaring. In fact, several classmates challenged him in our discussions by purposefully assuming the British position and charging the patriots with what amounted to high treason. Demonstrating shades of adolescent angst, Jeffrey was quick to pick up his incantation and defend it vigorously, more or less as he was doing in this performance task and retrospective interview. His awareness of multiple perspectives on the battle and on the Boston shootings did, however, allow him to understand that his interpretation was not necessarily the "right one" and that to maintain his position required evidentiary support rather than raw sentiment.

Jeffrey's is an intriguing case of how investigations that use both primary and secondary sources contribute to the development of a sense of historical context; engender the capacity to judge evidence validity, reliability, and political subtexts; and help students construct strong arguments for positions they choose to hold. Investigative approaches suggest a way to rein in bias by demanding research-based support, but that still may not be enough to restrain students such as Jeffrey. This issue needs further attention for what it may suggest about the power of a community that values evidence-based assertions over partisan displays to domesticate the latter to the former.

Kendra continued to struggle as a reader during the 4 months I was in the classroom. Like Candy and similarly to her initial performance task analyses, she relied heavily on comprehension and monitoring strategies as she attempted to make sense of the accounts. Seventy-seven percent of her online comments were either level 1 or level 2, with the majority being level 1 (see Table 6.2). However, by the time she reached Document 4 and the two images, she had constructed an initial interpretation of the event and began corroborating details across documents and then between the images and back to the documents in order to bolster it. Doing so allowed her to begin judging the validity of the images and make evidence-based interpretations about what had happened. After she had examined the second image, she stated:

> The pictures are the same thing. But the reason I think this is because of this Document 3, the newspaper account. It says down here—I'm reading the date, April 25, 1775—and this part was about them, you know, the British fighting the Americans. So these might be, they're like . . . oh, I know! The British are shooting the Americans back there (*pointing to the image*). Because this person right here had the gun powder and over here in this section, and over here, there's a lot of people over there. . . .
> The Americans weren't firing first. Okay, let me show you what

I mean. The British are firing at them (*pointing*). And they're
standing up, I guess standing to them, so the Americans
shoot back.

Tho, like Coral, was reserved during both performance tasks as well
as in class. When she did speak, she was understated and undemonstra-
tive, but often very incisive. Her approach to the endpoint task was also
much like Coral's. She was quick to infer and then assess where the action recounted in the documents appeared to be heading, vocalizing in
response to the minutemen testimony with, "Now, I think it's not a war,
but a fight. I think it's the British and the Americans, but I think I should
read it all over to think about that." Here she implies needing to obtain
more evidence before drawing any firm conclusions, an effort aimed at
preventing her from relying too much on an initial interpretation, thus
limiting her capacity to build her event knowledge by examining additional evidence (level 3). By early in the Lister narrative, she appeared
to be busy building knowledge of the Lexington battle and assessing
perspectives in accounts. For example, she noted that Lister's account
was rooted in a British view that differed markedly from the minutemen's
testimony. Again, she held back, withholding final judgment until she
had the opportunity to read and analyze all four documents. Finishing
the *London Gazette* account, she said, "They all have different points of
view probably, and like they see differently if they were there, and that's
why they told the stories differently. Maybe it's like [about] the time they
got there [i.e., arrived at the scene]; it's happening differently, so they
told that story."

At this point, Tho said that she was eager to get to the images because
they might help her make better sense of the action. However, upon seeing Image 1, she was disappointed and complained, "I can't see anything;
it's all blurry" (see Appendix B). Still puzzled, she began talking about the
second image with questions: "Why the two of this is different [*sic*], like
the pictures are different? Is it like different times, different places?" She
went on to describe details and looked over at Image 1 occasionally, as
though to compare the two. She noted, "It's the same thing [as Image 1].
People are fighting and dying . . . and that's it. I don't know. I can't tell
[what happened]."

In the retrospective interview, Tho went back to the documents and
explained that her indecision about arriving at a conclusive interpretation
was based on her lack of full trust in all the documents. She reiterated the
idea of different points of view and then stated that she was inclined to go
with the minutemen testimony, putting her faith in that primary source

because "they were there." After Fasulo, her interviewer, pointed out that Lister also claimed to have been there, Tho argued, "this was written in 1782, 7 years later . . . so he might have like forgot more than some other people that was there [*sic*]. Like if they pass something down to their son or something, the son might forget something. I can't trust this Document 2 a lot." In the end, she sided reluctantly with the minutemen's version: "So I'm not sure, but I think, this one [pointing to Document 1] you can understand more than this one [Document 2] and [with it] you can answer more questions about this battle."

Shifts in Students' Views of History

In the final May interview with the eight after the endpoint performance task was completed, we again returned to a set of questions similar to the ones we had asked at the outset in January. We sought to revisit their ideas about history as a subject matter and discipline, and to assess how those ideas had (or had not) shifted in the wake of being taught to be historical investigators. We asked similar questions and added several new ones: What do you think history is? Do you know what historians do? When historians disagree and argue with each other about what happened in the past, how do you think they finally decide what to write down? Why do historical investigators need to work with evidence? How can you decide whether the evidence is accurate and trustworthy or not? If you had to explain what happened in the past about a certain event, would you use both primary and secondary sources? Why or why not? In the study of history, why do you have to pay attention to the point of view of the people who have written primary sources? How about point of view in secondary sources? Again, I summarize what the students had to say, contrasting some of their ideas with what they reported in January.

All eight students defined history much as they had before. However, all but Jamie dropped the idea that it had to be about "big, memorable events." Several noted that even things that seemed unimportant could turn out to be relevant at some later point when historical investigators reexamined evidence from the past. As Ben pointed out, "Anything that happened in the past is history," and then suggested that that "anything" could become the subject of history if people took an interest in it, and even if it seemed trivial at the time. Jeffrey echoed this notion almost to the letter. In this sense, they had adopted the view of the social historians that history can be about almost anything that influences change over time, even when it appears to be relatively unimportant by present standards.

Students all knew at this point what historians did. All made mention of doing research, reading and studying documents as evidence, and exploring movies, pictures, and other "clues" to help them interpret what had occurred in the past. Alexandra mentioned that historians work with hypotheses, an idea similar to Davis's (1988) notion of conjectural logic, a process that sometimes involves making carefully reasoned inferences to fill in gaps when evidence is particularly thin.

In a notable shift in ideas about how historical investigators settle disputes, students displayed some fluidity in using the discourse of historical practice. Their responses were replete with comments about comparing and contrasting evidence among sources and accounts, attempting to sort out more powerful from less powerful interpretations, paying attention to how much evidence was used to buttress historical claims, and the like. Alexandra expressed an idea about corroboration of sources as a key to settling disputes by explaining that a justifiable interpretation had to be, in her words, "equivalent to the main evidence." Jeffrey hinted at the idea that, despite the need to carefully consult and corroborate sources, a resulting interpretation of what occurred would turn on an investigator's perspective and might not be accepted by all. As though he had himself participated in the Finlay–Davis debate over the "correct" use of evidence (see Chapter 1), Jeffrey argued, "She [one investigator] could have understood it one way and he [a second investigator] could have understood it another way. I'd depend on primary sources myself to decide."

All eight were quick to note that good historical investigators rely on the available evidence to construct their interpretations. They pointed out that evidence is crucial to building an understanding of the past and that without it, it is just someone's idea, and that idea could be very wrong. At the same time, deciding how to judge the trustworthiness of different types of evidence injected some angst into the responses, perhaps as a result of our trips across the bumpy interpretive landscape on which it was common to have difficulty drawing definitive conclusions (the Starving Time, the shootings in Boston). On this issue, Tho said she was not sure, but then said that she would check primary sources against other sources in an effort to corroborate an account. Kendra had difficulty articulating a response. With some additional probing of her ideas, she concluded that she would go back to the sources and study them again, in order to see how she could align them to infer a defensible interpretation. Alexandra, Ben, Coral, Jamie, and Jeffrey also noted that corroboration of details across accounts was the key. However, when pressed on this point, Coral observed that sometimes corroboration is difficult and you have to go with your best hunches, again an allusion to Davis's (1988) notion of conjectural logic. Candy looked up and simply said, "It's really hard!" Most of the students did appeal to the idea, which I had stressed in class, that the careful study and corroboration of the available evidence remained the best—but not always conclusive—course to follow in constructing and refining interpretations.

Regarding the question about preferences in the use of primary versus secondary sources, Alexandra indicated that she would draw from both, rationalizing this on the basis of the different perspectives each might provide. Tho echoed this concern. She then added, "I'm going to use the secondary source to check with the primary, and then the primary with the secondary source." Ben thought he would rely on primary sources because they are "closer to the truth; those people were actually there." Candy said she would use both since that way she would get more information. Much like Tho, Coral, and Jeffrey, Kendra made the case for the importance of drawing from both as a method of corroborating one's account, with a preference for placing greater trust in primary sources.

Generally, students expressed a clear understanding of the role point of view plays in understanding primary source material. Studying events in which the perspective of eyewitnesses bore heavily on building interpretations, such as the Starving Time or the "Boston Tea Party," sensitized students to the importance of establishing an understanding of both the specific subtext of an eyewitness and the larger historical context in which he or she lived. All eight referred directly or implicitly to the importance of identifying the source of a primary document. Alexandra noted that identifying the person who wrote it and that person's perspective "helps you understand better, and because [otherwise] you might misunderstand and misinterpret something." Reverting to his earlier argument about trusting eyewitnesses over secondary accounts, Ben said, "They have the power to convince you because they were there." His reasoning hinged on the idea that he could trust the point of view of someone who was there more readily than someone who was not because that was the best an investigator could hope for, the closest he could get to the actual event. Candy had difficulty with the question, talking around the idea that perspective was important in primary sources because historical actors often had good reason to "make things up." Through a series of analogies (two about the Boston "Massacre" and one about being in the school lunch room), Coral concluded that an interpretation of what occurs depends on your perspective and who you are. Jamie and Jeffrey responded with analogies similar to Coral's and drew the same conclusion. Kendra's response was akin to Ben's. Tho argued, "I think it's important to think about it because it's one way to check if they tell the truth or they lied at some point for some reason. And so, I think [perspective] is very important." Overall, the core of students' responses to these interview questions supported the patterns that emerged from the endpoint performance-task data.

LEARNING TO THINK HISTORICALLY
AND UNDERSTAND HISTORY

The results suggest that teaching these fifth-graders to engage in efforts to think about history using specialized investigative processes and critical intertextual reading practices met with some conditional successes. First, let me observe that, for the most part, the interpretations students constructed about the battle at Lexington reflect complex, conjectural, and heavily textured inferences not unlike the types experts draw after examining similar evidence. To conclude as Alexandra and Coral did, for example, that it is difficult to reach definitive conclusions about some historical events because the evidence is thin and conflictual is a significant cognitive accomplishment that may well be a crucial distinction between novice and more expert status in the history domain.

Second, let me also observe that sustained involvement in practicing history in this classroom helped expand these fifth-graders' strategic-knowledge repertoires. For example, initially students relied on a cluster of general reading strategies that, via classroom investigations, were enlarged to include more powerful history-specific critical reading and analytic practices. Borrowing language from Alexander's (1997) subject-domain learning model, the performance-task and interview data indicate that, in roughly 4 months of tackling the investigative approach, the students effectively moved from novices in the history domain, through acclimating to the domain's specific knowledge demands, and onto at least a level of strategic competence perhaps bordering on expertise.

Specifically with regard to this growth in strategic competence, opportunities to investigate the past introduced the young students to the practice of assessing the status of historical accounts. This involved identifying the nature of sources (primary, secondary) and cross-referencing them, checking and corroborating evidence as a means of refining interpretations, and reading and analyzing historical evidence critically. The students' investigative experience helped them acquire sensitivity to validity and reliability issues and problems related to drawing inferences from primary and secondary sources. The experience also helped them learn to identify the perspectives of the sources' authors and to realize how understanding those perspectives impacts the process of drawing conclusions, building interpretations, and then constructing evidence-based arguments about what occurred. It also sensitized students to the role their own interpretive position plays in constructing arguments.

The data indicate that the experience further helped students learn that some historical events raise interpretive questions that the available evidence cannot resolve and that some texts mask this outcome under the guise of the referential illusion. This awareness is a complex and significant cognitive accomplishment, one that many adults do not yet possess. Finally, the results indicate that the students developed a specialized vocabulary or discourse for talking about historical thinking and analyses (e.g., primary source, secondary source, perspective, evidence, interpretation) as they learned to read and examine accounts intertextually. All of these various accomplishments reflect the heuristics expert historians use in their investigative and constructive endeavors, indicating movement toward that type of expertise. As Lee and Ashby (2000) point out, giving students opportunities to learn this type of strategic-knowledge expertise allows them to "acquire the best intellectual toolkit we have for thinking about the human world over time" (p. 216).

With these fifth-graders (and their classmates, to the extent that these eight are representative of them), we witness appreciable growth in their capacity to think and reason historically. This appears to be especially the case with respect to their approach toward reading sources of historical evidence and evaluating their status. All eight showed important developments in acquiring a specialized vocabulary for sorting out, categorizing, and analyzing such sources. Based on studies of the analytic, interpretive, and procedural successes of historians who were expert investigators but not expert on a topic they were asked to investigate (e.g., Wineburg, 1998), we can speculate that the growth these students demonstrated in their capacities to analyze and construct carefully reasoned historical interpretations will enable them to become more accomplished historical thinkers and investigators in similar situations in the future.

As might be expected, the gains, though marked, were not the same for each student. The results demonstrate differences in the degree to which students expanded their strategic repertoires and their capacities to formulate textured evidence-based interpretations. In many respects, gains were tied to where students were in January. For example, the two students who began the study with general reading comprehension challenges (Candy and Kendra) did not progress as far as those who began as more accomplished readers. The native Spanish speaker, Candy, continued to struggle with investigative and analytic tasks, making some gains in her awareness of the specialized nature of thinking historically but remaining partially handcuffed by basic text-processing and word decoding difficulties. Kendra, despite showing considerable growth, experienced similar but less debilitating difficulties.

In a different vein, talkative, judgmental Jeffrey, who in many ways had mastered the analytic process and acquired the specialized domain-specific vocabulary, had some difficulty separating his propensity to make snap judgments from the more gradual process of building evidence-based claims via careful source analysis and corroboration of details. This was a function of his tendency to presentize his understanding; that is, failing to patiently plumb the historical context under investigation and instead using present-day assumptions and standards to draw conclusions. He was hardly alone in doing so. By the end, though, Jeffrey did indicate some awareness that he was rushing to judgment prematurely. This was a function of his new understanding of the unique characteristics of historical thought. These types of student differences, both subtle and more obvious, will need further analyses and attention in future research for what they suggest about how such investigative approaches must be tailored to better fit such students.

Given the diverse background of these students, it is tempting here to draw out significant differences in racial, ethnic, and gender terms. However, the interview and performance data I gathered in this study do not speak clearly on this matter. What the data do speak clearly about is that concentrated efforts to teach *all* my students to read, analyze, and think historically through a process of historical investigations moved *all* of them forward (assuming the eight are representative of the class). However, my approach produced no "superlative breakthroughs" in any one student's cognitive growth and movement toward expertise in history. Rather, the performance and interview data demonstrate growth that built upon what students brought with them to the experience.

When I met them in January, Alexandra and Coral—a White, European American girl and an African American boy, respectively—were what Brown and Campione (1990) have referred to as intelligent novices. Their rapid movement toward competence in the domain and their more than occasional flashes of expertise on the endpoint performance task suggests how my pedagogical approach effectively dovetailed with their previous success in school and their wealth of general strategic knowledge (intelligent novice status), irrespective of their race and gender. In retrospect, I now think Ben (Latino), Jamie (European American boy), Jeffrey (African American boy), and Tho (Asian American girl) were also intelligent novices in ways only a bit less sophisticated than Alexandra and Coral, but in other ways much more so than Candy (Latina) and Kendra (African American girl). Here again, despite differences in gender, ethnicity, and race, my pedagogical approach appeared to move these four other intelligent novices toward expertise in the domain as well, and also resulted in growth for Candy and Kendra (assuming the corroboration of performance-task and interview data is a valid measure of such growth, which I maintain it is).

Where the eight students were with respect to being more or less intelligent novices in January, I believe, is more telling about the growth of their academic development in history while I taught them than any other factor. However, saying this risks ignoring the fact that Candy and Kendra are both students of color. Their race and ethnicity may well be linked to social class, as is too often the case in American culture. Inquiries into their demographic backgrounds indicated that both came from homes where parents' income and education placed them in the lower middle class and close to working-poor status. Although for privacy reasons we did not ask students about this specifically, we can surmise that Candy's and Kendra's access to cultural and material resources was less than that of the other six primary informants. Access to cultural and material resources typically plays a role in success in school, and access is linked via social class to race and ethnicity, with minorities generally experiencing less such access.

Acknowledging this type of disparity means that I needed to devote more time and academic and cognitive resources to students such as Candy and Kendra in order to reduce the gap between them and their more intelligent novice counterparts. I did as much as I was able with these students over the course of the 4 months. However, I do not believe it was enough, judging by the discrepancies remaining in the endpoint performance-task data. Devoting considerable individualized time and energy to needy youngsters in urban classrooms with more than even 15 students is another major pedagogical dilemma teachers must manage. It is also a dilemma our society must confront and manage if we are serious about addressing the achievement gap that separates White students and students of color, the poor from the more fortunate. My experience in room 23 convinces me that, if we are serious, then we must invest the necessary resources in schools and classrooms (e.g., smaller class sizes, greater teaching expertise in those classes) where children with needs such as Candy and Kendra reside. However, this is only one of a number of unsettling issues that remain. I explore the others in the next chapter.

7

W(h)ither History
Education Revisited

In the opening chapter, I criss-crossed the terrain on which a number of challenges facing history education play out. Most of these challenges arise in relationship to the denial of reality–interpretation connection Scott (1996) refers to and the interpretive paradox it provokes. To review, Scott observes that the legitimacy and authority of historical investigators' interpretations of the past are said to be based on faithfulness to a reality that "lies outside, or exists prior to" (p. 1) those interpretations. Yet, at the same time, interpretations produce a reality via their own telling. History, Scott maintains, "functions through [this] inextricable connection between reality and interpretation" (p. 1), a connection that is denied because they are separable entities and we have no fail-safe procedures for determining when they actually amount to the same thing. The most we can presume is reasonable verisimilitude, but we cannot guarantee it. This leads to the interpretive paradox: the desire and effort to interpret the past *as it was* so we might better understand it, while realizing that doing so is beyond our reach because we are unable ever to be certain when we have succeeded.

Composed in the context of such challenges, and pursued with an investigative approach acknowledges the tensions surrounding the denial of that reality–interpretation connection, the study I have described speaks back to them. This is the subject of the final chapter. Specifically, I take up what I found to be the three most enduring and pervasive issues that affected the conduct of the study: (1) a cluster of teaching dilemmas brought on by practicing history while acknowledging the reality–interpretation paradox that inheres within it; (2) the resiliency of what I am calling the fundamentalist, "encyclopedia" epistemologies among some of my fifth-graders and the issues it raised for teaching the practice of investigating history; and (3) the knotty issues surrounding the process of building cognitive capacity among novices to historically contextualize their interpretations of documentary evidence and thus limit the degree to which they unfairly impose present standards on their understanding of past events.

Although these issues present undeniable challenges, teaching the process of learning history by doing it has several benefits that the results from this study indicate overshadow those challenges. I also examine what I consider the benefits to be. They follow from Scott's (1996) conviction—which I share—that, despite the difficulties it can produce, it is better to acknowledge and work with the paradox provoked by the denial of the reality–interpretation linkage than to ignore it. That acknowledgment means teaching history, rather than heritage, in the Lowenthalian sense. Finally, with a note of caution about the study's limits, I end by considering how my efforts here speak to the history education reform literature and the research that underpins it.

WITHER HISTORY EDUCATION?

Dilemmas in Teaching History Using Investigative Approaches

The issue of acknowledging and working with the reality–interpretation paradox Scott (1996) raises goes to the heart of the question: What should history education look like in the kinds of public school classrooms in which I taught? If we take Scott seriously, it means engaging in the practice of investigating history with children, and thereby exposing the referential illusion (i.e., the fantasy that historians' interpretations literally *mirror* a past reality) and the reality effect (Barthes, 1968, 1986) that follows from it (i.e., the sense that historical narratives directly speak the past back to us, despite the fact that this past is nonetheless lost *as it actually was*). This takes us to interesting but problematic places, as the 1954 *Harvard Guide to American History* warned it might: "If a time machine were available to carry the [historical investigator] back through the past at will, he would confront, on stepping off the machine, the very problems of interpretation he thought he left behind" (quoted in Berkhofer, 1995, p. 64). These places raise compelling dilemmas for teachers who choose to go there. Choosing implies that there are other classroom alternatives, such as participating in the referential illusion by allowing students to be seduced by textbook accounts that produce that mirage Barthes called the reality effect, which compromises the ability to learn to think historically. Though I maintain that this latter choice is ill advised, the former option, although superior, is not without its difficulties.

To pursue historical investigation can put teachers at odds with "official," heritage-based curriculum policy and standards targets. Those policies and targets in many parts of the United States contain long lists of historical topics to be taught under periodization schemes that can be found in the tables of contents of most school history textbooks. Why at odds? Why could a teacher not cover the substance of those lists and do it via historical investigation? From a range of interrelated ways of addressing these questions, I want to discuss several that I think of as most pressing in the wake of this study.

First, consider the issue of historical significance. No matter how one teaches history, choices must be made about what to teach. Investigators must investigate something. Those choices effectively involve defining what is historically significant. I explained in Chapters 4 and 5 that even when I worked from within a set of topics chosen for me by the school district, I continued to confront situations in which I had to make choices. The past and the stories we tell about it are too rich, too varied, and too many; we are always forced to choose among them. Making decisions about historical significance involves navigating a swamp; there is no way through it without entanglements. Gitlin's (1995) account of the California history textbook battles in *The Twilight of Common Dreams*, the *Enola Gay* controversy, and the flap over the original version of the National History Standards are case studies in point. These controversies arise when someone believes that history has veered from the path of *the* "official" narrative we should be telling, "the way it really was." Decisions about historical significance have serious consequences for identity politics and sociopolitical control.

To pursue the learning of history *by investigation* in the classroom involves choosing topics and events (see examples in Davidson & Lytle, 1992) that hone powerful investigative, domain-specific strategies and then use them to build deep historical understanding, thought, and critical-reading capacity. From this perspective, investigating the Starving Time or the Boston "Massacre" or Martin Guerre can be more compelling than inquiring into events—say, Paul Revere's famous ride or Jeb Stuart's legendary battle heroics—about which much more is known from the evidence and little is contested. In the school history classroom, digging deeply into the lives of people formerly disregarded as insignificant (e.g., midwife Martha Ballard), and downplaying the histories of traditional "national heroes" (e.g., George Washington), often yields more powerful learning opportunities because students are intrigued by the novelty and mystery of not knowing about such "hidden" historical agents, as was the case in room 23. Historical significance in these conditions tends to be arbitrated not so much by topics on the "official" curriculum list as by the degree to which mystery and contested interpretation dominate. Because of their focus on history in Lowenthal's (1998) sense—on learning it by doing it—investigative approaches often privilege historical events that are particular, local, unsettled, and open to reinterpretation. They are less concerned with the grand narratives and "official" nationalist stories that characterize many history education curriculum policies. Therefore, choices about historical significance that derive from placing a primary emphasis on investigation (rather than memorization) can place history teachers in conflict with those policies. But this is only part of the issue.

Second, consider that vexing clock, or what we might call the march of history itself. Even if we could find a way to fuse the teaching of a grand, heritage-based national narrative with an investigative approach, topical targets would need to shift. Investigating Native Americans through Watergate in a year's time, for example, would be inconceivable. As I think this study makes abundantly clear, teaching children to think historically, to reconstruct their epistemologies (i.e., to give up the illusion that history texts directly mirror a past reality), to learn expertise in historical inquiry, and to construct their own historical arguments is a slow, arduous process. The more novice the student, the more time and intensive energy it takes. Add to this students who speak English as a second language (Candy, Tho) and who have difficulty reading (Kendra). Individualized, time-intensive pedagogical strategies must be developed and deployed to teach them. Given the impartial, ceaseless ticking of the clock, a history curriculum that prides itself on "covering that long national 'freedom-quest' narrative" mitigates against a systematic reliance on the investigative approach and attention to the many subjective realities of classroom learning (uncertainty, unpredictability, the sometimes lethargic pace) it entails. My experience teaching the fifth-graders and the data generated from it tells me that with young, diverse novices such as the children in room 23, you simply cannot have it both ways.

In addressing this issue, Americans might turn to the British to learn something from the structure of their national history curriculum and its assessment targets (see Lee, 1995). Children there have opportunities to investigate history much earlier. Although during the Thatcher regime the government attempted to restore a focus on an "official," heritage-inspired national narrative, investigation into the past in England is still a privileged approach in the history curriculum and in teaching practice. That reliance on investigation may in part explain the relatively significant progress many British students display on measures of historical thinking, interpretation, and analysis as they move through school (e.g., Lee et al., 1996a). The British example may help us understand that, in order to learn to think historically, an obsession with asking children to commit a nationalist narrative to memory is a misguided approach.

And third, consider the heightened visibility of state-level accountability and high-stakes testing initiatives designed to reform education by executive mandate. In this fifth-grade design experiment the performance assessment tasks that asked the eight primary informants to read, analyze, and construct interpretations from historical documents show considerable promise as a testing technology within this sort of policy-making arena. My pedagogical decisions and teaching practices were aligned with the nature of those tasks. Rubrics were designed that contained characterization codes (see Appendix A) that were validly and reliably applied to students' vocalizations on the performance tasks. That data provided a window—albeit an imperfect one—into the cognitive processes the students used in learning to think historically, to read critically, to analyze and draw inferences, and to make evidence-based claims. As a culture, we purport to value this sort of thinking. Performance-assessment tasks such as the ones I employed suggest how that thinking can be measured.

Such assessment technologies are not new. They have been employed on voluntary Advanced Placement history examinations for years in the form of what are called document-based questions (DBQs). Only more recently have such performance tasks been built into some state's high-stakes testing programs (e.g., New York, Maryland), those required for all students at particular grade levels.

However, as I have noted, many policy makers in positions to make assessment decisions tend to be wary of these forms of assessments for at least two reasons. First, they are time-consuming to administer and produce detailed, rich data that can be expensive to score. Test-item raters must be educated to reliably apply carefully constructed measurement rubrics to student responses on the performance tasks. Even in small states such as Maryland, thousands of students take the state-mandated tests. Hundreds of raters are needed annually for the task of carefully scoring the items. Although the performances can measure sophisticated forms of historical thinking that demonstrate intellectual and cognitive acumen rather than simple recall, and therefore have the capacity to prompt history teachers to teach that type of acumen, the tasks are more costly to administer and judge than machine-scored multiple-choice items.

And second, apparently concerned about the importance of teaching "our" traditional nationalist narrative, some assessment policy makers prefer constructing tests that measure simple recall of official heritage-based heroes and the events that ostensibly made them so. In some places, these tests have been understood as *minimum*-competency measures. But as talk of holding all students to high educational and curricular standards has proliferated in recent years, it has pushed state policy makers to up the accountability ante on their tests. This often has meant adding more items and broadening the scope of the narrative to be studied and recalled (see Firestone, Fitz, & Broadfoot, 1999). Increasingly, the tests are designed not only to demonstrate to parents and constituents how children fare against the yardstick of those high standards (assuming the tests are valid measures of learning), but also to hold teachers accountable for what and how they teach. Property values rise and fall as a result of how people perceive that these teachers teach and their students score.

Although there are other possible ways of interpreting these movements, I, like Darling-Hammond (1991), read the landscape to be primarily about cost-based decisions, not educational ones. If the direction across the terrain involves high-stakes accountability policies applied to vast numbers of students (especially in states such as Texas where there is talk of measuring all students at every grade level), expense and efficiency become of paramount concern to policy makers. Reliable, machine-scored, low-cost historical-detail recall items thus frame many of the tests, despite their validity limitations (how much cognitive capacity do they actually measure?) and a record indicating how poorly many learners repeatedly score on them (Beatty, Reese, Persky, & Carr, 1996; Ravitch & Finn, 1987).[1] This is about a negotiation of cost efficiencies. That such choices continue to be made in many policy-making arenas remains an imposing challenge to encouraging the type of historical thinking measured by the performance tasks I employed. The experience in room 23 of aiming my teaching practices at what my performance assessment tasks would measure, and then studying what the fifth-graders learned as a result, convinced me that they were well worth the added time and expense required.

History teachers interested in practices that turn on historical investigation will no doubt be torn here as I was. Testing practices that have significant consequences, demand broad topic coverage, and measure bits and pieces of an "official," heritage-based narrative will put powerful pressure on them to teach to the tests. To assure that students can recall at least some details and heroes of the narrative, it is not difficult to understand that many resort to drill techniques. This takes precious time away from pursuing the types of historical inquiries and research processes outlined in this study. Even though I was not an employee of the school system in which I taught and in that sense "less accountable" for test results, I worried considerably, as I have shown, about how long it was taking me to move through the curricular territory. Students in room 23 were learning history, but not rapidly enough by typical curriculum and testing standards.

---

[1] Drawing from research on students' historical thinking, we might conclude that it is not that students don't know history; it is that the tests of recall do not measure how students learn it. Additional doses of the wrong medicine will not cure the patient.

These three areas will precipitate continuous classroom dilemmas for history teachers committed to teaching history through investigation. The best such teachers can hope for is to manage them in the near term and press for change on the long term. Although the issue of historical significance is unlikely ever to be resolved, the alignment of testing policies, curriculum standards, and classroom history materials (e.g., primary source documents) with messages about the importance of teaching historical thinking by asking students to do it would be an advantageous development. I want to believe that several elements described in this study point in the direction of that alignment.

Resilient "Encyclopedia" Epistemologies

Although I have discussed the resilience of my students' "encyclopedia" epistemologies in previous chapters, I see this issue as sufficiently crucial to raise it again here. Historical investigation, in my judgment, depends on a pragmatist's epistemological stance. Scott's (1996) paper "After History?"—from which I have been drawing repeatedly—is a handy primer on what I have in mind. I draw from the paper extensively here.

At the risk of belaboring the point, I want to say again: The past is lost to us; we cannot recover it "as it was." All that remain are artifacts and the residue of what went before us. We wish to reconstruct this past and be as faithful as we can to its reality. But all we can do is interpret those artifacts and that ancient residue. We cannot know for certain what went on in Jefferson's mind as he wrote the Declaration of Independence or what Truman felt when he chose to unleash the A-bomb on Japan. Even when personal diaries such as Ensign Lister's survive to the present, we must interpret them—and we do so mostly by our current lights, not by Lister's. No matter how we try, we cannot enter his psyche and know how things really were for him at Lexington Green. *We* imbue scattered artifacts and historical residue with meaning, and in the process—despite heroic efforts to do otherwise—*we* concoct more or less evidence-based fictions.

A pragmatist's epistemology acknowledges this tension, the unbridgeable divide that separates a reality back then from our interpretations of it now. As Scott (1996) observes, this is nothing new; historians have known it all along. Doing well at it involves reading well: Historical investigators must be able to read critically. If it is always-already interpretation, then we must seek out the best arguments. Investigators seek them not to fix or stabilize the past, because that is impossible. The lure of investigation, of digging about in the past, is to learn from it, to learn about our selves, to imagine a future derived from where we have been. This requires us to see history as a set of stories we construct and tell—and continually reconstruct and retell—about who we were and how they define who we see ourselves as now. They are tales that then enable us to project who we might be tomorrow.

A history textbook cannot halt this retelling, nor can the "official" heritage-based narrative of "our" common cultural accomplishments and aspirations. Neither has the power to end history, to tell things as they were once and for all time. These texts must be read and assessed as *someone's* interpretations and arguments about how things were—good, bad, or indifferent. And despite normative requirements for disinterest and detachment among historical investigators, no account or story or text could exist without at least some attachment and interest. And tomorrow, someone with different attachments and interests may wish to retell the story. My students certainly did.

However, as we have seen, some of those 10-year-olds remained convinced that one could fix the past, could nail down that one story that told things as they really had been. Some believed that encyclopedias and textbooks contained such accounts. The Truth was out there just waiting to be discovered. The investigator's task was to find that Truth, find that text that contained it.

Where and how do students acquire these encyclopedia epistemologies? Why are some so impervious to change? Despite attempting for more than 4 months to manage the dilemmas arising from those resilient epistemological stances, I have few answers to these questions. School is no doubt an influential factor. The importance placed on literal comprehension of text during emergent reading activities cultivates a belief that the meaning is in the text, that the text contains what really is. As they are learning to comprehend in such a manner, children encounter history textbooks that erase the historian author and produce belief in the reality effect—that all the words in the text map directly onto what's real. Many teachers give these textbooks elevated, but undeserved, epistemological status. Tests that require recall of details and events drawn verbatim from these history textbooks also reinforce their aerial status. And experiences away from school can additionally reinforce the encyclopedia epistemology.

As I concluded our unit on British colonization on the Atlantic seaboard, I observed my reconstituted resolve to work on shifting my students' epistemologies. That involved, I noted, teaching them to become more self-consciousness about how their own temporally anchored historical positionalities influenced where they thought historical knowledge came from, whose perspectives were involved in making sense of the past, and how those perspectives could be judged. I specifically designed learning opportunities with this resolve in mind as we investigated events leading up to the American Revolution. Yet data emerging from the endpoint performance assessment continued to reflect aspects of the encyclopedia epistemologies among some students. But why, in the face of a variety of such experiences designed to reinforce the idea that it is communities of historical investigators who debate and decide what to accept as valid (then later change their minds), some of my 10-year-old students' epistemologies remained so intractable continues to puzzle me. It is difficult to underestimate the challenge this matter of epistemological stance presents to teaching children to learn history by doing it.

The issue clearly needs further research. Learning to think historically and to engage in investigations of the past requires students to shift to a pragmatic epistemology (Dewey, 1931/1963). Without it, the challenge intensifies for teachers to help their students construct one, and the means of doing so is far from clear, as my muddied efforts suggest. History teachers committed to teaching history through investigation could be assisted by understanding more effective and time-saving strategies for bringing about such shifts. My experience with the fifth-graders in room 23 left me thinking that, in the short term and without this understanding, persistence with my pedagogical approach seemed to my only recourse. That persistence did help some children see history differently and acquire elements of the pragmatist's epistemology. However, it hardly moved them all. What this issue of resilience portends for students' future experiences of learning history in school is also not clear.

Learning to Historically Contextualize Interpretations

In bracing this issue in Chapter 1, I suggested that the challenge of contextualizing the past is very difficult because it is faced by all historical investigators—from the untested novice to the most seasoned expert—and it is largely undoable in any full sense. It is closely connected to the previous discussion of epistemology and also to the tension between a past reality and our interpretations of it.

By *historical contextualization* I mean the practice of interpreting people and events in terms of the historical context of the time in which they lived, not by our current standards and tastes. Judging the past by the present is often referred to as presentism. As we have seen, my students were no strangers to presentist assessments (e.g., Jeffrey's responses to the Lexington battle documents), despite my efforts to get them to understand the perspectives and points of view of people when they lived. Avoiding presentism entails understanding the assumptions, convictions, and philosophies of historical actors within *their* historical milieu. With regard to school settings, theorists have discussed the role of historical empathy—

investigators' putting themselves in the historical agent's place—in achieving that understanding and thus being able to contextualize the past one is investigating (see Ashby & Lee, 1987b; Davis, Yeager, & Foster, 2001; Shemilt, 1984; VanSledright, 2001). However, theorists also have questioned an investigator's capacity to attain this sort of empathy. Ashby and Lee (1987b) have attempted to chart its development and progression among grade school children. They concluded that historical empathy is a mysterious achievement.

Again, at the risk of belaboring another point, let me reconstruct the unresolved challenge we faced in room 23 regarding this issue. First, what made empathizing so difficult was that it demanded Herculean levels of examination of our assumptions and knowledge-based theories about the world, about the past, and about a possible future. These assumptions were so commonly taken for granted among the students and buried in the recesses of their lives that they frequently had difficulty imagining the right sorts of questions with which they could undertake this thorough self-examination. As their teacher, I had to be the source of those questions. However, my own taken-for-granted assumptions also bar me from knowing what they all might be.

Second, some theorists have noted that the type of empathy which begets historical contextualization requires close attention to the positionalities of the authors of historical texts and artifacts—this, it is argued, being the sine qua non of full historical understanding. Yet we lack the tools and unbroken evidence trails to accomplish this kind of empathy with the rigor necessary to promote full contextualization of the past. Even with sharp intellectual and investigative tools, sometimes the lack of evidence can thwart our best use of them. Imagining the motives, intent, and assumptions of historical agents turned out to be our best, but perhaps least trustworthy, tool in room 23.

Third, achieving a level of authentic empathy with those we investigated demanded that we bracket out our own historical positionalities in order to avoid the nasty habit of imposing our current presentist assumptions on our interpretations. "As the argument goes, this harnessing act enables us to fully contextualize the past, to get into the hearts and minds of our predecessors in ways that allow authentic empathic regard, to reconstruct historical agents' intentions and subsequent acts, and to develop a full understanding of the historical milieu in which these agents operated" (VanSledright, 2001, p. 61). But we found that the past of colonial North America was a foreign country (Lowenthal, 1985), that the act of checking our historical positionalities at the door and thus limiting the way we imposed them was impossible. As we tried to make sense of this world, our current sociocultural bearings were all we had to work from. Without them, there was no interpretation, no meaning-making process, and no understanding, historical or otherwise. There was no place to stand outside those bearings.

Yet I taught the fifth-graders that, despite these difficulties and limitations, the ability to avoid presentist judgments and to contextualize the past as much as possible is highly valued in the community of historical practice. As a result, I insisted that the students attend to it as they investigated the past. But how was I to achieve success among these novices? My efforts, as I noted, met with only partial success.

Part of what is at stake is how history teachers, as more knowledgeable others, model the art of historical contextualization for their students. I introduced this concern in Chapter 5. Should we model the building of context by beginning our investigations with narrative accounts and then move to primary source material, as I did with the fifth-graders? Or should it be the other way around, starting with primary sources, ordering them in a way that conveys a sense of chronology and implies narrative development? Each approach has its own set of advantages and limitations in teaching novices how to contextualize their investigations. This is another area that could stand further research.

Here again, perhaps what is required in the near term is pedagogical persistence—taking the time to structure investigative opportunities that entail self-examinations of the role contextualization plays in interpretation and stopping frequently to discuss the operation of this process. Teaching the vocabulary of contextualization and empathy might also be necessary. Because historical contextualization is so highly prized within the community of historians, it must not be neglected. However, as with the other challenges, this one will repeatedly influence the choices history teachers make about how to orchestrate their teaching practices, and it no doubt will raise classroom dilemmas that linger and press. As a result, it may cause some to move away from teaching history through investigation.

WHITHER HISTORY EDUCATION?

Despite the formidable challenges, there is every reason to pursue teaching history as investigation. My experience in room 23 taught me that its benefits clearly outweigh its difficulties. In fact, I found it exhilarating to address and manage the teaching dilemmas that the challenges provoked. However, beyond that, here are three advantages that this study indicates bear significant educational fruit and can serve to inspire more teaching of history as investigation into the past.

Understanding Themselves by Investigating Their Forebears

As I hope I have made clear, common practice today in teaching history in schools involves inviting students to participate in the referential illusion and inducing them to succumb to its reality effect. By inverting the typical foreground–background relationship between the products of investigation and the investigative act itself, and placing the investigation process front and center, history teachers expose the fact that the reality to which an interpretation refers is nothing other than someone's view of that reality. The inversion serves to unmask the illusion that the stories historians tell map directly onto the past, as though the telling was simply an unmediated conduit between past and present.

This process opens up a host of opportunities for children to learn about themselves. It enables them to see that we humans choose, create, and manipulate the stories we convey about ourselves and the ways we use them to live our lives. This is empowering because it teaches students that they, too, can have a hand in the process. It provides a window into understanding the ways in which human communities create rules and police the actions of their members. It then opens the window and encourages children to climb through, to participate in the action. To the extent that what they find there is democratic, children learn to participate in the activities of citizens in shaping such democracies. When they find undemocratic tendencies there, they learn ways to foil them. It is in these places that children discover that they have some power in formulating their own identities and destinies.

Participating in the referential illusion and yielding to its reality effect leads to the end of history and blocks participation in building community. If we think of history as the ceaseless investigation into who we were and thus are becoming, then we are engaged in a process of endlessly revising and remaking images of ourselves based on what has gone on before us. We do so because we anticipate different and better futures, imagine different communities. Achieving historical understanding is as much about the present and the future as it is about the past.

The consequence of succumbing to the reality effect—of accepting the idea that the products of historical investigation fix and stabilize a past reality—brings our investigations to an end. We would no longer need to revise, to revisit, to re-create, to reconceive. Who we are would be forever etched in time. History as I defined it above would cease. There would be no need to imagine a future; we would have arrived in the forever-present. The future would be obliterated. If, under this spell, history is over, then there is little need to investigate it because it can tell us nothing new about where we might go tomorrow. It renders us slaves to dogma generated by the illusion of a Truth we believe our immovable, static past conveys to us. The more intent we are in turning history to dogma, the more frequently schoolchildren (and many adults) find this dogma irrelevant and lifeless, and tell researchers repeatedly that it bores them witless (see Goodlad, 1984; Haladyna & Shaughnessy, 1985; VanSledright, 1997).

Doing history, engaging in those restless reexaminations of and investigations into the past, beckons the future. Our efforts to come to new interpretations of, say, the Starving Time or the Lexington "shot heard 'round the world," or the life of Martha Ballard, or the 2000 presidential election are driven by our desire to understand ourselves. "What will these new interpretations tell us about who we might be," we seem to be asking. This desire to question derives from the way we are compelled to imagine different futures, to improve our lot, to step forward from where we have been. Even nostalgia, that yearning for some idyllic past, anticipates the future with its desire to have those days return. Teaching children to look into the past, to dig it up, to investigate it opens pathways to the sort of self-understanding characterized by anticipation of a brighter future, a reconceptualization of identity, and the envisionment of hope. This is one of its principal benefits. It begs for light in classrooms. It asks us to displace our obsession with inert, heritage-based accounts that imply history has ended.

I find it ironic that, as the cheery, upbeat heritage truths (embodied in textbooks, for example) described by both Kammen (1997) and Lowenthal (1998) enter the classroom door, they whitewash and stabilize the past by disguising the human investigative machinery that produced them so well that they render what they purport to teach idle and lifeless. The heritage fashioner's sunny products—Bennett's (1994) "lasting visions of civilization," for example—clamor for classroom attention but in the end push children away because, as they proclaim their truth, they attempt to foreclose on children's excited and ceaseless searches for their futures as they explore the past. In stark contrast, historical investigations fuel that excitement as oxygen does a fire. This benefit appears undeniable.

The Motivational Lure of Historical Investigations

My students were deeply drawn into the process of investigating the past. This is the second benefit I wish to discuss. We know from the research that children frequently report finding the study of history to be a process of trying to remember other people's facts (Holt, 1990). They tell us that little could bore them as much. History as the restless excavation of the past in search of interpretations that might help us better understand ourselves today has the capacity to turn that boredom inside out.

Engaging children in historical investigations puts them largely in charge of their own learning. They become responsible for crafting interpretations and arguments about the past that reside alongside those created by others. In this way, they are connected directly to what may once have seemed to them a remote and meaningless set of events. The process also insists that in constructing their evidence-based versions—no matter how initially far-fetched—they draw on who they are because they cannot help but impose their assumptions and identities (i.e., historical positionalities) on the inferences they derive. In this act, despite the problems of presentism associated with it, children of the present beckon their ancestors from the past, rather than the other way around.

Students also find the process of wrangling over acceptable interpretations most compelling. Their interpretations intersect in a community of inquirers as they participate actively in it. They are empowered to consider and reconsider the rules by which they accomplish their efforts and construct their interpretations of the historical world, and thus their own. At the same time, they are held accountable to those rules. They are at the center of their own action rather than on the periphery, as passive recipients of the results of someone else's decision-making process. In this crucible, the students are more cognizant of how their identities can be shaped by the action. This is what draws them in—the possibility of having a more direct role in shaping and reshaping who they are.

Taking some responsibility for one's own learning can be daunting. However, in the safety of the classroom, where a teacher can assist should efforts be sidetracked, I can think of few more important experiences we would want to provide for our children on their way to becoming fully functioning adult learners. Investigating history provides one mechanism for enticing travel down that daunting path.

Historical Investigation as Critical Literacy

Each day it seems that we move closer to a completely information-dominated culture. The recent increase in the number of companies, marketers, government agencies, politicians, and research institutions doing business on the Internet, and the rising use of that medium by the public, demonstrates how reliant we have become on locating, consuming, and assessing information and then choosing how to use it. These developments require powerful reading strategies and critical-analysis capabilities by virtue of the sheer amount of information to which we must attend. However, data from the 1998 National Assessment of Educational Progress (NAEP) on how schoolchildren read show a consistent trend: By about fifth grade, students stop reading books and text unless they must

(Donahue, Voelkl, Campbell, & Mazzeo, 1999). Data from the NAEP also indicate that children lose interest in reading and find little joy in it at about this same point. These children, for the most part, become stunted in their reading development and rarely progress beyond basic reading capacity, creating what can be referred to as a plateau effect.

Efforts in school to push strategies for literal comprehension, although to some degree necessary, tend to make young children slaves to texts' putative meanings, as I described earlier. Children fail to notice that texts are written by humans for humans, for pleasurable reading purposes and to convey interpretations, ideas, and information about the world that may or may not be useful in enhancing intellectual acuity and solving problems. By the time children are the age of the students in room 23, many find reading first onerous and then unnecessary, because they are more easily drawn to the visual imagery on television, Play Station, and the Internet. They do not appear to realize that even attention to those images actually involves a form of reading because they have failed to learn how to read critically. Critical literacy—so fundamental to the vitality of democracy in an information culture, where it seems everyone wants the attention of your eyeballs—appears lost to many children by the time they are 10. These children appear stuck at the level of basic reading comprehension, beholden to literal meanings, and unable to ferret out those all-important author perspectives and subtexts.

Engaging children who encounter this plateau effect in acts of historical investigation holds significant promise for arresting the trend. First, my experiences with the fifth-graders demonstrated that, given an interesting problem to solve—a historical mystery or an interpretive conundrum—they took to the task of reading texts with considerable zeal. As we have seen, they were on impatient missions to dig up some answers, to understand what had occurred. Occasionally, it was difficult to get them out of those texts and images to talk about what they were reading. Jeffrey's and Coral's intense effort to understand the Starving Time, to read all the texts they could get their hands and eyes on, is a case in point.

Second, the results from the two performance tasks I asked the eight primary informants to undertake suggest that children even this young are capable of sophisticated types of reading. It does not seem to be a matter of a lack of intellectual ability, as some have maintained. Although my fifth-graders did not display the types of critical literacy that expert historians possess, in a relatively short period of time all made strides in being able to read more sensitively and analytically. Perhaps two crucial aspects of their growth in capacity to read critically involved the ways in which they showed greater reliance on reading *inter*textually and detecting the subtexts and perspectives of the authors who had written these texts. It is difficult to know what type of transfer this form of reading may have in other learning contexts at or away from school. That a number of students displayed interest in being able to read critically and intertextually, found it powerful, and were able to be taught how in just over 4 months suggests that it may well carry over to other settings.

It is difficult to overstate the importance that learning to read critically has for the emerging generation of young adults in information-dominated cultures. The invitation teachers have to transform an otherwise inert school subject such as American history into an opportunity to teach this type of critical literacy should not be foregone. We owe it to our children. In fact, using historical investigations to teach critical reading may be one the greatest warrants we can muster for offering history courses in school. For me, it was the only warrant that mattered in the end. Although it may have seemed otherwise, I was little interested in turning my students into miniature historians. Rather, I deliberately sought to teach them the analytic strategies used by historians because of their extensive value in educating thoughtful, reflective young citizens who can detect snake-oil sales spin and reveal a disguised agenda. This type of opportunity to teach critical literacy, and the warrant that buoys it, is perhaps the most powerful benefit of engaging young children in the practice of doing history.

From where I sit looking back on the results of this study, the challenges—though compelling—are overshadowed by the three benefits just considered. The history education goals we set for our children, to the extent that they point toward these benefits and the classroom teaching practices that support them, move us toward a more powerful form of educational opportunity than ones that merely ask children to reproduce inert accounts of the past. In this sense, the National History Standards' (NCHS, 1994) concern with the importance of teaching students to learn history by doing it seems to be well placed. And the results from this study indicate that fifth-grade is not too early to begin. I can only imagine what a steady diet of this type of history in school would do to enhance the overall intellectual acumen of future adults.

Many of the challenges I have described hinge on decisions about how much we are willing to invest in history education. For example, the performance tasks that the results from this study indicate are necessary components for assessing historical thinking are simply more expensive to administer and score. Another example would entail supplying teachers with the source materials necessary to engage their students in historical detective work. A third instance involves the professional educational opportunities teachers may need in order to learn more about how to turn their history classrooms into communities of inquirers. And a fourth would turn on reconceptualizing how we prepare teachers to teach in history classrooms that make carrying out investigations into the past a principal pedagogical practice. This latter one alone would take a serious financial commitment.

If we accept the idea that the benefits of learning history by doing it are impressive and therefore worth pursuing, then I take this question of investment to be an issue of moral commitment to children. If we are convinced that what children gain by a move in this direction is inspiring and improves significantly upon common practice, then we must be willing to support it. The fifth-graders in room 23 welcomed the challenge. Will we?

USING THE PAST TO IMAGINE THE FUTURE:
A CAUTIONARY NOTE

Having said all of this, I must end with a cautionary observation. I am arguing for a serious discussion and possible reconceptualization of the way we teach history in schools and of how we understand what history ought to look like in classrooms, especially those in the middle grades, where children initially encounter the systematic study of U.S. history. My claims for the benefits of doing things differently are based on the results of a 4-month teacher-research design experiment in one fifth-grade classroom and on a careful analysis of the data that experiment produced. Although those results align with much of the research on teaching and learning history discussed in Chapter 1 and with the vision of history in the National History Standards, the fact remains that it is only one study. There are few others in the literature. What happened in Kendall Elementary School in southern Maryland may or may not be what happens under similar circumstances in Marshall Elementary School in northern California. In short, we need additional studies of this kind in order to lend further support to the claims and implications I have drawn.

As Alexander (2000) has pointed out, one reason that we continually tinker around the educational margins but seldom undertake serious educational reform has to do, in part, with our lack of a theory of academic development. Despite accumulations of vast amounts of research on how children and adults learn, we have yet to construct a vision of what this might look like in academic domains, such as history, and developmentally, across grade levels from elementary through high school. I contend that this study can be conceived as one marker on that path toward understanding academic development in the domain of history. Wilson's (1990) design experiment in a history/geography classroom of third-graders and her analysis of what they were learning as a result of her teaching practices may be thought of as another. Both attempt to chart—albeit tentatively—what historical thinking looks like among young novices under pedagogical conditions designed to enhance it. Those results then speak to what we know about historical thinking among experts, the gulf that separates the two, and, by implication, how to traverse that gulf.

No doubt, there are other such studies of this nature yet to be reported. However, we need many more to chart novice-to-expert learning trajectories in history. Charting those trajectories could be enhanced by longitudinal designs that explore learning occurring under particular pedagogical approaches (e.g., historical investigation), say, across grades 4 through 8. If other such designs examined development in the history domain in classrooms where more traditional approaches were in place, we would then acquire even greater substantive grounds on which to draw comparisons. This in turn would make possible a yet more ecologically sound basis on which we could tout the benefits of one over the other.

Here is another area in which how we choose to spend scarce educational dollars may matter. Currently, there is little research money to fund these sorts of studies in the history domain. Such studies in mathematics and in the sciences are relatively easily procured because the National Science Foundation (NSF) seems to have no shortage of funds. The National Endowment for the Humanities only recently began funding educational studies, and the amount of funds they possess for educational research pales by comparison to those available from the NSF. Those interested in researching academic development in history typically must seek support from private foundations and, in the process, compete with researchers doing every other sort of research in a variety of domains.

I suspect that until more systematic research occurs and additional studies such as this one and those with longitudinal designs begin to populate the literature, we will continue to tinker at the margins of history teaching practice. In the meantime, many of our children will likely miss out on the powerful advantages that those encounters with history can produce. If nothing more, of course, history teaches us that we can choose, if we wish, to have things differently.

Appendix A

Research Method

TEACHING PRACTICE DATA COLLECTION
AND ANALYSIS PROCEDURES

To gather data on how I planned to teach, what then occurred in the classroom, and my interpretation of those occurrences, I used several methods. First, I wrote out all my lesson plans meticulously, so that I would have a record of my planning practices. Second, once in the classroom, I videotaped all the lessons. I also asked my research assistant to visit the class on average about once every eight class sessions and take field notes, as a means of triangulating my recollections of events with hers and with the videotape record of those lessons. And third, I maintained a detailed journal in which I recorded my thoughts about how things were progressing, my reactions to each class episode, and notes about students, curriculum resources, and the like.

To analyze this data for the purpose of generating a written record of classroom events along with interpretive commentary, I digitized all my daily lesson plans and my journal entries. Also, with the help of my research assistant, I created a catalogue of each videotape and transcribed what I considered to be particularly interesting or relevant lessons. My criteria for relevance was based on implications of classroom events for the research questions I was attempting to address with respect to the theory of historical thinking I was employing. I triangulated my lesson plans and journal entries with the videotape catalogue, the transcribed lessons from those tapes, and my assistant's field notes as a means of developing an understanding of all the lessons I conducted. My descriptions of classroom events and dialogues that occurred in Chapters 3, 4, and 5 are based on this record and my analysis of it.

Part of teaching involves keeping track of students' efforts to learn the ideas presented in the classroom. To augment my understanding of how my daily teaching practices intersected with the development of students' historical understandings, I also collected their assignments, essays, log books, Research Logs, newspaper articles and illustrations, and the like, and made copies. Anything that students produced effectively became data. I used this data to inform my characterizations of classroom events and as background for understanding results from the two performances tasks students undertook.

PERFORMANCE-TASK DATA-COLLECTION PROCEDURES

In Chapter 6, I discussed the nature of the initial and endpoint performance tasks I asked eight primary informants from room 23 to engage in. Here I provide additional detail about the nature of the data collected and how they were analyzed.

The initial January performance task was preceded by tape-recorded interviews in which I gathered detailed demographic information (age, birth date, parents' occupations and education, race/ethnicity, etc.) from the eight students and also queried them about their understanding of history, the nature of historical knowledge, and related questions. After the second performance task in May, I again interviewed the eight about their views of history, the nature of historical knowledge, how historians settle disputes about evidence, and so on. Such data were designed to shed light on how the students responded to the performance tasks and how their ideas about history changed, both key measures of the educational efficacy of the pedagogical theory underpinning my investigative approach and my intent to enhance students' historical thinking. All interview data were transcribed verbatim. From the interviews about who the students were, I built demographic portraits of the eight, and then added summaries of their views of history at both the beginning and endpoint of the study. My research assistant, Fasulo, also interviewed the remaining 15 students to obtain detailed demographic information from them so that I could build such portraits of all the students.

The initial performance task involved the tape-recorded reading of two documents concerning the shooting in Boston in March, 1770, which later became known in the American colonies as the Boston Massacre (excerpt from Hakim text and Captain Thomas Preston's account; Appendix B). The eight informants were given the documents one by one and asked to think out loud as they read. Students did this individually, accompanied only by either myself or Fasulo. Before they began, students engaged in a practice exercise in which they read a small portion of a unrelated history text and were coached in the activity of speaking out loud about what they were thinking as they read. We did not proceed to the initial task until students could accomplish the practice exercise to our satisfaction. This meant, for example, getting comfortable stopping at the points in the text where I had placed red dots, signifying that they were to pause at that juncture and talk about what was going on in their heads. On average, the red dots appeared approximately at the end of every two to three sentences and always at the end of each paragraph.

Before they began reading the first Boston Massacre document, students were told that they would be reading two texts about shootings that occurred in Boston, Massachusetts, in March 1770, prior to the American Revolutionary War. Their purpose was to figure out what happened, who did the shooting, and why.

As is common practice in think-aloud protocol research, we had the students proceed without interruption except to ask when necessary "What are you thinking now?" if they failed to pause at a red dot. This uninterrupted process was referred to as the "online" portion of the task. Following their reading of the two documents, we asked several questions, such as: Which document did you like the most and why? Did you notice any differences between the two? Who were the authors of the two documents? What difference does it make where the author's information comes from? Which document did you think told the story most accurately? Such follow-up questioning processes were referred to as "retrospective interviews."

After this procedure was completed, the eight were individually told that they would now be shown three images of that shooting to further assist them in making sense of the event (Figures B.1, B.2, and B.3 in Appendix B). We asked them to talk out loud about what they were thinking as they looked at the images. The purpose of using the images was to aid the process of constructing an understanding of events by presenting additional evidence. I wanted them to further demonstrate how they were thinking about different types of evidence and using it to construct an interpretation of what had occurred. I thought it also might be helpful for the students who were reading below grade level to have an opportunity to "see" the event as well as read about it.

We let them work their way through the images, encouraging them only as necessary to speak up with prompts such as "What are you thinking now?" (online portion). After they had completed the image examinations, we followed up in a retrospective interview with questions such as: Can you order the images from most accurate to least accurate? Why is Image X more accurate to you than the other images? Do you notice any differences in the images? The images all describe the same Boston Massacre, so why are there differences? Where do the images come from, do you think? How do they compare to the documents?

For the second performance task, the same procedures were employed. This time, we used four texts and two images that dealt with the battle at

Lexington Green (minutemen testimony, excerpts from British Ensign Lister's diary, two brief newspaper accounts; see Appendix B).

The purpose of changing the focal event was to fashion a degree of parallelism in the way the procedure was administered initially. That is, students reported having heard of the Boston Massacre and a few remembered seeing a picture of it before they engaged in the first performance task. However, the prior knowledge they had to draw on in analyzing the documents was somewhat limited. In our study of the causes of the American Revolution in class, we had noted in a general sense the shots fired at Lexington as one of many possible causes of the American Revolution. Only Ben and Jamie had looked more deeply into the details and read a couple of sources, none of which were reused for this performance task. As with' the Boston Massacre, the Lexington event contained a similar riddle element: Who gave the order to fire? Therefore, primarily because the answer to the question was inconclusive and because students' prior knowledge was relatively limited, it seemed a reasonable event to pair this with the first task. The specific goal was to attempt to equalize the degree to which the eight students could rely on their prior knowledge of events to read, compare, contrast, source, and corroborate the texts and images of the battle at Lexington. If their lack of knowledge of the two events were effectively equivalent, then, in analyzing the data, concentration could be placed on the specific processes (e.g., monitoring comprehension, corroboration, judging of perspective) students relied on during the tasks. In part, this demand was met. However, the eight did know that the skirmish at Lexington Green was termed the first battle of the Revolution and that it was a puzzle who fired first. Ben and Jamie held a slight edge with regard to having more ideas about it.

PERFORMANCE-TASK ANALYSIS PROCEDURES

To develop a coding scheme for understanding what students were doing as they read through the documents and images, I began with Pressley and Afflerbach's (1995) general scheme for characterizing how readers read texts. As I noted in Chapter 6, it was difficult to rely for a set of codes solely on the research studies that specify what expert historical investigators do when they work through historical evidence (Leinhardt & Young, 1996; Wineburg, 1991). Because this research is silent on what novices do, and because novices, by definition, do not employ the heuristics and strategies that experts do, I needed to begin with a set of general codes that could be applied to novice-level historical investigators. Then, to round out the coding scheme, I could draw from the expert research to create a continuum of strategic-reading approaches—from general to history-specific—I observed among the eight. I clarify how this system evolved in what follows.

Pressley and Afflerbach (1995) reanalyzed all previous studies that had used verbal-report (or think-aloud) protocols to understand what readers do when they read. From this reanalysis, they constructed three general reading strategies that readers who routinely made sense of texts rely upon: (1) They draw from their prior knowledge to make meaning from a text; (2) they use a variety of comprehension and monitoring strategies, such as rereading, summarizing, questioning, and predicting or inferring as they read the text; and (3) they conduct what I will call here "*intra*textual evaluating." That is, these readers vocalize, for example, judgments of character actions, affective reactions to the text's contents, and questions or assessments directed at the author's word choices, style, and so forth (e.g., "Oh my gosh, this is terrible! This part doesn't make any sense.").

Using this general characterization to understand how my eight fifth-graders were reading the documents proved only partially adequate (note that I also considered the images as texts to be read). Historical thinking that produces understanding, the research tells us, requires the analyses and *evaluative comparisons* of multiple sources of evidence (diary accounts, letters, books, images, and artifacts) with respect to how these sources cohere and thus can be used to corroborate claims in constructing an evidence-based interpretation of an event. These analyses and crucial evaluative comparisons help readers judge historical agents' perspectives, understand the status of accounts, and establish historical context (e.g., Lee & Ashby, 2000; Leinhardt & Young, 1996; Wineburg, 1991; 1998). Therefore, to make sound sense of the past, historical investigators cannot rely only on *intra*textual analyses and evaluations; they must also engage in what might be called *inter*textual readings. To the three global reading strategies of Pressley and Afflerbach (1995), I added a fourth, specialized historical-reading strategy, which I called *inter*textual evaluations.

Intertextual evaluations include such analytic procedures as judging an image as a piece of evidence against other accounts or images, assessing the perspective and possible intention of an author and/or historical agent, and evaluating the actions and intentions of historical agents in a text or image against the actions of agents in other event-related texts or images. I worked from the idea that young history readers who demonstrate the first three types of reading strategies defined by Pressley and Afflerbach (1995) *but also* add the fourth—critical intertextual evaluations—to their repertoire are *beginning to read more expertly in the subject*—and thus think more historically. However, rather than simply imposing these characterizations of reading on the students' verbal reporting as they read the Boston "Massacre" and Lexington battle texts, I also searched the data themselves for the best fit between student vocalizations and my characterization of them. This allowed me to further refine and modify the types of reading procedures I had thus far developed: prior knowledge (PK), comprehension monitoring strategies (CMS), *intra*textual evaluations (IAE), and *inter*textual evaluations (IEE).

Typical of novices encountering a historical event for the first time, my eight readers vocalized little prior knowledge about either the shootings in Boston or the battle at Lexington. As a result, I subsumed prior knowledge into the category of reading termed comprehension and monitoring strategies. I reasoned that drawing from prior knowledge (the little there was that was evident in the students' readings) was a strategy they used to comprehend the texts they encountered, and thus it more accurately described a general comprehension and monitoring strategy. By studying the students' vocalizations closely, it became clear that only after they had begun examining a second document (text) in a set, and occasionally only after seeing the first of the images, did they begin to draw on a form of prior historical knowledge. In a sense, the eight readers were building knowledge of the Boston "Massacre" and Lexington battle events as they read, constructing it piece by piece as they drew from their varying successes exercising comprehension-monitoring strategies. When the students would attempt to corroborate details in their growing understanding of the event in question by pointing to what they had read in a preceding document or seen in an image, I called this process event-knowledge accretion (EKA). This was an effort to develop a more specific characterization of what they were doing as they read through the documents.

Comparing and contrasting sources made possible by event knowledge accretion signaled a move from reliance on *intra*textual analytic strategies to *inter*textual forms. To capture this shift, I redrew my understanding of the students' reading approaches along two large and distinctly different types of responses to the documents: *intra*textual analyses (IAA) and critical *inter*textual analyses (CIEA). For these novices, analyzing a source *intra*textually (IAA) was simply good, general reading practice, a necessary but insufficient condition for conducting historical investigations. Critical *inter*textual analyses (CIEA) come closest to what historical investigators must do to successfully engage historical documents and evidence: comparing, contrasting, corroborating details contained within the documents and evaluating—against others—an author's or artist's perspective and its reliability on the basis of assessing his or her partisan position and allegiance. This way of reading must occur with a view to understanding the historical context in which an event occurred. The process allows the investigator to systematically test and refine his or her interpretation.

Movement from the plane of general *intra*textual reading practice to that of critical *inter*textual analysis signifies the type of growth in the reading of documents (texts) that is necessary for the development of historical understanding. It also can signal the beginning steps of a shift away from a fundamentalist, "encyclopedia" epistemology, the stance, as we have seen, that often characterized the intellectual framework with which novices approach historical documents.

To give a sense of the movement from intratextual analyses (IAA) to that of the more expert, critical intertextual analyses (CIEA), I constructed my coding categories along a four-level continuum. Figure A.1 describes the final coding scheme categories by level and by location on the continuum.

Using this refined coding scheme pictured in Figure A.1—with the two major categories (IAA and CIEA) and the four subcategories (CMS, IAE, EKA, CIEE)—I systematically coded all the performance-task data, both initial and endpoint. A simple sentence unit uttered by a student and appearing in his or her transcript constituted one vocalization. Multiple vocalizations were referred to as frequencies. I then put the coded data away for 4 months. After that period, I reprinted all the transcripts of the performance tasks and recoded that data again without reexamining my first round. This allowed me to do a type of reliability check. It produced a coding agreement match from first to second analysis of 87%. I resolved the disagreements over which code to apply by arguing the decision back and forth with myself. This tack pushed me to further clarify and slightly expand the characteristics of performances described in each subcategory.

Overall, the application of the coding process allowed me to infer how the eight students approached the reading and analysis of the historical documents, both initially and then at the endpoint. One can think of the four levels as locations on a continuum that describe general to subject-specific strategies readers utilize as they read and analyze historical evidence on a topic about which they are gaining knowledge. Movement back and forth across the continuum (or the lack thereof) depends on comprehension of text, critical-reading capability and strategy use, and event-knowledge accretion.

To illustrate, a novice history reader/investigator (one of my fifth-graders in this case) begins by using the more global comprehension and monitoring strategies (CMS, or level 1) to make sense of an initial documentary text or image. Upon making some meaning from the text or image, she then moves to make judgments that situate it in her understanding, as specified in level 2 (IAE). As she encounters more evidence from additional documents and images provided as part of the task, she

Global reading strategies   *History-specific reading strategies*

Intratextual Analyses (IAA)   Critical Intertextual Analyses (CIEA)

LEVEL 1

Vocalization Type: Comprehension Monitoring Strategies (CMS)

- Checking/pointing out details
- Rereading portions of document/image
- Questioning the document/image
- Summarizing about a document passage or image depiction
- Predicting/inferring about a document/author purpose
- Checking fit with understanding or lack thereof

LEVEL 2

Vocalization Type: Intratextual Evaluations (IAE)

- Judging who characters are and actions in text/image
- Assessing text language/image depiction effectively
- Judging whether the text/image makes sense
- Questioning/evaluating the author/artist/title/ caption (e.g., style, syntax, color)

LEVEL 3

Vocalization Type: Event Knowledge Accretion (EKA)

- Checking where source(s) come(s) from, identifying the nature of a source(s) relative to other sources
- Corroborating/checking details against those gleaned from other accounts/images, using account to add to knowledge of event, checking fit of details from one document/image to another
- Building an initial interpretation from accreted knowledge

LEVEL 4

Vocalization Type: Critical Intertextual Evaluations (CIEE)

- Judging validity and reliability of source vis-à-vis other sources
- Assessing and judging the subtext against other subtexts
- Assessing actions/intentions of the historical agents with respect to other accounts
- Testing and refining the interpretation

Figure A.1. Coding scheme used for analyzing fifth-graders' vocalizations on performance tasks.

begins responding to it by drawing from her growing event knowledge (EKA or level 3), whereby she checks sources and corroborates details (data-gathering and interpretive heuristics employed by expert historians). Finally, she begins to evaluate the evidence *intertextually* (CIEE, or level 4) with respect to validity, reliability, subtextual, and agency concerns, as a means of constructing and verifying an event interpretation. The third level, and particularly the fourth, suggest a specialized critical-reading approach, bordering on that evidenced by historians. Although the model indicates that young children can learn to read much more expertly (levels 3 and 4), they typically do not do so without having opportunities to learn such expert reading processes. Figure A.1 depicts how the students' online comments show movement and growth along the continuum.

Appendix B

Documents and Images Used in the Two Performance Tasks

Document 1

THE BOSTON MASSACRE

Joy Hakim

On a freezing March day in 1770, one of the king's soldiers was looking for work to earn some extra money. Someone started making fun of him and told him to get a job cleaning toilets. [. . .] One thing led to another and there was a fight.

That started things. Soon a noisy, jeering group of mischief-makers gathered in front of the Boston Custom House. They began pushing and shoving and throwing stones and pieces of ice at the British sentry. He got knocked down and he called for help. Captain Thomas Preston came to the rescue with eight British soldiers.

There is some confusion about what happened next. The mob is said to have taunted the redcoats, yelling, "Fire! Fire!" Captain Preston is said to have yelled, "Hold your fire!" Then a British soldier was hit with a big stick. He claimed he heard the word "fire," so he fired his gun into the crowd. The street gang moved forward; the redcoats panicked and fired at unarmed people. Five Americans died; seven were wounded.

None of them was a hero. The victims were troublemakers who got worse than they deserved. The soldiers were professionals . . . who shouldn't have panicked. The whole thing shouldn't have happened.

From Hakim, J. (1993b). *From colonies to country* (pp. 64–65). New York: Oxford University Press.

Document 2

BRITISH CAPTAIN THOMAS PRESTON'S ACCOUNT OF THE BOSTON MASSACRE

On the 2nd [of March] . . . two [soldiers were] going through . . . [a factory where they made rope]. The rope-makers insultingly asked them if they would empty a [toilet]. This . . . had the desired effect [of angering] the soldiers, and from words they went to blows. Both parties and finally the soldiers retired to their quarters. [But] single quarrels could not be prevented, [because] the [Boston people are] constantly . . . abusing the soldiery.

On Monday night about 8 o'clock two soldiers were attacked and beat. [. . .] About 9 [o'clock] some of the guard came to and informed me the [Boston people] were assembling to attack the troops. . . . As I was captain of the day, [I went] to the main guard. On my way there I saw the people in great commotion, and heard them use the most cruel . . . threats against the troops. In a few minutes . . . , about 100 people passed . . . and went towards the Custom House where the King's money is. They . . . surrounded the [soldier] posted there, and with clubs and other weapons threatened . . . him. I was soon informed by a townsman their intention was to carry off the soldier . . . and probably murder him. This I feared might be [the first step in the people trying to take the King's money.] I . . . sent . . . 12 men [with guns] to protect both the sentry and the King's money. . . .

The mob still [grew] . . . , striking their clubs . . . one against another, and calling out, "Come on you rascals, you bloody backs, you lobster scoundrels, fire if you dare, . . . damn you, fire! We know you dare not. . . . " Some well-behaved persons asked me if the guns were [loaded]. I replied, "Yes." They then asked me if I intended to order the men to fire. I answered, "No, by no means. . . ." While I was speaking, one of the soldiers received a severe blow with a stick, stepped a little on one side, and instantly fired. . . . [I asked him] why he fired without orders. [He said,] "I was struck with a club on my arm. . . . [If I had been struck on the head, I would have died.]"

. . . A general attack was made on the [soldiers] by a great number of heavy clubs and snowballs. . . . Our lives were in imminent danger. . . . Instantly, three or four of the soldiers fired, one after another, and [then] three more [firings] in the same confusion and hurry. The mob then ran away, except three unhappy men who [were shot dead]; one more is since dead, three others are [almost dead], and four slightly wounded. The whole of this [happened] in almost 20 minutes. [When I asked] the soldiers why they fired without orders, they said they heard the word fire, and supposed it came from me. This might be the case. . . . Many of the mob

Figure B.1. Boston "Massacre," Image 1. Courtesy National Archives and Record Administration, College Park, Maryland.

Figure B.2. Boston "Massacre," Image 2. Courtesy National Archives and Record Administration, College Park, Maryland.

Figure B.3. Boston "Massacre," Image 3. Engraving by Paul Revere. Courtesy U.S. Library of Congress.

called out fire, fire, but I [told] the men that I gave no such order; that my words were, don't fire, stop your firing.

From British Public Records Office, C. O. 5/759. Reprinted in Jensen, M. (Ed.). (1964). *English historical documents,* (Vol. IX). London: Falmer.

ENDPOINT PERFORMANCE TASK

Document 1

TESTIMONY FROM 34 MASSACHUSETTS MINUTEMEN ABOUT EVENTS AT LEXINGTON GREEN

We, Nathaniel Mulliken, Philip Russell, [and 32 other men present at Lexington when shots were fired], all of [legal] age, and [who live in]

Lexington, . . . do testify and declare, that on the 19th of April [1775], about 1 or 2 o'clock in the morning, being [told] that . . . a body of [British] regulars were marching from Boston towards Concord, . . . we were alarmed . . . and having met at the place of [Lexington Green], we were dismissed by our Captain, John Parker, for the present, with orders to be ready to [march] at the beat of the drum. . . .

We further testify . . . that about 5 o'clock in the morning, hearing our drum beat, we proceeded towards the Green, and soon found that a large body of [British] troops were marching towards us. . . . Some of our company [of Minutemen] were coming up to the Green, and others had reached it, at which time [our] company began to [break up], [and while] our backs were turned on the troops, we were fired on by them, and a number of our men were instantly killed and wounded. . . . Not a gun was fired by any person in our company on the [British] regulars to our knowledge before they fired on us, and they continued firing until we made our escape.

Lexington, Massachusetts, April 25th, 1775.
Nathaniel Mulliken, Philip Russell, and 32 other men . . .
Duly Sworn before three Justices of the Peace [or Judges]

Document reprinted in Sawtell, C. (1968). *The nineteenth of April, 1775: A collection of first hand accounts.* Lincoln, MA: Sawtells of Somerset.

Document 2

PERSONAL NARRATIVE OF ENSIGN JEREMY LISTER, BRITISH ARMY

To the best of my recollection, about 4 o'clock in the morning, being the 19th of April, the front 5 companies was ordered to load, which we did. . . . It was at Lexington when we saw one of their companies drawn up in regular order [facing us]. Major Pitcairn of the [British] Marines, second in command, called to them to break up, but their not seeming willing, he demanded that we [stay in] our [lines], which we did, when they gave us . . . fire, then ran off to get behind a wall.

We had one man wounded . . . in the leg. His name was Johnson. Also Major Pitcairn's horse was shot in the flank; we returned their [fire], and before we proceeded on our march from Lexington, I believe we killed and wounded 7 or 8 men.

Ensign Jeremy Lister, youngest of the British officers at Lexington, in a personal story of events at Lexington Green, 1782. Document reprinted in Lister, J. (1931). *Concord fight.* Cambridge, MA: Harvard University Press.

Document 3

FROM THE *SALEM GAZETTE*, SALEM, MASSACHUSETTS COLONY, APRIL 25, 1775

The troops came in sight just before sunrise . . . the [British] Command-
ing Officer accosted the [colonial] militia in words to this effect: "Disperse
you rebels, damn you, throw down your arms and disperse;" upon which
the [American] troops [cheered], and immediately one or two [British]
officers discharged their pistols, which were instantaneously followed by
the firing of four or five of the soldiers, and then there seemed to be a
general discharge from the whole body [of British troops]. Eight of our
men were killed and nine wounded.

Document reprinted in Bennett, P. (1970). *What happened on Lexington Green.*
Menlo Park, CA: Addison-Wesley.

Figure B.4. Lexington battle, Image 1. Courtesy National Archives and Record
Administration, College Park, Maryland.

Figure B.5. Lexington battle, Image 2. Courtesy National Archives and Record Administration, College Park, Maryland.

Document 4

FROM THE LONDON GAZETTE, LONDON, ENGLAND, JUNE 10, 1775

Six companies of light infantry . . . at Lexington found a body of the country [or colonial] people under arms, on a green close to the road. And upon the King's troops marching up to them in order to [ask] the reason of their being so assembled [with their guns], they [ran] off in great confusion. And several guns were fired upon the King's troops from behind a stone wall, and also from the meeting house and other houses. . . . [As a result] of this attack by the rebels, the troops returned the fire and killed several of them.

Document reprinted in Bennett, P (1970). *What happened on Lexington Green*. Menlo Park, CA: Addison-Wesley.

Appendix C

Documents Used for In-Class Investigation of the Jamestown Starving Time

Student Resource: Document 1

THE STARVING TIME IN JAMESTOWN
THE WINTER OF 1609–1610

Some . . . say the Starving Time was an Indian war against the English invaders. The Powhatan may have decided to get rid of the settlers by starving them. Powhatan refused to trade with them. He laid siege to Jamestown. That means armed Indians wouldn't let anyone in or out. The settlers couldn't hunt or fish. They could hardly get to their pigs and chickens. The gentlemen ate the animals that were in the stockade—without much sharing. That made the others very angry. Soon there was nothing for anyone to eat.

A few escaped. "Many of our men this Starving Time did run away unto the savages, who we never heard of after," [Captain] Percy wrote.

Finally, in May 1610, two English ships tied up at Jamestown's docks. Of the 500 people that were in Jamestown in October when John Smith left for London, only 60 were still [there].

From Hakim, J. (1993a). "The Starving Time." In *Making Thirteen Colonies* (p. 33). New York: Oxford University Press.

Student Resource: Document C-1

EXCERPT 1

Governor George Percy c. 1605:
It pleased God after awhile, to send those people which were our mortall enemies to releeve us with such victuals, as Bread, Corne, Fish, and Flesh in great plentie, which was the setting up of our feeble men, otherwise wee had all perished. Also we were frequented by divers Kings in the Countrie, bringing us store of provision to our great comfort.

EXCERPT 2

Captain John Smith in 1624:
What by their crueltie, our Governours indiscretion, and the losse of our ships, of five hundred within six moneths after Captaine Smiths departure [October 1609–1610], there remained not past sixtie, men, women and children. This was that time, which still is to this day [1624] we call the starving time; it were too vile to say, and scarce to be beleeved, what we endured; but the occasion our own, for want of providence industrie and government, and not the barrenesse and defect of Countrie, as is generally supposed.

EXCERPT 3

William Simmonds in 1612:
It was the spaniards good hap to happen upon these parts where infinite numbers of people, whoe had manured the ground with that providence that is afforded victuall at all times; and time had brought them to that perfection [that] that they had the use of gold and silver, and [of] the most of such commodities as their countries affoorded: so that what the Spaniard got was only the spoile and pillage of those countrie people, and not the labours of their owne hands.

But had those fruitfull Countries beene as Salvage [i.e., savage], as barbarous, as ill-people, as little planted laboured and manured, as Virginia; their proper labours, it is likely would have produced as small a profit as ours.

Excerpts taken from Pearson, J., & Watkins, B. (1991). *Early Jamestown: A unit of study for grades 5–8* (p. 36). Los Angeles: National Center for History in the Schools. (Reproduction rights are provided for all excerpts.)

Student Resource: Document C-2

MODERN VERSION OF EXCERPTS OF ACCOUNTS FROM THE EARLY YEARS

EXCERPT 1

Thanks to God, our deadly enemies saved us by bringing food—great amounts of bread, corn, fish, and meat. This food saved all of us weak and starving men. Otherwise we would all have died. Leaders from other tribes also brought us food and supplies which made us comfortable

EXCERPT 2

Six months after Captain Smith left, the cruelty of the [Powhatans], the stupidity of our leaders, and the loss of our ships [when they sailed away] caused 440 of the 500 people in Jamestown to die. . . . We still call this the "Starving Time." What we suffered was too terrible to talk about. But the fault was our own. We starved because we did not plan well, work hard, or have good government. Our problems were not because the land was bad, as most people believe.

EXCERPT 3

It was the Spaniards' good luck to find lands where there were huge numbers of people who worked so hard that there was always food. These people were so advanced they developed the use of gold and silver and other things their land provided. The Spanish pillaged and robbed these people. They did not work for what they got. If these rich counties had been as savage, as barbarous (uncivilized), as poorly planted and with as few people as Virginia, then the Spanish would not have made more profits than we made.

Modern excerpts taken from Pearson, J., & Watkins, B. (1991). *Early Jamestown: A unit of study for grades 5–8* (p. 37). Los Angeles: National Center for History in the Schools. (Reproduction rights are provided.)

Student Resource: Document A-1

Captain John Smith in 1612:
Each household knoweth their owne lands and gardens, and most live of their owne labours. For their apparell, they are some time covered with

the skinnes of wilde beasts, which in winter are dressed with haire, but in sommer without. The better sort use large mantels of deare skins not much differing in fashion from the Irish mantels. . . .

Their buildings and habitations are for the most part by the rivers or not farre or distant from some fresh spring. Their houses are built like our Arbors of small young springs [saplings?] bowed and tyed, and so close covered with mats or the bark of trees very handsomely, that not withstanding either winde raine or weather, they are as warme as stooves, but very smoaky; yet at the toppe of the house there is a hole made for the smoake to goe into right over the fire. . . .

Men women and children have their severall names according to the several humour[s] of their parents. Their women (they say) are easilie delivered of childe, yet doe they love children verie dearly. To make them hardy, in the coldest morning they wash them in the rivers, and by painting and ointments so tanne their skins after [a] year or two, no weather will hurt them. The men bestow their times in fishing, hunting, wars, and such manlike exercises. Scorning to be seen in any woman like exercise; which is the cause that the woman be verie painfull and mean often idle. The women and children do rest of the worke. They make mats, baskets, pots, morters; pound their corn, make their bread, prepare their victuals, plant their corne, gather their corne, beare al kind of burdens, and such like. . . .

Their fishing is much in Boats. These they make of one tree by bowing [i.e., burning] and scratching away the coles with ston[e]s and shells till they have made it in [the] form of a Trough. Some of them are an elne [i.e., and ell, a unit of measure to 45 inches] deepe, and 40 or 50 foot in length, and some will beare 40 men; but the most ordinary are smaller, and will beare 10, 20, or 30. According to their bignes. Instead of oares, they use paddles and sticks, with which they will row faster than our Barges. . . .

Excerpt taken from Pearson, J., & Watkins, B. (1991). *Early Jamestown: A unit of study for grades 5–8* (pp. 21–22). Los Angeles: National Center for History in the Schools. (Reproduction rights are provided.)

Student Resource: Document A-2

MODERN VERSION OF JOHN SMITH'S DESCRIPTION OF THE POWHATANS

Each family has its own land and gardens. They do their own work.
For clothes they wear animal skins. In winter they wear skins with fur and hair left on, but in summer they wear leather. More important people wear cloaks made of deer skins that look like the cloaks the Irish wear. . . .

They build their homes near rivers or springs. They tie long slender branches together in bundles and weave them into a frame for a house, like a giant basket. They lay mats or bark over this frame. The houses are warm and snug, but very smokey, even though they leave a hole above their fireplaces for smoke. . . .

Their houses are surrounded by their own fields and gardens. The farmland can be a small plot or large fields. Sometimes their houses are grouped together, separated only by groves of trees. Near their homes are piles of wood for burning in their home fires. . . .

Parents give children several names. Women have babies easily, and love them very much. To make babies strong, on the coldest mornings they wash them in rivers. They also put oils and lotions on the skin of their babies to protect them against the weather.

Men fish, hunt, and go to war. Women often work while the men are idle. Women and children do all the other work. They make mats, baskets, pots, and grinding tools, grind corn into flour, bake bread, and do all the cooking. They also do the farming, planting, raising, and gathering of corn. Women do the hauling and all other heavy work. . . .

They use boats for fishing. The boats are made by burning out the center of the tree. They scrape away the burned coals with stones and shells to form a long hollow trough. These boats can be almost four feet deep and 40 or 50 feet long. Some hold 40 men, but most are smaller, holding 10 to 30 men. They use paddles instead of oars and travel quickly. . . .

Modern version taken from Pearson, J., & Watkins, B. (1991). *Early Jamestown: A unit of study for grades 5–8* (pp. 23–24). Los Angeles: National Center for History in the Schools. (Classroom reproduction rights are provided.)

References

Afflerbach, P., & VanSledright, B. (2001). Hath! Doth! What? The challenges middle grade students face when they read innovative history text. *Journal of Adolescent and Adult Literacy, 44,* 496–707.

Alexander, P. A. (1997). Mapping the multidimensional nature of domain learning: The interplay of cognitive, motivational, and strategic forces. *Advances in Motivation and Achievement, 10,* 213–250.

Alexander, P. A. (2000). Toward a model of academic development: Schooling and the acquisition of knowledge. *Educational Researcher, 29,* 28–33, 44.

Ankeney, K., Del Rio, R., Nash, G., & Vigilante, D. (1996). *Bring history alive! A sourcebook for teaching United States history.* Los Angeles: National Center for History in the Schools.

Ankersmit, F., & Kellner, H. (Eds.). (1995). *A new philosophy of history.* Chicago: University of Chicago Press.

Ashby, R., & Lee, P. (1987a). Discussing the evidence. *Teaching History, 48,* 13–17.

Ashby, R., & Lee, P. (1987b). Children's concepts of empathy and understanding in history. In C. Portal (Ed.), *The history curriculum for teachers* (pp. 62–88). London: Falmer.

Ashby, R., & Lee, P. (1996, April). *Children's ideas about testing historical claims and of the status of historical accounts.* Paper presented at the annual meeting of the American Educational Research Association, New York.

Bain, R. (2000). Into the breach: Using theory and research to shape history instruction. In P. Stearns, P. Seixas, & S. Wineburg (Eds.), *Knowing, teaching, and learning history: National and international perspectives* (pp. 331–352). New York: New York University Press.

Barthes, R. (1968). The reality effect. In T. Todorov (Ed.), *French literary theory today: A reader* (R. Carter, Trans.; pp. 11–17). Cambridge, UK: Cambridge University Press.

Barthes, R. (1986). The discourse of history. In *The rustle of language* (R. Howard, Trans.; pp. 128–139). New York: Hill & Wang.

Barton, K. (1996). Narrative simplifications in elementary students historical thinking. In J. Brophy (Ed.), *Advances in research on teaching,* (Vol. 6) (pp. 51–84). Greenwich, CT: JAI Press.

Barton, K. (1997). "I just kinda know": Elementary students' ideas about historical evidence. *Theory and Research in Social Education, 24,* 407–430.

Barton, K. (2001). "You'd be wanting to know about the past": Social contexts of
children's historical understanding in Northern Ireland and the USA. *Comparative Education, 37,* 89–106.

Barton, K., & Levstik, L. (1998). "It wasn't a good part of history": National identity and students' explanations of historical significance. *Teachers College Record,
90,* 478–513.

Beatty, A., Reese, C., Persky, H., & Carr, P. (1996). *NAEP 1994 U.S. history report
card: Findings from the National Assessment of Education Progress.* Washington,
DC: U.S. Department of Education.

Bennett, P. (1970). *What happened on Lexington Green.* Menlo Park, CA: Addison-
Wesley.

Bennett, W. J. (1994, November). *To reclaim a legacy: A report on the humanities in
higher education.* Washington, DC: National Endowment for the Humanities.

Berkhofer, Jr., R. F. (1995). *Beyond the great story: History as text and discourse.* Cambridge, MA: Harvard University Press.

Bodnar, J. (1992). *Remaking America: Public memory, commemoration, and patriotism
in the twentieth century.* Princeton, NJ: Princeton University Press.

Brophy, J., & VanSledright, B. (1997). *Teaching and learning history in elementary
schools.* New York: Teachers College Press.

Brown, A. (1992). Design experiments: Theoretical and methodological challenges
in creating complex interventions in classrooms. In G. Salomon (Ed.), *Distributed cognition: Psychological and educational considerations* (pp. 188–228). New
York: Cambridge University Press.

Brown, A., & Campione, J. (1990). Communities of learning and thinking, or a
context by any other name. *Contributions to Human Development, 21,* 108–126.

Bruner, J. S. (1960). *The process of education.* Cambridge, MA: Harvard University
Press.

Bruner, J. S. (1996). *The culture of education.* Cambridge, MA: Harvard University Press.

Coltham, J. B. (1971). *The development of thinking and the learning of history.* London: Historical Association.

Cronon, W. (1992). A place for stories: Nature, history and narrative. *Journal of
American History, 78,* 1347–1376.

Cuban, L. (1991). History of teaching in social studies. In J. Shaver (Ed.), *Handbook of research on social studies teaching and learning* (pp. 197–209). New York:
Macmillan.

Cummins, D., & White, W. (1980). *Inquiries into American history: The American
Revolution.* Encino, CA: Glencoe.

Darling-Hammond, L. (1991). The implications of testing policy for quality and
equality. *Phi Delta Kappan, 73,* 218–224.

Davidson, J. W., & Lytle, M. H. (1992). *After the fact: The art of historical detection*
(Vol. 1). New York: McGraw Hill.

Davis, N. Z. (1983). *The return of Martin Guerre.* Cambridge, MA: Harvard University Press.

Davis, N. Z. (1988). "On the lame." *American Historical Review, 93,* 572–603.

Davis, O. L., Jr., Yeager, E., & Foster, S. (Eds.). (2001). *Development of historical empathy: Perspective taking in social studies*. Lanham, MD: Rowman Littlefield.

Dewey, J. (1963). *Philosophy and civilization*. New York: Capricorn Books. (Original work published 1931)

Discovery Communications. (1996). *The Revolutionary War* [Video]. Bethesda, MD: Author.

Donahue, P., Voelkl, K., Campbell, J., & Mazzeo, J. (1999). *NAEP 1998 reading report card for the nation*. Washington, DC: U.S. Department of Education.

Edinger, M. (2000). *Seeking history: Teaching with primary sources in grades 4–6*. Westport, CT: Heinemann.

Epstein, T. (1998). Deconstructing differences in African American and European American adolescents' perspectives on United States history. *Curriculum Inquiry, 28,* 397–423.

Epstein, T. (2000). Adolescent perspectives on racial diversity in U.S. history: Case studies from an urban classroom. *American Educational Research Journal, 37,* 185–214.

Finlay, R. (1988). The refashioning of Martin Guerre. *American Historical Review, 93,* 553–571.

Firestone, W., Fitz, J., & Broadfoot, P. (1999). Power, learning and legitimation: Assessment implementation across levels in the United States and the United Kingdom. *American Educational Research Journal, 36,* 759–793.

Fordham, S. (1996). *Blacked out: Dilemmas of race, identity, and success at Capital High*. Chicago: University of Chicago Press.

Ghere, D., & Spreeman, J. (1998). *Causes of the American Revolution: Focus on Boston*. Los Angeles: Organization of American Historians and the Regents, University of California.

Gitlin, T. (1995). *The twilight of common dreams: Why America is wracked by the culture wars*. New York: Metropolitan Books.

Goodlad, J. I. (1984). *A place called school: Prospects for the future*. New York: McGraw-Hill.

Grant, S. G. (2001). It's just the facts, or is it? The relationship between teachers' practices and students' understandings of history. *Theory and Research in Social Education, 29,* 65–108.

Grant, S. G., & VanSledright, B. (2001). *Constructing a powerful approach to teaching and learning in elementary social studies*. Boston: Houghton Mifflin.

Hakim, J. (1993a). *Making thirteen colonies*. New York: Oxford University Press.

Hakim, J. (1993b). *From colonies to country*. New York: Oxford University Press.

Haladyna, T., & Shaughnessy, J. (1985). Research on student attitudes toward social studies. *Social Education, 49,* 692–695.

Hallam, R. N. (1971). Thinking and learning in history. *Teaching History, 2,* 337–346.

Hanna, P. (1963). Revising the social studies: What is needed. *Social Education, 27,* 190–196.

Holt, T. (1990). *Thinking historically: Narrative, imagination, and understanding*. New York: College Entrance Examination Board.

Iggers, G. G. (1997). *Historiography in the twentieth century: From scientific objectivity to postmodern challenge*. Hanover, NH: Wesleyan University Press.

Jensen, M. (Ed.). (1964). *English historical documents* (Vol. IX). London: Falmer.

Kammen, M. (1991). *Mystic chords of memory: The transformation of tradition in American culture*. New York: Vintage.

Kammen, M. (1997). *In the past lane: Historical perspectives on American culture*. New York: Oxford University Press.

Kobrin, D. (1992). It's my country, too: A proposal for a student historian's history of the United States. *Teachers College Record, 94*, 329–342.

Kozol, J. (1992). *Savage inequalities: Children in America's schools*. New York: HarperPerennial.

Lampert, M. (1985). How do teachers manage to teach? *Harvard Educational Review, 55*, 178–194.

Lee, P. J. (1995). History and the national curriculum in England. In A. Dickinson, P. Gordon, P. Lee, & J. Slater (Eds.), *International yearbook of history education* (Vol. 1) (pp. 73–123). London: Woburn.

Lee, P. J. (1998). History across the water: A U.K. perspective on history education research. *Issues in Education, 4*, 211–220.

Lee, P. J., & Ashby, R. (2000). Progression in historical understanding among students ages 7–14. In P. Stearns, P. Seixas, & S. Wineburg (Eds.), *Knowing, teaching, and learning history: National and international perspectives* (pp. 199–222). New York: New York University Press.

Lee, P. J., Ashby, R., & Dickinson, A. K. (1996a). Progression in children's ideas about history. In M. Hughes (Ed.), *Progression in learning* (pp. 50–81). Clevedon, UK: Multilingual Matters.

Lee, P. J., Ashby, R., & Dickinson, A. K. (1996b). Children making sense of history. *Education, 3–13, 24*, 13–19.

Leinhardt, G., & Young, K. M. (1996). Two texts, three readers: Distance and expertise in reading history. *Cognition and Instruction, 14*, 441–486.

Levstik, L. (1996). NCSS and the teaching of history. In O. L. Davis, Jr. (Ed.), *NCSS in retrospect* (Bulletin No. 92) (pp. 21–34). Washington, DC: National Council for the Social Studies.

Levstik, L., & Barton, K. (1996). They still use some of their past: Historical salience in elementary children's chronological thinking. *Journal of Curriculum Studies, 28*, 531–576.

Levstik, L., & Barton, K. (1997). *Doing history: Investigating with children in elementary and middle schools*. Mahwah, NJ: Erlbaum.

Lister, J. (1931). *Concord fight*. Cambridge, MA: Harvard University Press.

Lowenthal, D. (1985). *The past is a foreign country*. Cambridge, UK: Cambridge University Press.

Lowenthal, D. (1998). *The heritage crusade and the spoils of history*. Cambridge, UK: Cambridge University Press.

Masur, K. (1999, December). Edmund Morris's *Dutch*: Reconstructing Reagan or deconstructing history? *Perspectives: American Historical Association Newsletter, 37*, 3–5.

Morris, E. (1999). *Dutch: A memoir of Ronald Reagan*. New York: Random House.

National Center for History in the Schools (NCHS). (1994). *National standards for United States history: Exploring the American experience*. Los Angeles: UCLA.

Novick, P. (1988). *That noble dream: The "objectivity question" and the American historical profession.* Cambridge, UK: Cambridge University Press.

O'Connor, K. (1991). *Narrative form and historical representation: A study of American college students' historical narratives.* Paper presented at the Conference for Pedagogic Text and Content Analysis, Harnosand, Sweden.

Pearson, J. (1991). *William Penn's peaceable kingdom: A unit of study for grades 5–8.* Los Angeles: National Center for History in the Schools.

Pearson, J. (1992). *A society knit as one: The Puritans, Algonkians, and Roger Williams: A unit of study for grades 5–8.* Los Angeles: National Center for History in the Schools.

Pearson, J., & Watkins, B. (1991). *Early Jamestown: A unit of study for grades 5–8.* Los Angeles: National Center for History in the Schools.

Poster, M. (1997). *Cultural history + postmodernity: Disciplinary readings and challenges.* New York: Columbia University Press.

Pressley, M., & Afflerbach, P. (1995). *Verbal protocols of reading: The nature of constructively responsive reading.* Hillsdale, NJ: Erlbaum.

Ravitch, D., & Finn, C., Jr. (1987). *What do our 17-year-olds know? A report on the first National Assessment of History and Literature.* New York: Harper and Row.

Sawtell, C. (1968). *The nineteenth of April, 1775: A collection of first hand accounts.* Lincoln, MA: Sawtells of Somerset.

Scott, J. W. (1996, February). *After history?* Paper presented at History and the Limits of Interpretation: A Symposium, Rice University, Houston. (available online at <www.ruf.rice.edu/~culture/papers/Scott.html>)

Segall, A. (1999). Critical history: Implications for history/social studies education. *Theory and Research in Social Education, 27,* 358–374.

Seixas, P. (1993). Historical understanding among adolescents in a multicultural setting. *Curriculum Inquiry, 23,* 301–327.

Seixas, P. (1994). Student's understanding of historical significance. *Theory and Research in Social Education, 22,* 281–304.

Seixas, P. (1996). Conceptualizing the growth of historical understanding. In D. Olson & N. Torrance (Eds.), *The handbook of psychology in education.* Oxford: Blackwell.

Seixas, P. (1999). Beyond "content" and "pedagogy": In search of a way to talk about history education. *Journal of Curriculum Studies, 31,* 317–337.

Shemilt, D. (1980). *History 13–16 evaluation study.* Edinburgh: Holmes McDougall.

Shemilt, D. (1984). Beauty and the philosopher: Empathy in history and classroom. In A. Dickinson, P. Lee, & P. Rogers (Eds.), *Learning history* (pp. 39–84). London: Heinemann.

Shemilt, D. (1987). Adolescent ideas about evidence and methodology in history. In C. Portal (Ed.), *The history curriculum for teachers* (pp. 62–99). London: Falmer.

Shulman, L. (1987). Knowledge and teaching: Foundations of a new reform. *Harvard Educational Review, 57,* 1–22.

Smith, J., & Niemi, R. (2001). Learning history in school: The impact of course work and instructional practices on achievement. *Theory and Research in Social Education, 29,* 18–42.

Stahl, S., Hynd, C., Britton, B., McNish, M., & Bosquet, D. (1996). What happens when students read multiple source documents in history? *Reading Research Quarterly, 31,* 430–456.

Taylor, D. (1991). *Learning denied.* Portsmouth, NH: Heinemann.

Tyack, D., & Tobin, W. (1994). The "grammar" of schooling: Why has it been so hard to change? *American Educational Research Journal, 31,* 453–479.

VanSledright, B. (1995). "I don't remember—the ideas are all jumbled in my head": Eighth graders' reconstructions of colonial American history. *Journal of Curriculum and Supervision, 10,* 317–345.

VanSledright, B. (1996). Closing the gap between disciplinary and school history? Historian as high school history teacher. In J. Brophy (Ed.), *Advances in Research on Teaching* (Vol. 6) (pp. 257–289). Greenwich, CT: JAI Press.

VanSledright, B. (1997). And Santayana lives on: Students' views on the purposes for studying American history. *Journal of Curriculum Studies, 29,* 529–557.

VanSledright, B. (1998). On the importance of historical positionality to thinking about and teaching history. *International Journal of Social Education, 12,* 1–18.

VanSledright, B. (2001). From empathic regard to self-understanding: Im/positionality, empathy, and historical contextualization. In O. L. Davis, Jr., E. Yeager, & S. Foster (Eds.), *Development of historical empathy: Perspective taking in social studies* (pp. 51–68). Lanham, MD: Rowman Littlefield.

VanSledright, B., & Afflerbach, P. (2000). Reconstructing Andrew Jackson: Elementary teachers' readings of revisionist history texts. *Theory and Research in Social Education, 28,* 411–444.

VanSledright, B., & Frankes, L. (2000). Concept- and strategic-knowledge development in historical study: A comparative exploration in two fourth-grade classrooms. *Cognition and Instruction, 18,* 239–283.

VanSledright, B., & Kelly, C. (1998). Reading American history: The influence of using multiple sources on six fifth graders. *The Elementary School Journal, 98,* 239–265.

Wertsch, J. V. (1998). *Mind as action.* New York: Oxford University Press.

Wilson, S. (1990). *Mastodons, maps, and Michigan: Exploring uncharted territory while teaching elementary school social studies* (Elementary Subjects Center Rep. No. 24). East Lansing, MI: Center for the Learning and Teaching of Elementary Subjects, Michigan State University.

Wineburg, S. (1991). On the reading of historical texts: Notes on the breach between school and academy. *American Educational Research Journal, 28,* 495–519.

Wineburg, S. (1998). Reading Abraham Lincoln: An expert/expert study in historical cognition. *Cognitive Science, 22,* 319–346.

Wineburg, S. (2001). *Historical thinking and other unnatural acts: Charting the future of teaching the past.* Philadelphia: Temple University Press.

Wolcott, H. (1995). *The art of fieldwork.* Walnut Creek, CA: Altamira Press.

Index

About the Author

Bruce VanSledright teaches at the University of Maryland, College Park. A former American history teacher, he currently conducts research on the teaching and learning of history in public schools. Much of his research has been case-based studies of how teachers go about teaching the subject. His reports on how students learn history have focused on the ways in which those students develop historical understandings by reading documents and texts.